How to Get a Free College Education and a Job You Love

Jonathan Machtig

Brett Machtig

MGI Publications

Bloomington MN

MGI Publications

Bloomington MN

ISBN 978-1-954236-03-5

NOTE: Material discussed is meant for general illustration and/or informational purposes only and it is not to be construed as specific investment advice. Although the information has been gathered from sources believed to be reliable, please note that individual situations can vary and decisions should only be made with individual professional advice.

Advisory services through Capital Advisory Group Advisory Services LLC and securities through United Planners Financial Services of America, a Limited Partnership. Member FINRA and SIPC. The Capital Advisory Group Advisory Services, LLC (CAG) and United Planners Financial Services are not affiliated.

© 2022 by MGI Publications, Jonathan Machtig and Brett Machtig. All rights reserved.

Published 2022. First Printing March 2022.

No part of this publication may be reproduced, distributed, or transmitted in any form or by any means, including photocopying, recording, or other electronic or mechanical methods, without the prior written permission of the publisher, except in the case of brief quotations embodied in critical reviews and certain other noncommercial uses permitted by copyright law.

About the Authors

Jonathan Machtig works as a Chess Department Director for Star Education. Star Education provides after-school programs for 10,000 California-based students K-12. Jonathan's hobbies include reading, music, and chess. Jonathan attended Musician's Institute in Los Angeles and Salt Lake School for the Performing Arts.

Brett Machtig serves on the Normandale College Business Advisory Committee as well as The National Security Forum for the United States Department of Defense. Brett is the founding partner of The Capital Advisory Group and has written more than 22 books on finance, history, negotiation, and art. His hobbies include history, collecting antique books, and a lifetime of study. www.brettmachtig.com

Contents

Forward   7

Introduction   11

Section I

The Best Occupational Tracks From Trade Schools to Advanced Degrees

   1.1 What Are the Best Paying Technical School Professions?   21

   1.2 What Are The Best Paying Professions Requiring Just A Two-Year Associate's Degree?   41

   1.3 What Bachelor's Degree Careers Pay Higher Incomes?   51

   1.4 Beyond The Undergraduate Degree   67

Section II

What Majors Offer The Greatest Challenges After Graduation And How to Minimize Your College Costs

   2.1 Which College Majors Have The Lowest Median Earnings?   79

2.2 Which College Majors Have The Highest Unemployment?	81
2.3 How Can You Most Effectively Reduce the Cost of College	85
2.4 Can The Military Help You Reduce The Cost of Higher Education?	93

Section III

Keys to Success In Higher Education Before, During, and After

3.1 How Can I Best Prepare For Getting Into College?	101
3.2 What Are The Keys For Success While Attending College?	107
3.3 What Are The Keys to Financial Success After College?	117

Section IV

Other Key Advice And Resources

4.1 How to Use On-Line College Resources to Help Your Experience	129
4.2 What Are The Best Applications for Preparing for College?	135

4.3 When Should You Consider Going Back to College to Learn a New Profession?	139
4.4 Greatest Tips For Going to School Later in Life	151
4.5 How to Pick the Best College for You	155
4.6 Best Books On Where to Get Help	161
4.7 Colleges Who Offer Debt Free College Educations	173

Conclusion 181

Section V

Bonus Material: Excerpts From *Your Guide to Financial Freedom*

5.1 How to Plan	185
5.2 The Single Most Important Factor to Financial Success	205

Section VI

Colleges Indexes

6.1 Top Rated Colleges in the US by Region - East — 222

6.2 Top Rated Colleges in the US by Region - Midwest — 224

6.3 Top Rated Colleges in the US by Region - South — 226

6.4 Top Rated Colleges in the US by Region - West — 228

6.5 Top Hardest Colleges to Get Accepted in the US — 230

6.6 Top 50 Highest Mid-Career Paying Colleges — 240

6.7 United States Colleges and Universities by State — 246

Forward

I have been involved in writing college curriculum training financial life skills for more than 20 years. I have noticed a trend where students are being negatively impacted by the financial costs of college. Also, workers fear the cost and the stress of going back to school to get re-education in a new profession.

I have written one book designed to help students thrive financially after they have already graduated, so we will not repeat the financial lessons taught in A Twenty-Something's Guide to Financial Freedom, co-written by Brett Machtig, Josh Gronholz and the esteemed Henry H. Parker, Ph.D.

A Twenty-Something's Guide to Financial Freedom was written to teach students one of the most important secrets in life: how to let money make money for you. By contrast, this book is designed to simply help you get the most out of college or other higher education, while incurring the least amount of cost to you and your family. It also will help you in your education planning and monitoring.

COVID-19 has really changed the landscape of work and school. Although we expect this to change going forward, we expect that the use of "on-line" classes will continue to expand in the coming years for many colleges that are struggling financially.

In talking with many successful business owners and Fortune

500 executives, less emphasis is placed on college degrees as a requirement to gain employment. This is not to suggest that you no longer should go to college, but to consider the financial costs and make sure your ultimate career path can cover the cost of the education. In fact, employers like Google & Amazon have structured their own alternative education paths instead of requiring you to go to college.

In the past many have looked back on the socialization and life lessons learned in college as some of the best life lessons learned. If college will allow more freedom to do remote on-line course work, consider living in a location that can provide these life lessons, hopefully where on-line access speeds can help your classwork.

Elon Musk will soon roll out his Starlink internet network. This network will give previously unavailable parts of the world options for those who need internet to work or do on-line classes. On-line classwork and resulting careers can provide some great lifestyle options.

As an example, for health reasons, I travel halfway across the world to live in Thailand for a month per year. There, I have found excellent internet service and a very healthy environment where I can write and spend quality time with my family.

The point of this book is to help you find a job that you love so that it feels like your life's calling. Jonathan Machtig found it teaching music and chess. I found my life's calling helping others to find a way to live from the returns on their savings. In both cases, we are eager to start the day and pour our love, time, and energy into helping others.

Hopefully, this book will give you the tools to live the life of your dreams. You can choose the area you want to work and how to get the most out of your educational path.

College Grads are Suffering in Debt.

"Some debts are fun when you are acquiring them, but none are when you set about retiring them."

—Ogden Nash

Introduction

It's 2021 and Americans are burdened by more student loan debt than ever. Among the Class of 2018, 69% of college students took out student loans and they graduated with an average debt of $29,800, including both private and federal debt. Meanwhile, 14% of their parents took out an average of $35,600 in federal Parent PLUS loans.

You've probably heard another scary statistic: Americans owe over $1.56 trillion in student loan debt, spread out among about 45 million borrowers or about $521 billion more than the total U.S. credit card debt for the same time frame.

Attending college can cost on average $26,000 per year for undergraduates at a four-year institution, based on Nation-

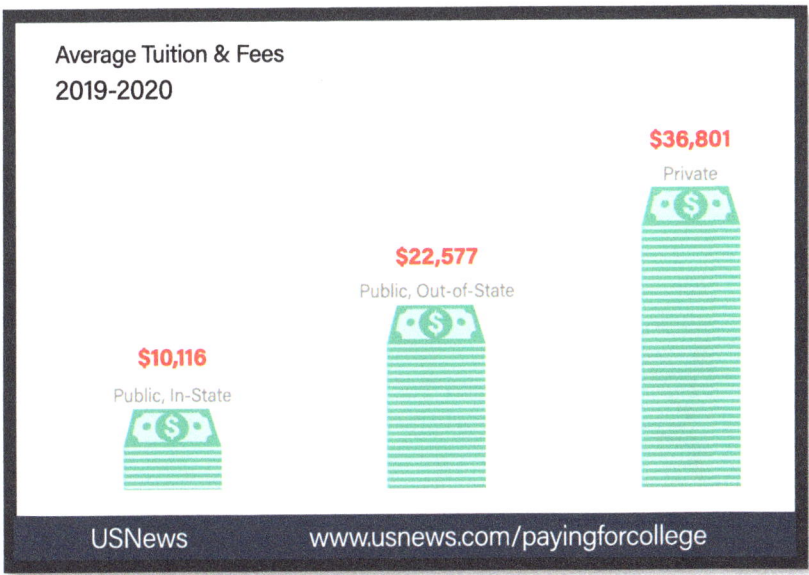

al Center for Education Statistics data for 2015-2016. The ever-increasing college costs probably have most of us scratching our head wondering if a college degree is really worth it. Congress is looking into some student loan reduction plans, but whatever they come up with, it will only deal with a small portion of the student loan liability.

Will we really get a return on our investment in that college degree? Before we answer that question, let's take a look at what the real price tag for college actually is these days.

The Average Cost of Tuition

According to the College Board, the average cost of tuition and fees (fees may include the library, campus transportation, student government, and athletic facilities) for the 2016–2017 school year was $33,480 at private colleges, $9,650 for state residents at public colleges, and $24,930 for out-of-state residents attending public universities per year.

These numbers do not include housing, meals, books or school supplies which could easily add another $10,000 to $16,000 a year. If you add room and board to yearly tuition

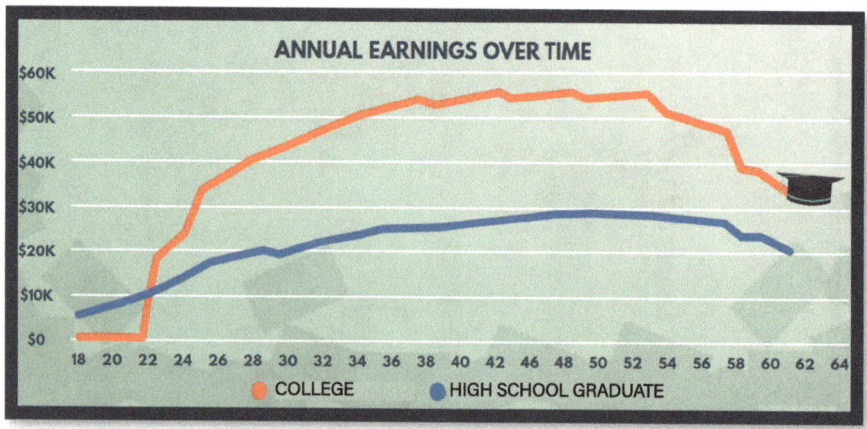

Advisory services through Capital Advisory Group Advisory Services LLC and securities through United Planners Financial Services of America, a Limited Partnership. Member FINRA and SIPC. The Capital Advisory Group Advisory Services, LLC (CAG) and United Planners Financial Services are not affiliated.

and fee averages, a private nonprofit four-year college costs $45,370, while a public four or five year costs $20,090. Many majors like engineering, accounting, architecture and nursing require five-years in a college program to attain the bachelor's degree. Now, multiply those numbers by four or five years of college, and you are looking at a really hefty college bill. For example, four years in a public college would cost $80,360, or five years in a private college would cost $226,850! It's no wonder that the student debt crisis has toppled $1.5 trillion.

Footing the bill for college can be a tough pill to swallow when you couple the costs with the fact that many graduates are out of work. While I'm not recommending students pick up unnecessary student loan debt, I do think that there is enough evidence to encourage students to go to college.

It's possible that your student may join the ranks of highly successful entrepreneurs who don't have college degrees, but there is just a very small fraction of people who are going to become the next Bill Gates, Steve Jobs, or Richard Branson. These success stories are few and far between, and what these business leaders lacked in formal education, they more than abundantly made up for in entrepreneurial skills, busi-

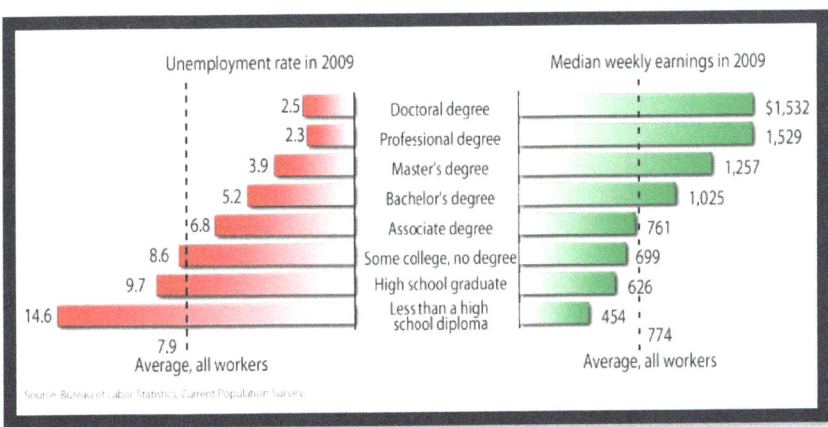

Advisory services through Capital Advisory Group Advisory Services LLC and securities through United Planners Financial Services of America, a Limited Partnership. Member FINRA and SIPC. The Capital Advisory Group Advisory Services, LLC (CAG) and United Planners Financial Services are not affiliated.

ness savviness, drive, and passion.

Data Indicates That a College Degree Is Still Worth the Investment

According to the Bureau of Labor Statistics, the pay gap between those with a four-year degree and those with a high school degree is at a record high. Those with a four-year college degree earn a median weekly salary of $1,137, whereas employees with a high school degree average $678. The difference is even higher when comparing employees with doctoral degrees (the median weekly salary is $1,623) and those with some or no college degree (the median weekly salary is $738). *https://www.bls.gov/web/empsit/cpseea05.htm

In fact, not only will college graduates make more money, but also not going to college could cost you dearly to the tune of $1 million in lifetime wages. While you may wonder if these numbers apply to only graduates of Ivy League schools, the Economic Policy Institute numbers show that the benefits of college don't just go to graduates of elite colleges, but to all college graduates with a four-year degree. Those with a high school degree face, on average, a higher 17.9 percent unemployment versus an average lower 5.6 percent for college graduates. Also nearly one in seven high school graduates is stuck in a part-time job with entry-level wages and very few options for full-time employment.

Hypothesis Statement

This is a "how-to" so you can get the most from higher education at whatever level of education you desire. This book is about how to do just that, get more from your high school, technical school or college degree, and to do it without sad-

---

Advisory services through Capital Advisory Group Advisory Services LLC and securities through United Planners Financial Services of America, a Limited Partnership. Member FINRA and SIPC. The Capital Advisory Group Advisory Services, LLC (CAG) and United Planners Financial Services are not affiliated.

dling yourself with loads of debt after graduating. It is about getting a job you can embrace that can support your ideal lifestyle. It is about making you "in demand and relevant" in today's economy.

How far do I need to go after High School?

As you can see, the more education you have, the more you can make and the less likely you are to be unemployed.

But if you go beyond the averages, it is possible to get too much education without work experience to justify the salary expense to an employer and you can become unemployable for the wages required at that education level. Research undertaken proves that unemployment and underemployment of graduates are devastating phenomenae. A high incidence of either are indicators of poor institutional direction, ineffectiveness, and inefficiency.

Since the beginning of the economic recession in the US economy in 2007 and later to the 2020 graduates, an increasing number of graduates have been unable to find permanent positions in their chosen field. According to statistics, the unemployment rate for recent college graduates has been higher than all college graduates in the past decade, implying that it has been more difficult for graduates to find a job in recent years. One year after graduation, the unemployment rate of 2007-2008 bachelor's degree recipients was 9%. Underemployment among graduates has also been high. Educated unemployment or underemployment is due to a mismatch between the aspirations of graduates and employment opportunities available to them. The many who lack a marketable profession, often find themselves the first to lose their jobs.

Advisory services through Capital Advisory Group Advisory Services LLC and securities through United Planners Financial Services of America, a Limited Partnership. Member FINRA and SIPC. The Capital Advisory Group Advisory Services, LLC (CAG) and United Planners Financial Services are not affiliated.

Aggravating factors for unemployment are the rapidly increasing quantity of international graduates competing for an inadequate number of suitable jobs, schools not keeping their curriculum relevant to the job market, the growing pressure on schools to increase access to education to all (which usually requires a reduction in educational quality), and students being constantly told that an academic degree is the only route to a secure future. This is less true today, but good grades are still considered a must in "first job" employment requirements.

It also might be caused from students picking careers based on what they like to study rather than how many of a particular profession are needed in the current economy.

College and Universities cost thousands of dollars a semester, and this has gone up 1,120 percent in the last thirty years. Students have been given the impression that employers are looking for people who, through tests and grades, have demonstrated that they are high achievers. In many recent surveys, that has been proved. Employers are looking for people who have learned how to work well with others, and have gained substantial communication skills as well as critical thinking abilities.

Current statistics show graduates are not meeting employers needs and the recently increased minimum wage will make the first-job hires even more expensive. For example, since many graduating students are struggling to pay off their student loans, graduates are accumulating debt and struggling to pay back their loans. Fifteen percent of the student borrowers default within the first three years of repayment. Many resort to returning to live with their parents and having to work multiple part-time jobs. Loans average about $20,000 - $30,000. Higher education becomes an investment in which students are expecting to find a job with enough

Advisory services through Capital Advisory Group Advisory Services LLC and securities through United Planners Financial Services of America, a Limited Partnership. Member FINRA and SIPC. The Capital Advisory Group Advisory Services, LLC (CAG) and United Planners Financial Services are not affiliated.

income to pay off the loans in a timely manner. To top it off, COVID-19 has made finding a job paying enough to allow timely loan repayment, even more difficult.

College is an investment that students need to discern whether it will be beneficial or not, and whether it will help to advance their career in the long run. In the next chapters we will explore where the best opportunities exist at each level of higher education, from technical trade schools all the way through advanced degrees.

While you are searching for the college that is right for you please watch for these colleges. We ranked the worst colleges in America for 2021. Each college was scored and ranked based on a number of different factors including: the graduation rate, quality of education, the school's reputation, the percentage of graduates who find jobs, and cost.

- Alabama State University
- Black Hill State University
- Coppin State University
- DeVry University
- Fayetteville State University
- Florida Memorial University
- Grambling State University
- Lindsey Wilson College
- Mayville State University
- Morris College
- Nazarene Bible College
- New England College
- Philander Smith College
- Saint Augustine's University
- Shaw University
- Stratford University
- The Art Institute of Atlanta
- The University of Maine at Augusta
- The University of Montevallo State
- The University of South Carolina Aiken
- University of the District of Columbia
- University of the Southwest
- Waldorf University
- Wesley College
- Western International University

Advisory services through Capital Advisory Group Advisory Services LLC and securities through United Planners Financial Services of America, a Limited Partnership. Member FINRA and SIPC. The Capital Advisory Group Advisory Services, LLC (CAG) and United Planners Financial Services are not affiliated.

Section I

The Best Occupational Tracks from Trade Schools to Advanced Degrees

"Not all knowledge comes from college and not all skills come from degrees."

—Mike Rowe

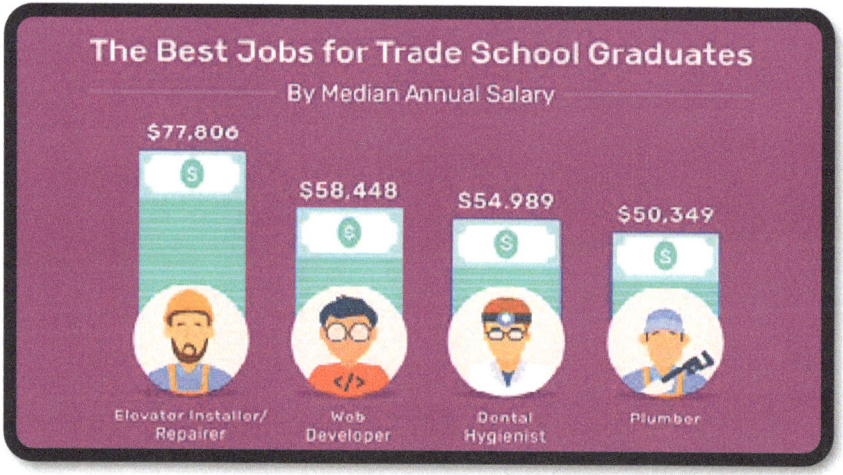

"Sometimes the best school, is the school of hard Knocks; if we can survive the curriculum."

—Brett Machtig

1.1 What Are the Best Paying Technical School Professions?

If you decide that going to college is not for you, here are some high-paying career options in trade schools.

Air Traffic Control A.S. Degree - (Median Annual Salary – $124,540). As air travel and drone traffic increases, the need for safe management of air traffic also grows in the 2020's. Air traffic controllers are the aviation professionals who monitor planes and communicate with pilots about when to take off and land safely in a given region. They analyze flight paths, issue flight path changes, and use radar equipment to direct aircraft movement. Air traffic controllers also coordinate all ground traffic for flight crew, maintenance, and baggage transport vehicles. Active listening, concise speaking, and on-demand operational analysis skills are needed for this job. If you believe that you have what it takes to work in the fast-paced world of an air traffic controller, you'll want to apply to an air traffic control degree program. In addition to the FAA's system to control all flights in the U.S., they will soon roll out

NOTE: This is a challenging and high-stress occupation.

systems to control drone package delivery and unmanned drone traffic, so demand will continue to increase for these jobs.

A two-year, associate degree is the minimum that you'll need to get started in the air traffic control career field. The Federal Aviation Administration (FAA) Air Traffic Collegiate Training Initiative partners with 36 schools across the nation to deliver industry-approved training for tomorrow's air traffic controllers. During your air traffic control degree program, you'll study topics such as flight operations, navigation, and air traffic control technology. Some specific courses that you'll take include aviation weather, aviation regulations, aviation safety, and exploration of aircraft.

Since you'll need to be certified by the FAA to work as an air traffic controller, your degree program prepares you to pass its certification exam. The FAA poses strict job requirements for air traffic controllers. In addition to getting an associate degree in air traffic control through one of the FAA's approved programs, you'll be required to pass a medical exam, a background security check, and a pre-employment test. You also must get an official school recommendation and be hired with the agency before your 32nd birthday. The job currently offers great pension and an early retirement age.

An alternative path for this career training is through the military. All branches of the military have aircraft and they train their own air traffic controllers.

National Elevator Industry Educational Program - (Median Annual Salary – $79,780). Due to Americans' collective preference to skip the stairs and take the elevator, mechanics are in high demand nationwide. While you'll need an extensive set of technical and physical fitness skills to land this lucrative job, you won't need a four-year degree. Aspiring elevator mechanics step onto this career path through ap-

---

Advisory services through Capital Advisory Group Advisory Services LLC and securities through United Planners Financial Services of America, a Limited Partnership. Member FINRA and SIPC. The Capital Advisory Group Advisory Services, LLC (CAG) and United Planners Financial Services are not affiliated.

prenticeship programs like the one that's offered by the National Elevator Industry Educational Program (NEIP).

The NEIEP is a school that works with trade associations, labor unions, and employers to recruit and train mechanical tradespersons. Its elevator mechanic apprenticeship program lasts for five years and covers all that you need to know about installing, maintaining, and repairing elevators. In the current NEIEP apprenticeship program, you'll have one year of probationary employment; the first six months include online coursework. Some classes that you'll take are electrical system fundamentals, workplace safety, and introduction to mechanical systems. The last four years of your apprenticeship program involve on-the-job training and advanced electrical and mechanical courses.

Many states require licensure for elevator mechanics due to public safety concerns. After completing the five-year NEIEP apprenticeship program, a graduate usually takes his licensing test and works as a full-fledged elevator mechanic. Learning while you work in a high-paying career field appeals to many people. However, NEIEP's recruitment process isn't an easy one. You must apply for the program, and the organization only takes applications at certain times of the year. You must be at least 18 years old and have a high school diploma, or its equivalent, to apply. After a successful application submittal, you'll be invited to take a mechanical aptitude test

Advisory services through Capital Advisory Group Advisory Services LLC and securities through United Planners Financial Services of America, a Limited Partnership. Member FINRA and SIPC. The Capital Advisory Group Advisory Services, LLC (CAG) and United Planners Financial Services are not affiliated.

so that NEIEP can see if you're a good candidate for its program. An aptitude test score of at least 70 percent allows you to move on to the interview process.

Military Veterans get preference for the NEIEP's apprenticeship program, and the International Union of Elevator Constructors (IUEC) is a key contact for former service members. The IUEC supports the Helmets to Hardhats program that helps former military members use their GI bill funds to get training in skilled trades.

Dental Hygiene A.S. Degree - (Median Annual Salary – $74,820). If you've ever experienced the pain of infected teeth or gums, you'll appreciate the contributions that dental hygienists make to the field of dentistry. You probably know that many tooth and gum problems stem from poor oral hygiene and aren't surprised that there is a high demand for dental hygienists. However, the yearly salaries that these dental professionals command may surprise you. Dental hygienists do dental preventive maintenance.

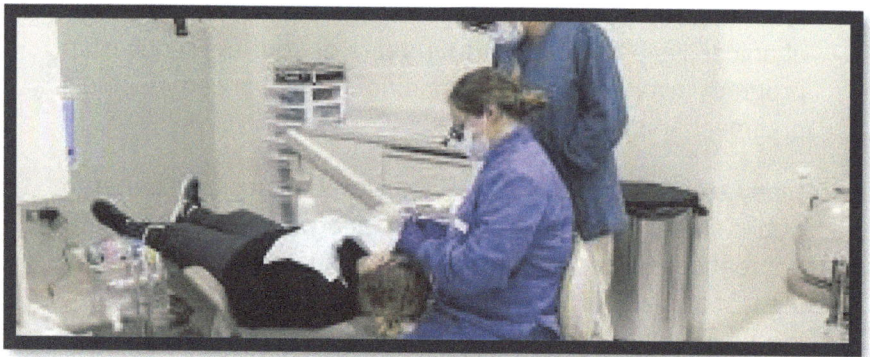

In addition to professionally removing plaque and tartar from teeth, they educate patients about proper brushing and flossing methods. To prepare for a career in dental hygiene, you'll need at least an associate degree in the subject. Human anatomy, microbiology, dental radiography, and oral pathology are some of the courses that you can expect to take in a typical

---

Advisory services through Capital Advisory Group Advisory Services LLC and securities through United Planners Financial Services of America, a Limited Partnership. Member FINRA and SIPC. The Capital Advisory Group Advisory Services, LLC (CAG) and United Planners Financial Services are not affiliated.

two-year, dental hygiene degree program. Upon graduation, you'll know about dental care techniques and treatments. You'll understand the industry's safety standards and laws. Employers at dental offices, public health clinics, and managed care facilities will also have confidence in your ability to manage and safeguard patient records according to national laws.

Dental Hygiene A.S. degree programs come in conventional and online classroom formats. What this degree program offers in schedule flexibility, it makes up for in course rigor. To work as a dental hygienist, graduates must pass a licensing exam.

Most educational programs are loaded with mathematics and science courses to prepare aspiring dental hygienists for that career-launching test. Most schools also require that you pass a background check as part of the program admittance process. When deciding on a dental hygiene school, there are a few elements that make some programs stand out from the rest. Choose one that's accredited by the American Dental Association's Commission on Dental Accreditation (CODA). You'll need credentials from an approved CODA program to sit for your licensing exam. Dental hygienist programs that partner with dental clinics offer benefits that others do not. Hands-on training at a dental clinic prepares you to ace your licensing test and real-world dental care.

NOTE: The Army, Navy and Air Force also train and have their own dental hygienists. This can be an alternate path to receive this training.

Diagnostic Medical Sonography A.S. Degree - (Median Annual Salary – $67,080). We credit advancements in medical technology for the longer life spans of today's population. One example of this is found in the field of diagnostic medical sonography. You can't treat an ailment if you don't know that it exists. Medical sonographers use imaging devices to detect anomalies in the human body or confirm normal conditions. You'll need a two-year Associate of Science in Di-

Advisory services through Capital Advisory Group Advisory Services LLC and securities through United Planners Financial Services of America, a Limited Partnership. Member FINRA and SIPC. The Capital Advisory Group Advisory Services, LLC (CAG) and United Planners Financial Services are not affiliated.

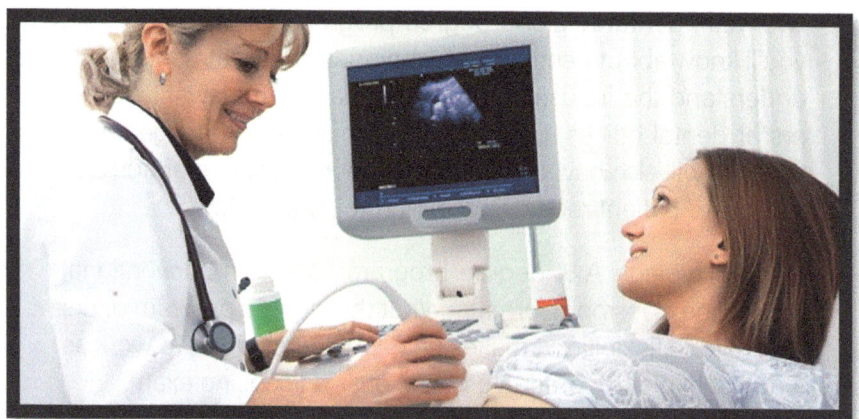

agnostic Medical Sonography degree to operate the imaging equipment for diagnostic medical tests. This degree program includes basic course work in math, human anatomy, physics, and medical terminology.

During your first semester of studies, you'll also take classes in communication and medical ethics to prepare you for interaction with patients in clinical settings. Specialized imaging and sonography training make up most of the remaining course work in these programs. Sonography degree graduates learn how to get, view, and assess medical images. They acquire in-depth knowledge in physics and physiology.

Most students complete medical sonography degree programs in two years or less. You can find diagnostic medical sonography programs in both traditional classroom and online formats. While most degree-seekers in other subjects enjoy the convenience of online courses, many sonography students choose to take classes on school campuses. Medical sonography requires its practitioners to have hands-on training and applied skills. You'll most often gain those skills through in-person, laboratory-style classes.

If you choose an online medical sonography degree program, make sure that it includes some first-hand learning opportunities in a lab setting or as part of an internship. Diagnostic

Advisory services through Capital Advisory Group Advisory Services LLC and securities through United Planners Financial Services of America, a Limited Partnership. Member FINRA and SIPC. The Capital Advisory Group Advisory Services, LLC (CAG) and United Planners Financial Services are not affiliated.

medical sonographers use imaging technology in a variety of healthcare situations from detecting blood clots in an active senior to checking in on a developing baby in the mother's womb. It's no wonder that this job is one of the fastest growing occupations in the nation.

Aviation Maintenance Technology A.S. Degree - (Median Annual Salary – $63,060). Things are looking up for job-seekers who graduate with aviation maintenance technology degrees. This is a two-year degree program that prepares you to troubleshoot, repair, and do preventive maintenance on airplanes. As air travel continues to play an important role in global logistics and leisure travel, aviation maintenance technology will take center stage in the industry. Employment as an aviation maintenance technician at airlines, aircraft manufacturers, and government agencies require formal education, credentials, and experience. Prior to COVID-19, there was a tremendous shortage of pilots. Today there is still a lot of opportunity in the field of aviation because of the expansion of drone traffic. Consider getting trained on both airplanes and drones.

The two-year aviation maintenance technology degree allows you to gain everything that you'll need to enter the aircraft maintenance career field. Besides course work in aviation systems, physics, and mathematics, you'll gain the knowledge to

---

Advisory services through Capital Advisory Group Advisory Services LLC and securities through United Planners Financial Services of America, a Limited Partnership. Member FINRA and SIPC. The Capital Advisory Group Advisory Services, LLC (CAG) and United Planners Financial Services are not affiliated.

pass the FAA Airframe and Power plant certification exam. Most FAA-sponsored degree programs include hands-on courses or internships in real-world settings that help you to gain the experience that employers want from their top employment candidates. Some specific courses that you can expect to take in an aviation maintenance technology degree program include aviation electrical and instrument systems, aircraft composite structures, and power plant line maintenance.

Aviation maintenance is heavily regulated to protect the safety of pilots, crew, and passengers. As a result, most aviation maintenance degree programs include classes about repair station operations, aircraft regulations, and technical report writing. While there are many aviation maintenance degree programs from which to choose, only FAA-approved programs will open the door to an aviation maintenance career. The military offers an alternate path for entry into aviation maintenance. Its aviation maintenance technicians undergo intense training, get valuable on-the-job experience, and sit for industry-recognized certification exams that result in credentials that can be used for civilian employment later.

Training and hands-on experience can also be achieved through the US Military Services. All departments of the Service use aircraft and drones, especially the Navy, Marines, and Air Force. The Army uses rotorcraft and drones mostly.

Home Inspection Certificate Program - (Median Annual Salary – $59,700). A retired couple falls in love with a vintage home in their new community. It's the right size, character, and price for their budget. They didn't get to be well-heeled retirees by throwing their money away. The couple wants to know more about the home's history and structure before they sign a contract. They call a home inspector to give them insight into the condition of the home's wiring, pipes, and foundation. This couple is not alone, and people just like them help to grow the demand for qualified home inspectors.

Advisory services through Capital Advisory Group Advisory Services LLC and securities through United Planners Financial Services of America, a Limited Partnership. Member FINRA and SIPC. The Capital Advisory Group Advisory Services, LLC (CAG) and United Planners Financial Services are not affiliated.

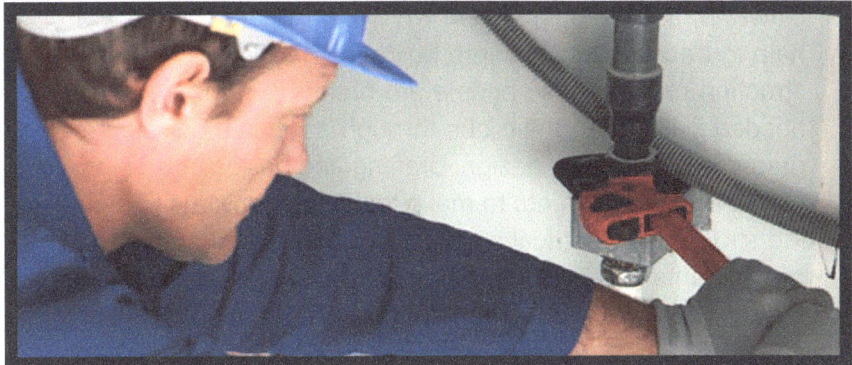

A certificate in home inspection is the key to getting work in this field. During a home inspection training program, you'll take classes about residential construction interiors, exteriors, and structures. You'll learn how to assess the condition of residential electrical, plumbing, and heating and cooling systems according to industry regulations. Some courses get you ready to do challenging home inspections via instruction about using drones to get aerial pictures of roofs for safer, more accurate assessments. You can complete most home inspection training programs in two years of part-time study or eight months of full-time study. Accreditation is an important attribute of a legitimate home inspection training program.

An accredited home inspection training program has been evaluated by an independent industry organization to make sure that its courses are appropriate and of high quality. In most states, you'll need a license to conduct home inspections as an independent contractor for home buyers, financial institutions, and insurance companies. A good home inspection program needs to prepare you to take your licensing exam. You also need to check the credentials and experience of the course instructors because they can't teach what they don't know.

Drafting and Design A.A.S Degree - (Median Annual Salary – $55,550). When it comes to real estate development, architects and general contractors get all the attention.

Advisory services through Capital Advisory Group Advisory Services LLC and securities through United Planners Financial Services of America, a Limited Partnership. Member FINRA and SIPC. The Capital Advisory Group Advisory Services, LLC (CAG) and United Planners Financial Services are not affiliated.

However, there are lesser-known design tradespersons who help to translate designs into building specifications for construction crews. These people are drafters, and they get the needed skills to do their jobs through associate degree programs in drafting and design. Drafting and design degree programs prepare students to make technical drawings of building structures, electrical systems, plumbing, and mechanical components for residential and commercial properties. Since sustainability is a requirement for many modern building projects, you'll likely learn how to depict photovoltaic systems within your building diagrams.

Specific courses that you can expect to take during a drafting and design degree program include engineering concepts and methods, introduction to geographic information systems, engineering graphics, and computer-aided design. You can choose to specialize in areas of drafting and design such as mechanical drafting, architectural drafting, and graphic design. With this degree you'll find work in multiple sectors such as construction, urban planning, and manufacturing. Outstanding drafting and design programs offer work-study projects or internships that help you to gain real-world experience. Look for ones that have job placement programs.

Plumbing Technology A.S. Degree - (Median Annual Salary – $53,910). If you're like everyone else, you take running water, flushing toilets, and heated rooms for granted. Plumbers are the tradespeople who make these modern necessities possible for homes and businesses across the globe. Plumbers install and repair the pipes that bring water and gas to buildings as well as sewage and waste water services. Getting a two-year associate degree in plumbing is the first step to landing a job in this field. Plumbing degree programs cover the installation and maintenance of plumbing lines and fixtures, water pumps, and sewer lines. You'll also take classes about heating, ventilation, and air conditioning systems.

Advisory services through Capital Advisory Group Advisory Services LLC and securities through United Planners Financial Services of America, a Limited Partnership. Member FINRA and SIPC. The Capital Advisory Group Advisory Services, LLC (CAG) and United Planners Financial Services are not affiliated.

Most plumbing degree programs include these specific courses:

- Plumbing technology
- Electricity fundamentals
- Occupational safety
- Plumbing fixture installation

While it's logical to think that you can only take a plumbing degree program in a classroom setting because of the hands-on nature of the subject, there are online plumbing degree programs. The appeal of these degree programs is convenience and flexibility since they feature mobile-friendly and interactive learning platforms that allow you to learn when and wherever you want. Most people opt for traditional classroom training when it comes to getting a plumbing degree.

Many schools offer hybrid courses that allow you to take plumbing theory via online platforms and to attend class in person for hands-on training. Plumbing degree programs usually take two years or less to complete. You'll need a state license to practice plumbing, and good plumbing degree programs include courses and projects that prepare you for your licensing exam. Check the licensing exam elements for your state to see if your chosen plumbing degree program covers those topics.

Petroleum Technology A.S. Degree - (Median Annual Salary – $53,300). While the demand for alternative energy is growing, fossil fuel-based systems still dominate the world's industrial landscape. The oil sector needs skilled persons to help find and extract oil, gas, and mineral deposits to fuel the world's cars, ships, and aircraft. An associate degree in petroleum technology will get you started on this career path. During a petroleum technology degree program, you'll take courses in petroleum geology, geophysics, and petroleum and natural gas chemistry. Your program will also cover topics such as environmental safety, oil drilling, and principles of

Advisory services through Capital Advisory Group Advisory Services LLC and securities through United Planners Financial Services of America, a Limited Partnership. Member FINRA and SIPC. The Capital Advisory Group Advisory Services, LLC (CAG) and United Planners Financial Services are not affiliated.

well control. When deciding on a petroleum technology degree program, choose one that has lots of industry partners. Some schools have built-in networks and affiliations that make finding jobs easier for their graduates than for graduates of other schools. If they offer alternative energy training in solar, nuclear or wind power, consider these sub-specialties because they will continue to grow much faster than the petroleum specialties.

Once trained, you can buy a business from a retiring baby boomer and make even more!

Paralegal Studies A.A. Degree - (Median Annual Salary – $50,940). Legal codes are meant to protect the innocent, punish guilty people, and bring remedies for injustices. Law offices that handle large case loads often rely on paralegals to help lawyers with legal research, court document preparation, and other administrative duties.

While there isn't a national standard for paralegal work, industry organizations such as the National Association of Legal Assistants and the National Federation of Paralegal Associations have set worthwhile de-facto career success criteria for paralegals over the years.

While you can learn the legal concepts for paralegal work in a job setting, most law offices only hire a paralegal who has completed at least a two-year, associate degree in paralegal studies. They often prefer candidates who also have paralegal certifications, and most paralegal degree programs offer classes that prepare you to take certification exams. In these degree programs, you'll learn about court proceedings, trial exhibit preparation, and case research. Some specific courses that you can expect to take in a paralegal studies program include contract law, civil litigation, and ethics.

Most paralegal degree programs also cover these common legal specialties:

Advisory services through Capital Advisory Group Advisory Services LLC and securities through United Planners Financial Services of America, a Limited Partnership. Member FINRA and SIPC. The Capital Advisory Group Advisory Services, LLC (CAG) and United Planners Financial Services are not affiliated.

- Real estate law
- Corporate law
- Labor law
- Education law
- Intellectual property law

While job growth rates for paralegals are expected to be much faster than average when compared to other occupations in the United States, just having a paralegal degree isn't always enough to get a job in the legal field. Good paralegal degree programs include internships. Besides offering valuable experience, these internships provide you with networking opportunities at local law offices. Consider a program that offers internships as part of their curriculum.

Military Service Technical Training - (Median Annual Salary – $61,487). As mentioned, service in the US Military can also be an avenue to gain valuable technical training that can be easily transferred into a lucrative civilian career. These trades can range from aviation related fields to firearms repair, engine and big truck repair, gas turbine engine operations and repair, heavy equipment operations, weather prediction and forecasting, electronics, computer programming and repair, HVAC system repair, welding, steam plant operations and repair, and even nuclear power plant operations.

An additional possible benefit from military training is that significant amounts of it have been evaluated for college credit that can be accepted by many civilian colleges. For example: The US Navy's Nuclear Power School has been evaluated for college credit worth 60 semester hours. (Note: The US Navy Nuclear Power training program is considered to be the most academically challenging of all military training programs across all of the US armed forces.)

Advisory services through Capital Advisory Group Advisory Services LLC and securities through United Planners Financial Services of America, a Limited Partnership. Member FINRA and SIPC. The Capital Advisory Group Advisory Services, LLC (CAG) and United Planners Financial Services are not affiliated.

If you choose the military as your path, there are some things you will want to consider:

Pros: You will be paid while attending this training and supplied with uniforms, housing, and board. You will get training and real hands-on experience in the field you enter. You will have the distinction of being a veteran when you leave the service with the respect and perks that accompany it. If you choose to stay in the service after your initial enlistment period is over, you could retire with a military pension after only 20 years.

Cons: You will be required to work and perform menial tasks, especially while a junior enlisted member. Boot camp is required in all services, is challenging, and not normally considered fun, but is of short duration, usually 6 to 8 weeks, depending on which military branch is chosen. Failure to successfully complete your military occupational specialty school will result in your being reassigned to a position of the military's choosing, which could be in a field that you do not want, and which may not translate to a civilian job you desire. Failure is not a good option.

If you are interested in a military training path, do your homework. Check all the services and zero in on the occupation you want. You will have to score well on the military written entrance exam (ASVAB) to ensure you are eligible for the specialty you have chosen. There are guides and practice ASVAB exams on-line to help you prepare for this test.

There also needs to be an opening for the military specialty you have chosen. If no openings are available in your chosen field, your entrance could be delayed until an opening is available, or you might have to choose a backup plan.

After completing your ASVAB exam, you will spend time with a military recruiter. Recruiters have quotas they must fill, and some military specialties always have openings and a higher recruiting point value for them, so that they could try and

Advisory services through Capital Advisory Group Advisory Services LLC and securities through United Planners Financial Services of America, a Limited Partnership. Member FINRA and SIPC. The Capital Advisory Group Advisory Services, LLC (CAG) and United Planners Financial Services are not affiliated.

convince you to enter an occupation field that is not what you want. If you qualify for your chosen field, get the recruiter to put it in writing in your enlistment contract. This prevents you being sidetracked into an occupational field and training you do not want, but which the military needs filled.

Lastly, if you enlist in the military go in with a positive attitude and devote your efforts to listening and following instructions. Try and do the best you can with every assignment with the goal of excelling in everything you do. This will go a long way toward impressing your supervisors and ensuring you are in line for promotions and any available additional training.

Niche.com's 2020 Best Trade Schools in Minnesota

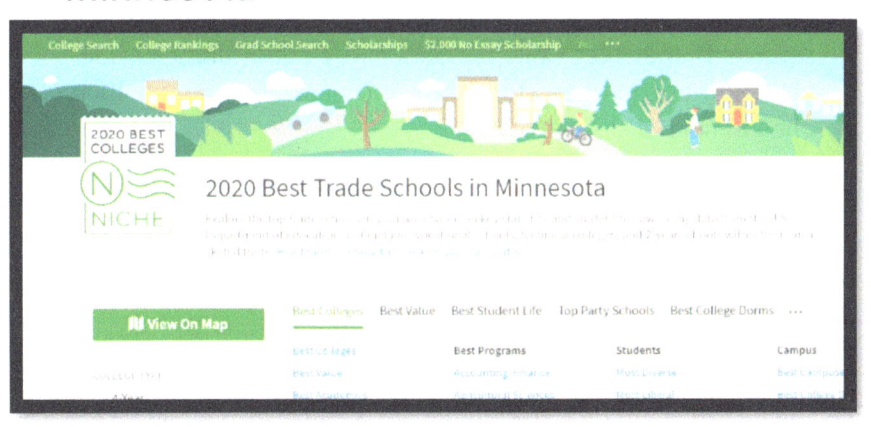

Niche.com is a great resource to find the best technical school in your area, based on the best colleges ranked by "Best Value," "Best in your Major," "Best College Dorms," and dozens of other criteria and demographics. Niche.com's list includes vocational schools, technical colleges, and two-year schools with a focus on a skilled trade. Use Niche.com to explore the top trade schools in your area based on key statistics and student reviews using data gathered from the U.S. Department of Education.

www.niche.com/colleges/search/best-trade-schools/s/minnesota/
https://www2.ed.gov/rschstat/

Advisory services through Capital Advisory Group Advisory Services LLC and securities through United Planners Financial Services of America, a Limited Partnership. Member FINRA and SIPC. The Capital Advisory Group Advisory Services, LLC (CAG) and United Planners Financial Services are not affiliated.

Ridgewater College

Ridgewater College is a two-year college located in Wilmar, MN. [www.ridgewater.edu] Ridgewater College offers over 100 degrees and certificates in a wide range of academic areas. We can help you find the right academic path for you. We know that choosing a degree option can be confusing, and would love to walk you through the process.

Certificates, diplomas, and degrees differ in the time it takes to earn each as well as the credits required in order to graduate. Each of these academic achievements is suitable for certain specific fields or career goals.

Student life is rich with opportunities for extracurricular activities and interests. The tuition can't be beat for the value you receive. Ridgewater College offers every opportunity for success and encourages students to be passionate about their chosen field of study.

Ridgewater's general standards and costs:

- Overall Niche Grade: B+
- 100% Acceptance Rate
- Cost: $11,161 Net Price

Minnesota State Community and Technical College

Minnesota State Community and Technical College is a two-year college located in Fergus Falls, MN. [www.minnesota.edu] Minnesota State Community and Technical College is a public community and technical college with multiple campuses in Minnesota. The college is a member of the Minnesota State Colleges and Universities system.

Here are some student comments about their experience at M State:

Advisory services through Capital Advisory Group Advisory Services LLC and securities through United Planners Financial Services of America, a Limited Partnership. Member FINRA and SIPC. The Capital Advisory Group Advisory Services, LLC (CAG) and United Planners Financial Services are not affiliated.

M State Sophomore: *"M State is a wonderful college to attend whether you just graduated high school, you're in the workforce and need more education, or you are trying to climb the ladder in your current career."*

"The Professors at M State are active listeners to each individual. They are always willing to lend a helping hand so students can excel! Also, because class sizes are smaller, professors are able to get more one-on-one time with students. During class hours lectures are thorough and very easy to understand. Whenever students do not understand, Professors are available and easy to talk to!"

"Every staff member at M State works their hardest to make sure students get the best out of their education. They go to great lengths to ensure the best college experience into every student! The professors, advisers, administrators, and other staff all work together to ensure quality!"

Minnesota State's general standards and costs:

- Overall Niche Grade: B
- 100% Acceptance Rate
- Cost: $9,662 Net Price

Dakota County Technical College

Dakota County Technical College is a public two-year technical college located in Rosemount, Minnesota inside the Minneapolis/St. Paul metropolitan area. [www.dctc.edu] DCTC belongs to the Minnesota State Colleges and Universities System and is one of five stand-alone technical colleges in the state.

Below are some student comments about DCTC:

DCTC Freshman: *"I have just completed my first year at DCTC. It's a great campus, small enough to get to know students and* teachers actually know your name. It provides great facilities, however it does not have on campus accommodation. I feel this would be a great draw card to new students or encourage more international students."

"I have found a few teachers treat those in the athletic program with disdain. Not all athletes are stupid. We do want to learn but we also have found passion with our choice of sport. The athletic tutors have been amazing, helping to juggle workloads, training and traveling."

Dakota County Technical's general standards and costs:

- Overall Niche Grade: B
- 100% Acceptance Rate
- Cost: $11,457 Net Price

Final Words on Technical School Opportunities

While no one can predict economic conditions with exact accuracy, you can position yourself to take advantage of opportunities if you have the right training and credentials. The described degree, certification, and apprenticeship programs allow you to gain marketable, ready-to-use skills for the current and future job market. They deliver high returns on time and financial investments that are hard to get from traditional four-year university degree programs.

If you want to become a doctor, majoring in biology is a solid choice as an undergraduate since you'll learn about the functions of living organisms, including human beings, in great depth. And should you choose to not go on to medical school after all, you can still earn a very good salary as a biologist in bio-technical, medical and other industries with a starting salary around $40,000 and over $71,000 at mid-career (or even more as a microbiologist).

While getting into law school doesn't usually require a specific major, having critical reading and writing skills are essential and these can be developed and honed in majors like English, political science, and marketing and communications, among others.

As we've already discussed, English majors aren't completely left behind when it comes to earning potential after completing an undergraduate degree. Political science and marketing and communications majors also enjoy good salaries, earning around $40,000 at the start of their careers and up to double this amount at mid-career.

We will next explore college opportunities not requiring a Bachelor's degree.

Advisory services through Capital Advisory Group Advisory Services LLC and securities through United Planners Financial Services of America, a Limited Partnership. Member FINRA and SIPC. The Capital Advisory Group Advisory Services, LLC (CAG) and United Planners Financial Services are not affiliated.

"Money is usually attracted, not pursued."

"Don't let money run your life, let money run your life better."

—John Rampton

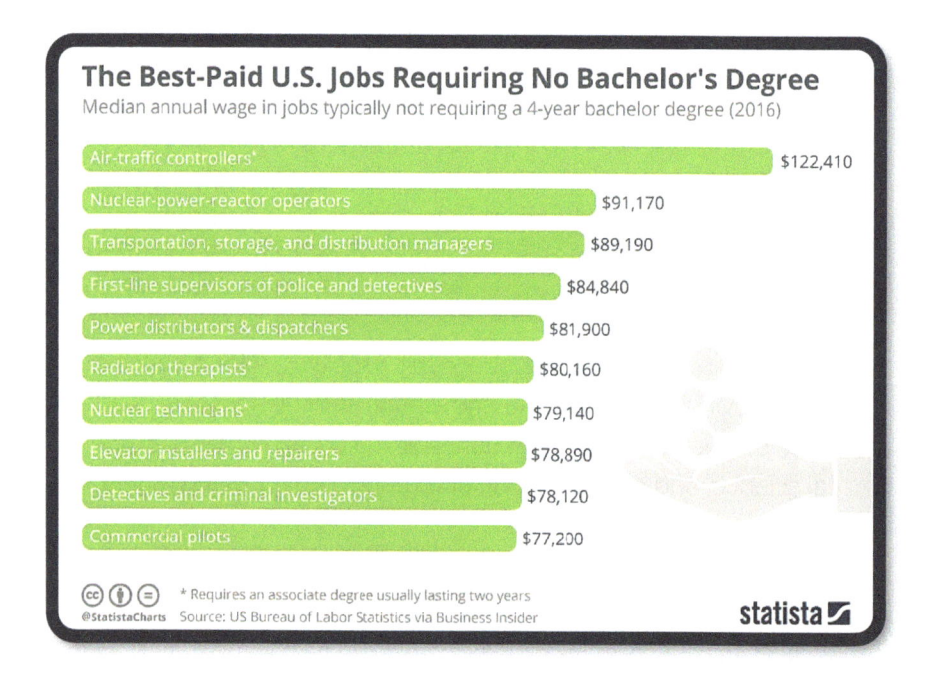

The Best-Paid U.S. Jobs Requiring No Bachelor's Degree
Median annual wage in jobs typically not requiring a 4-year bachelor degree (2016)

Job	Median Annual Wage
Air-traffic controllers*	$122,410
Nuclear-power-reactor operators	$91,170
Transportation, storage, and distribution managers	$89,190
First-line supervisors of police and detectives	$84,840
Power distributors & dispatchers	$81,900
Radiation therapists*	$80,160
Nuclear technicians*	$79,140
Elevator installers and repairers	$78,890
Detectives and criminal investigators	$78,120
Commercial pilots	$77,200

*Requires an associate degree usually lasting two years
Source: US Bureau of Labor Statistics via Business Insider
@StatistaCharts — statista

"Don't think that money does everything or you are going to end up doing everything for money."

—Voltaire

1.2 What Are The Best-Paying Professions Requiring Just a Two-Year Associate's Degree?

Historically, healthcare has been the most lucrative associate degree option that was guaranteed to earn you a good wage. However, these rankings show that technology-focused majors can also be a good option for high salary earnings. That being said, health-related subjects have a higher than average percentage of alumni who say that their work is very meaningful.

Of course, not all associate degrees lead to high salaries. An early childhood education program usually leads to low salary potential, but most graduates do love the work saying that their jobs make the world a better place.

So if you are short on time, want to get your career started quickly or just don't think a four-year school is right for you, one of the associate degree options on this list may be a smart choice. Also, today some high-schools allow you to attend college. Both my daughters took this option and will have associate degrees when they graduate from High School - for <u>free</u>. Not only can it save you money, but it can also potentially get you into a better college if you go on for further education.

Physician Assistant Studies - Students who enroll in physician assistant studies programs learn skills necessary to work as a physician assistant in a medical facility or clinic setting and it requires an Associate Degree; starting pay is $55,600, by mid-career it is paying $98,300.

Radiation Therapy - A radiation therapy degree includes coursework in oncology, pathology, radiation physics and treatment planning. Typically, they will also be required to have hands-on experience in a clinical setting and it requires an Associate Degree. Starting pay is $61,400, by mid-career it is paying $93,300, and has a 92% placement.

Software Engineering - Students who enroll in software engineering programs learn how to develop new ways for software to function. Classes include coding and mathematical courses to help students pursue this major. Common employers of software engineers include Microsoft, Google, Intel, Amazon, and other enterprise-level tech companies and it requires an Associate Degree. Starting pay is $48,100, by mid-career it is paying $90,700 and has a 33% placement.

Where you go to college does matter here, so consider colleges specializing in software engineering.

Other high-paying professions that require only an Associate's Degree:

Degree Major/Specialty	Starting Pay	Mid-Career Pay	Placement %
- Project Management	$48,900	$89,300	n/a
- Computer Science	$40,600	$83,700	48%
- Fire Protection Engineering	$37,100	$83,100	n/a
- Instrumentation Technology	$36,700	$81,700	63%
- Biomedical Engineering	$44,000	$80,900	n/a

Advisory services through Capital Advisory Group Advisory Services LLC and securities through United Planners Financial Services of America, a Limited Partnership. Member FINRA and SIPC. The Capital Advisory Group Advisory Services, LLC (CAG) and United Planners Financial Services are not affiliated.

Finding the Best Two-Year Colleges

Here are some of the top-rated two-year colleges criteria we use to rate institutions. Consider adding your own criteria to refine your options, like proximity to family, vegan restaurants close by, or one that excels in your favorite sports.

Factor	Description	Weight
Academics Grade	Niche Academics grade, which incorporates factors such as acceptance rate, quality of professors, as well as student and alumni surveys regarding academics at the school.	40.0%
Value Grade	Niche Value grade, which incorporates statistics such as average loan amount, alumni earnings and student surveys regarding value.	27.5%
Professors Grade	Niche Professors grade, which incorporates factors such as number of awards won by faculty, student-faculty ratio, as well as student surveys regarding professor quality.	7.5%
Campus Grade	Niche Campus Quality grade, which incorporates factors such as quality of campus food and housing, as well as student surveys regarding facilities on campus.	5.0%

Advisory services through Capital Advisory Group Advisory Services LLC and securities through United Planners Financial Services of America, a Limited Partnership. Member FINRA and SIPC. The Capital Advisory Group Advisory Services, LLC (CAG) and United Planners Financial Services are not affiliated.

Diversity Grade	Niche Diversity grade, which incorporates factors such as ethnic composition of the student body, proportion of international students and out-of-state students, as well as student surveys regarding diversity on campus.	5.0%
Student Life Grade	Niche Student Life grade, which incorporates statistics such as safety, diversity, athletics and student surveys regarding student life.	5.0%
Student Surveys on Overall Experience	Niche survey responses scored on a 1-5 scale regarding the overall experience of students and alumni at each school.	5.0%
Local Area Grade	Niche Local Area grade, which incorporates factors such as median rent, local crime rates, access to amenities, as well as student surveys regarding the local area around campus.	2.5%
Safety Grade	Safety grade, which incorporates factors such as campus crime rate, local crime rate, as well as student surveys regarding health and safety services on campus.	2.5%

Advisory services through Capital Advisory Group Advisory Services LLC and securities through United Planners Financial Services of America, a Limited Partnership. Member FINRA and SIPC. The Capital Advisory Group Advisory Services, LLC (CAG) and United Planners Financial Services are not affiliated.

Northland Community & Technical College

Northland Community & Technical College is a two-year college located in Thief River Falls, MN. [www.northlandcollege.edu] Northland is rated the 92nd best community college in America. Below are some student comments about Northland:

UND Junior: *"So far, Northland is a world different from UND, where I spent three previous years. You don't feel like a number at Northland. It is incredibly easy to communicate with your teachers and administrators. Your advisor and teachers actually remember your name! The facility is up to date with relevant technology. Parking is a breeze! Fellow students are friendly too."*

"This is a great place to lower your educational cost and time while still getting cutting edge education and hands-on relevant courses that translate into an immediate career after completing your specific degree. I highly recommend this college over UND."

Northland's general standards and costs:

- Overall Niche Grade: B
- 100% Acceptance Rate
- Cost: $10,263 Net Price

Advisory services through Capital Advisory Group Advisory Services LLC and securities through United Planners Financial Services of America, a Limited Partnership. Member FINRA and SIPC. The Capital Advisory Group Advisory Services, LLC (CAG) and United Planners Financial Services are not affiliated.

Minnesota West Community & Technical College

Minnesota West Community & Technical College is a two-year college located in Granite Falls, MN. Minnesota West is the 116th best community college in America.

Below are some student comments about Minnesota West:

MN West Sophomore: *"Minnesota West is a nice community college. It's local for me so it's a perfect fit to jump-start my college career. I'm going to be graduating soon and go to a four-year degree college. My credits will transfer well, all things seem to be looking good. There's not much more I could ask for from them. The teachers I've had have been good, and the people I've interacted with seem friendly."*

"Overall, I do like the college. I've take almost all of my classes online and my experiences with that have been very satisfying. I would recommend this college to people who are interested."

Minnesota West's general standards and costs:

- Overall Niche Grade: B
- 100% Acceptance Rate
- Cost: $9,946 Net Price

Advisory services through Capital Advisory Group Advisory Services LLC and securities through United Planners Financial Services of America, a Limited Partnership. Member FINRA and SIPC. The Capital Advisory Group Advisory Services, LLC (CAG) and United Planners Financial Services are not affiliated.

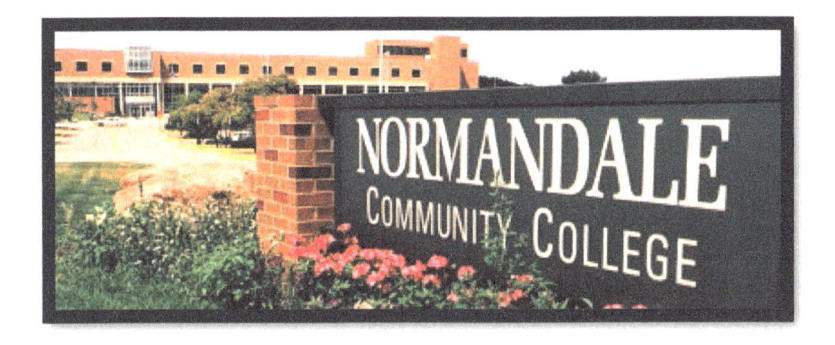

Normandale Community College

Two-Year College Bloomington, MN
www.normandale.edu

#225 Best Community Colleges in America

Normandale Community College is the largest community college in Minnesota with an enrollment of close to 15,000 students and a Continuing Education and Customized Training (CECT) division that provides our workforce with competitive skills, yet, it still maintains a small college feel in the world-class City of Bloomington. Normandale is also home to an extraordinary Japanese Garden which has become a destination and a beautiful community resource they are proud to host.

This book's co-author, Brett Machtig has served on Normandale's business advisory board since 2016. Both of Brett's daughters attended Normadale College, enrolling in their sophomore year of high school. Brett's youngest daughter, Abby wants to be a doctor and graduated with an associate degree that greatly accelerated her college at a fraction of the cost.

Advisory services through Capital Advisory Group Advisory Services LLC and securities through United Planners Financial Services of America, a Limited Partnership. Member FINRA and SIPC. The Capital Advisory Group Advisory Services, LLC (CAG) and United Planners Financial Services are not affiliated.

Below are some student comments about Normadale:

NCC Sophomore: *"My experience with Normandale overall has been excellent. The community is warm and welcoming, the teachers are knowledgeable and accessible, and the opportunities for growth are incredible.*

The opportunities for bonding as a campus are less plentiful than in four-year colleges (from what I've heard/seen) but in turn, there is a greater focus on learning and achievement. A truly wonderful college and experience, for a fraction of the price of most other colleges."

Normandale's general standards and costs:

- Overall Niche Grade: B
- 100% Acceptance Rate
- Cost: $11,169 Net Price, $0 if in the local high school program

"Vitally important [for the young] is to realize the value of education and then to cultivate earnestly, aggressively, ceaselessly the habit of self-education."

—B.C. Forbes

"The art of money is not [just] making it, but in keeping it."

—Proverb

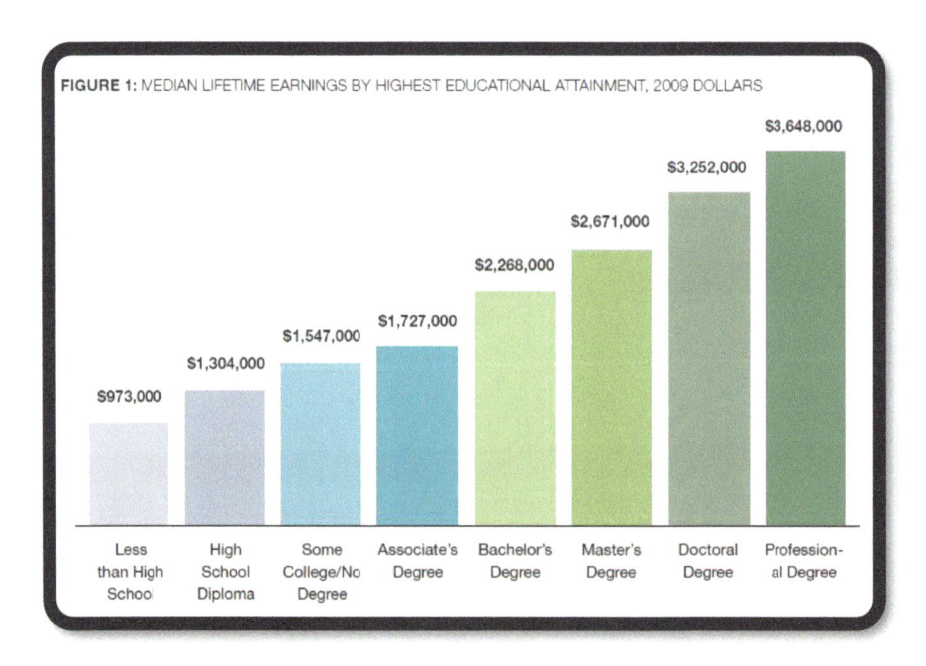

FIGURE 1: MEDIAN LIFETIME EARNINGS BY HIGHEST EDUCATIONAL ATTAINMENT, 2009 DOLLARS

Education Level	Median Lifetime Earnings
Less than High School	$973,000
High School Diploma	$1,304,000
Some College/No Degree	$1,547,000
Associate's Degree	$1,727,000
Bachelor's Degree	$2,268,000
Master's Degree	$2,671,000
Doctoral Degree	$3,252,000
Professional Degree	$3,648,000

"Education is the passport to the future, for tomorrow belongs to those who prepare for today."

—Malcom X

1.3 What Bachelor's Degree Careers Pay Higher Incomes?

What colleges are worth more in getting a job? Now that we've seen that a college degree is (more than) worth it, let's look at how the major you select can make a difference to your earnings down the road. A study released by Georgetown's Center on Education and the Workforce reveals that the difference in lifetime wages for different majors is enormous. In fact, the difference between lifetime wages for the highest and lowest paying majors is $3.4 million!

In keeping with current trends, the College Salary Report shows that the best bachelor degrees are mostly STEM-focused, meaning they are focused on science, technology, engineering or math. STEM degrees continue to be some of the highest paying degrees on the College Salary Report year after year. The top three highest paying college Bachelor's Degree majors include:

Petroleum Engineering - At the very top of the list is petroleum engineering, yielding a base salary of nearly $100,000 for recent graduates. The oil and gas industry is a hot one as companies around the world seek new petroleum resources and how to mine and use them as efficiently as possible and petroleum engineers provide the know-how when it comes to geology, drilling and other fields to accomplish their work.

Chemical and Electrical Engineering - Chemical and electrical engineering jobs are next, earning recent graduates base salaries around $61,000, which grow to over $100,000 at mid-career. Graduates in these disciplines can find employment in a wide variety of fields, from developing and improving consumer products like laundry detergent and cosmetics to designing automated production systems for factories.

Aerospace Engineering - Elon Musk needs you! Aerospace engineering is another field that has generally commanded good salaries for graduates, though a severe cut in funding of the federal space program in the U.S. will likely have a large negative impact on job prospects in this field. However, there are other organizations that require the expertise and knowledge of aerospace engineers to build and refine all types of aircraft for consumer, commercial, and military use. Majors in this difficult discipline can expect to earn just over $60,000 to start and surpass $100,000 per year at mid-career.

Computer Engineering and Computer Science - Given the prominence of computers, cell phones and other electronic devices in so many jobs and everyday use at home, the software and peripherals needed for them are extremely important as well. This is where computer engineering and computer science majors come in, developing the software and firmware that drive electronic devices and computers as well as the hardware, peripherals and accessories that interface with them.

Majors in these fields can expect to earn around $60,000 after completing an undergraduate degree, which will grow close to $100,000 at mid-career.

Information Technology and Information Systems - Note that computer engineering and computer science are different from information technology and information systems majors. The fields of information technology and information systems deal primarily with the application of computer systems in businesses, from systems that manage automated production lines to the email and other communication and management systems used within a company. These fields, while still challenging, don't require the same type of knowledge and expertise as computer engineering and computer science majors and their starting salaries are around $48,000.

Applied Mathematics - At the top of the earnings list when it comes to math-related fields is applied mathematics, with graduates earning over $50,000 when starting out and pulling in close to $100,000 at mid-career. Applied mathematicians can work in several fields building mathematical models to solve business problems or predict behavior or the results of systems and processes.

Statistics - Statistics is another field where college graduates have the earning potential to stay in the black with starting salaries around $50,000 for recent graduates and in the low-$90,000s at mid-career. Statisticians focus on the collection, organization, and analysis of data and can work in a variety of industries from pharmaceutical to insurance companies and many others. This major also requires strong computer knowledge and skills since the data analysis is primarily completed using complex computer programs.

Finance - If you'd rather use your math skills to manage money, a major in finance may be right up your alley and will put you on track to earn around $46,000 per year after graduation and up to nearly $90,000 at mid-career. Finance majors go on to work in financial institutions, government agencies and companies in every industry to analyze and report on assets and liabilities.

Fashion Design -Fashion design is a field that requires a bit more than the ability to put together a well-coordinated outfit. Fashion and its trends can be an indirect gauge of what's going on in cultures and societies around the world. It takes a unique eye to identify these trends and the business sense to capitalize on them to make a successful fashion designer. Upon graduation, starting salaries aren't stunning off the bat (around $35,000) but this salary can double by mid-career. There is also a higher under employment in this field, as many graduates find jobs in retail, instead of fashion design.

English literature - Many people lament the generic-sounding English degree and it's often stereotyped as a major that doesn't do a good job of preparing graduates for a real job. While most stereotypes have a grain of truth to them, they're never entirely accurate.

English majors can study literature and other types of writing from cultures around the world in multiple eras and build strong writing skills along the way as well. These abilities can easily translate to jobs in journalism, publishing, and other areas where writing or the evaluation of written material is key and can earn graduates under $40,000 shortly after graduation and over $65,000 per year at mid-career.

Advisory services through Capital Advisory Group Advisory Services LLC and securities through United Planners Financial Services of America, a Limited Partnership. Member FINRA and SIPC. The Capital Advisory Group Advisory Services, LLC (CAG) and United Planners Financial Services are not affiliated.

Health Sciences - Many health-related professions will be required as our population gets older.

Here are just a few:

Specialty	Median Income	High Income	Low Mid-Career
Pharmacist	$122,499	$134,956	$109,993
Laboratory Services Dir.	$108,232	$137,376	$86,205
Surgical Physician Assistant	$99,313	$124,285	$70,138
Nurse Practitioner	$96,850	$112,869	$83,259
Chief MRI Technologist	$80,887	$93,096	$66,049
Pathology Assistant	$76,666	$102,143	$36,781
Audiologist	$74,385	$88,096	$62,856
Respiratory Therapist	$72,380	$86,629	$57,592
Cyto-technologist	$69,190	$81,864	$57,358

Advisory services through Capital Advisory Group Advisory Services LLC and securities through United Planners Financial Services of America, a Limited Partnership. Member FINRA and SIPC. The Capital Advisory Group Advisory Services, LLC (CAG) and United Planners Financial Services are not affiliated.

The Best Four-Year Colleges in the State of Minnesota

Here are some of the top rated four-year colleges in Minnesota, based upon the criteria on page 33. The same methodology is used to produce the Overall Niche Grade for each ranked school. Statistics obtained from the U.S. Department of Education represent the most recent data available, as self-reported by the colleges.

Advisory services through Capital Advisory Group Advisory Services LLC and securities through United Planners Financial Services of America, a Limited Partnership. Member FINRA and SIPC. The Capital Advisory Group Advisory Services, LLC (CAG) and United Planners Financial Services are not affiliated.

Carleton College

Four-Year College, Northfield, MN
www.carleton.edu

#1 Best College in Minnesota
The Top Rated School

- World-Class Academics - Carleton is renowned for its rigorous liberal arts curriculum and excellence in undergraduate teaching.

- A Friendly, Vibrant Campus - Carleton students balance academics with a full life outside the classroom, through hundreds of student groups and campus activities.

- Affordable to All - Carleton offers some of the best financial aid in the U.S. They are committed to meeting 100% of financial need for all admitted students, all four years.

- Global Opportunities - More than 70% of Carleton students study abroad — from Paris and London to Dakar and Shanghai.

Carleton Sophomore: *"Carleton has wonderful faculty and their selling point would definitely be the academics. Carleton is also very generous with giving financial aid to students, which has helped me tremendously. Although it is secluded in a small town, I find this to be very good for my safety (honestly, you'll probably be too busy being on campus to even want to go to the cities). I think the dorms are above average for a lot of colleges in America. I've visited many, and Carleton's "worst dorm" (which I lived in) was very nice. Overall, great school! Can't wait to finish my degree."*

"A+" Overall Niche Grade, 21% Acceptance Rate, $28,148 Net Price, 1360-1530 SAT Range

---

Advisory services through Capital Advisory Group Advisory Services LLC and securities through United Planners Financial Services of America, a Limited Partnership. Member FINRA and SIPC. The Capital Advisory Group Advisory Services, LLC (CAG) and United Planners Financial Services are not affiliated.

Macalester College

Four-Year College, Saint Paul, MN
www.macalester.edu

#2 Best College in Minnesota

Macalester was founded in 1874 on a firm belief in the transformational power of the liberal arts education. Since then, the students and alumni have demonstrated that power as a force for positive change, in turn attracting a growing community of learners from around the world.

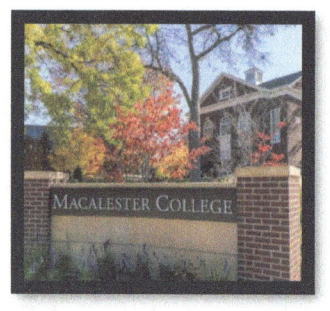

Today Macalester is recognized as a global leader among liberal arts colleges, with the highest standards for scholarship and a continuing commitment to internationalism, multiculturalism, and service to society.

Macalester Sophomore: *"Macalester is excellent academically. The professors are intelligent, engaging, and eager to help students pursue their interests."*

"The location in the twin cities is helpful for finding internships and volunteer opportunities. While the campus is close to downtown Saint Paul, it is located in a very safe residential neighborhood, which means that much of the student life is focused on campus. The athletics are considerably good for a division three school."

"There are also a wide range of clubs and other activities for students to be engaged in. The school could be much more diverse, but it is more diverse than other liberal arts colleges I have visited. Overall, it is an excellent school!"

"A+" Overall Niche Grade, 41% Acceptance Rate, $30,672 Net Price, 1300-1480 SAT Range

---

Advisory services through Capital Advisory Group Advisory Services LLC and securities through United Planners Financial Services of America, a Limited Partnership. Member FINRA and SIPC. The Capital Advisory Group Advisory Services, LLC (CAG) and United Planners Financial Services are not affiliated.

University of Minnesota - Twin Cities

Four-Year College, Minneapolis, MN
twin-cities.umn.edu

#3 Best College in Minnesota

Student Life:

- 23 Varsity athletic teams
- 3,400 Students in Greek Life
- 900+ Student Organizations
- 90% First-year students living on campus
- 21% Students of color
- 31,455 undergraduate students (as of Fall, 2018)
- 16,038 graduate and professional students (as of Fall, 2018)

Citizens of the World:

- 130 Nations represented on campus
- 7,212 International students
- 2,576 U students studying abroad

Advisory services through Capital Advisory Group Advisory Services LLC and securities through United Planners Financial Services of America, a Limited Partnership. Member FINRA and SIPC. The Capital Advisory Group Advisory Services, LLC (CAG) and United Planners Financial Services are not affiliated.

Award-Winning Faculty - the 3,900 faculty include members of the National Academy of Sciences, the National Academy of Engineering, and the Institute of Medicine, plus the American Academy of Arts and Sciences, among other bodies. Current and former faculty have won Guggenheim Fellowships, MacArthur Fellowships ("genius grants"), Nobel Prizes, and other significant honors.

Their staff are known for being exceptionally dedicated—committed to the University of Minnesota's mission and to each other. While nationwide the average time spent with an employer is four years, employees stay at the University of Minnesota for an average of eight years. They stay because they know their work matters.

UofM Alum: *"I loved attending University of Minnesota. It had everything that I wanted to study and that was a lot! During my time there, I studied American Indian studies as well as Ojibwa language, Spanish, and Portuguese. I also studied Psychology and received my Master's degree in Social Work.*

Since University of Minnesota has one of the largest study abroad programs in the country, I was able to study abroad 3 times and really hone my Spanish and Portuguese speaking skills. I also loved living on campus. The Twin Cities have a lot to do and it is exciting to live in such [a] progressive city!"

"A+" Overall Niche Grade, 50% Acceptance Rate, $16,808 , Net Price 1270-1480 SAT Range

St. Olaf College

Four-Year College, Northfield, MN
wp.stolaf.edu

#4 Best College in Minnesota

Founded in 1874 by Norwegian Lutheran immigrants, St. Olaf is a nationally ranked liberal arts college of the ELCA located in Northfield, Minnesota. There are 3,040 Students on a 350 acre campus.

Here are the statistics of the 2020 freshman class:

- Number Applied 5,949
- Number Enrolled 786
- Median Combined SAT Score 1260
- Median ACT Score 29
- Average High School GPA 3.64
- First Generation 18% Freshman

St. Olaf Student: *"St. Olaf College is an extremely competitive college to get into being one of the best institutions in Minnesota as well as nationally. St. Olaf has a top notch Music Department and program that parallels prestigious conservatories with internationally touring Choirs, Bands and Orchestras. While the college is religiously affiliated, the school is liberal and accepting. The cafeteria is easily one of the best in the country and the campus is stunning and modern. Academic rigor is at a very high level and demands the very best of students. St. Olaf College has been the right choice for me."*

"A" Overall Niche Grade, 43% Acceptance Rate, $27,587 Net Price, 1150-1400 SAT Range

Gustavus Adolphus College

Four-Year College, Saint Peter, MN
gustavus.edu

#5 Best College in Minnesota

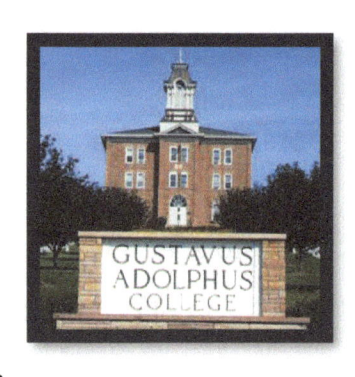

Gustavus Adolphus College is a highly selective, private, coeducational, residential liberal arts college affiliated with the Evangelical Lutheran Church in America (ELCA). Founded in 1862, it has valued its Lutheran and Swedish heritages throughout its history. The college is guided by five core values: excellence, community, justice, service, and faith.

Student Life

- More than 120 special interest groups and organizations
- Five daily Sabbath services, a Sunday worshiping community service, and one evening praise service weekly
- 12 student-run religious organizations
- More than 75% of Gustavus students participate in service each year, either through service programs or service-learning
- 75% participation in more than 30 intramural activities and 9 club sports
- Fulbright, Goldwater, Marshall, Rhodes, Truman, National Science Foundation, and NCAA Postgraduate fellowship winners

Faculty

- Full-time faculty of 184; 40 part-time
- 78% of faculty members hold tenure-line positions; 64 per-

Advisory services through Capital Advisory Group Advisory Services LLC and securities through United Planners Financial Services of America, a Limited Partnership. Member FINRA and SIPC. The Capital Advisory Group Advisory Services, LLC (CAG) and United Planners Financial Services are not affiliated.

cent are tenured.

- 100% of tenured faculty members hold the terminal degree in their fields.
- Student-to-faculty ratio: 11:1
- Average class size: 18

Campus Facilities

- 340 beautifully landscaped acres
- Designated in 2015 by the Carnegie Foundation as a "community-engaged campus"—the highest national distinction available for a college.

Gustavus Freshman: *"Gustavus is a fantastic place for an undergraduate degree. What attracted me most to the school was the strong community and support for all students. The professors really care [about] your success, and they care about you as a person."*

"Anyone on campus will refer you to the best place of help for what you need."

"The food is really good, as far as college cafeterias go. The campus is in a nice small town, 15 minutes from Mankato and one hour from the twin cities. My favorite place on campus is definitely the arboretum!"

"A" Overall Niche Grade, 68% Acceptance Rate, $29,894 Net Price 1080-1340 SAT Range

IVY League Colleges

There are a few colleges where attending will add tremendously to your income. Here are the top schools by income of the average graduate:

	College	Starting	Mid-Career
1	Harvey Mudd College	$91,400	$162,500
2	Massachusetts Institute of Technology	$88,300	$158,100
3	United States Naval Academy	$79,600	$152,600
4	Princeton University	$77,300	$150,500
5	California Institute of Technology	$87,600	$150,300
6	Harvard University	$76,400	$147,700
7	Stanford University	$81,800	$147,100
8	Santa Clara University	$71,100	$146,300
9	United States Military Academy	$81,100	$146,300
10	Babson College	$73,000	$146,200
11	Colgate University	$69,700	$144,800
12	Stevens Institute of Technology	$75,800	$144,300
13	SUNY Maritime College	$74,500	$143,400
14	University of Pennsylvania	$73,700	$142,900
15	Colorado School of Mines	$75,800	$142,800
16	Williams College	$67,600	$142,300
17	Dartmouth College	$73,300	$141,400
18	Yale University	$72,700	$141,300
19	Swarthmore College	$67,700	$141,000
20	Albany College of Pharmacy and Health Sciences	$77,700	$140,800
21	Washington and Lee University	$66,500	$140,600
22	United States Air Force Academy	$77,600	$140,400
23	Lehigh University	$70,300	$139,800
24	University of California-Berkeley	$72,600	$138,800
25	Claremont McKenna College	$70,700	$138,500

Advisory services through Capital Advisory Group Advisory Services LLC and securities through United Planners Financial Services of America, a Limited Partnership. Member FINRA and SIPC. The Capital Advisory Group Advisory Services, LLC (CAG) and United Planners Financial Services are not affiliated.

	College	Starting	Mid-Career
26	United States Merchant Marine Academy	$84,300	$138,500
27	Webb Institute	$81,500	$137,900
28	Rose-Hulman Institute of Technology	$76,600	$137,700
29	Georgia Institute of Technology-Main Campus	$74,500	$137,300
30	University of Notre Dame	$68,300	$136,900
31	Brown University	$69,900	$136,700
32	Carnegie Mellon University	$78,600	$136,500
33	Haverford College	$61,300	$136,300
34	Cooper Union for the Advancement of Science and Art	$69,300	$136,100
35	Worcester Polytechnic Institute	$74,600	$135,500
36	Rensselaer Polytechnic Institute	$72,600	$135,200
37	Duke University	$72,300	$135,000
38	Georgetown University	$67,200	$134,500
39	Rice University	$72,400	$134,100
40	Clarkson University	$66,800	$133,100
41	Cornell University	$71,600	$133,100
42	California State University Maritime Academy	$69,800	$132,900
43	Columbia University in the City of New York	$73,700	$132,100
44	Lafayette College	$68,400	$131,800
45	Bucknell University	$67,700	$129,500
46	Brandeis University	$61,400	$129,400
47	Samuel Merritt University	$93,900	$129,300
48	Charles R Drew University of Medicine and Science	$85,700	$129,300
49	University of California-San Diego	$65,000	$128,900
50	Manhattan College	$64,300	$128,700

Advisory services through Capital Advisory Group Advisory Services LLC and securities through United Planners Financial Services of America, a Limited Partnership. Member FINRA and SIPC. The Capital Advisory Group Advisory Services, LLC (CAG) and United Planners Financial Services are not affiliated.

"Your life is your story, and the adventure ahead of you is the journey to fulfill your own purpose and potential."

—Kerry Washington

"It is good to have an end to journey toward, but it is the journey that matters, in the end."

—Ursula K. Le Guin

"[On graduating college] your family is extremely proud of you. You cannot imagine the sense of relief they are experiencing. This is the most opportune time to ask for money."

—Gary Bolding

1.4 Beyond the Undergraduate Degree

There are several lucrative fields that require a graduate degree, including professions in the medical and legal fields. Your undergraduate major can help you prepare for graduate studies in these fields, so if your eye is on one of these areas in the long run and you're willing to put in the extra time and effort to complete a master's degree (or higher) to get into one of these professions, choose wisely now.

Source: https://www.payscale.com/college-salary-report

Some claim "times" have changed. A master's degree is the new bachelor's degree. According to the Digest of Education Statistics, about the same number of people have a master's today than had a bachelor's in 1967. Thirty years ago, a bachelor's degree distinguished you in the marketplace. That's no longer the case. The fact is you may not qualify for certain positions with only a bachelor's degree. And when they think about an advanced degree, people are looking for master's degrees that pay.

From 1985-2015, the number of master's degrees awarded has more than doubled, and many are focused on master's degrees that pay off. Master's degree programs are growing and evolving, with degrees now offered in nearly every field of study. Master's degrees can be professional or academic.

Professional degrees are designed for employment or advancement within a given field. Academic degrees are designed for intellectual growth and may be a prerequisite for doctoral work. Master's degrees may take anywhere from one to three years to complete.

People choose to pursue a master's degree for a number of reasons. Some choose to put off the job search and continue their education. Others may be forced to stay in school due to the economy and poor job prospects. Many people want to keep their training and skills current and/or become more marketable for career advancement. Having a master's degree may set you apart from other candidates when applying for jobs, like a bachelor's once did.

Perhaps one of the biggest reasons people decide to get a master's is to boost their salary. Studies show that people with advanced degrees earn more on average than those with bachelor's degrees.

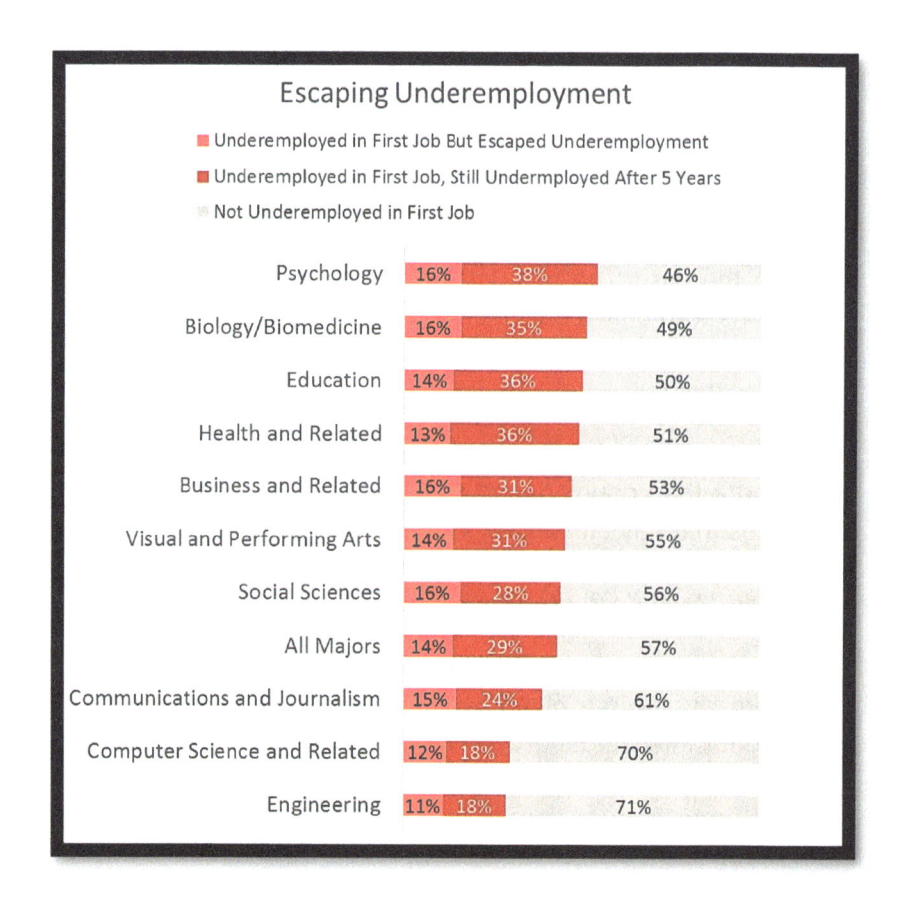

Escaping Underemployment

- Underemployed in First Job But Escaped Underemployment
- Underemployed in First Job, Still Underemployed After 5 Years
- Not Underemployed in First Job

Major	Escaped	Still Underemployed	Not Underemployed
Psychology	16%	38%	46%
Biology/Biomedicine	16%	35%	49%
Education	14%	36%	50%
Health and Related	13%	36%	51%
Business and Related	16%	31%	53%
Visual and Performing Arts	14%	31%	55%
Social Sciences	16%	28%	56%
All Majors	14%	29%	57%
Communications and Journalism	15%	24%	61%
Computer Science and Related	12%	18%	70%
Engineering	11%	18%	71%

In 2012, the median of earnings for young adults with a master's degree or higher was $59,600, 27 percent more than the median for those with a bachelor's degree, according to the National Center for Education Statistics. Be sure to do a cost-benefit analysis before deciding on a master's program.

There's no guarantee that a master's will make you more money or land your dream job, even if the degree you pursue is on a list of the highest-paying master's degrees. In some professions, advanced degrees are becoming mandatory, including teaching, social work, and psychology.

In these cases, master's degrees are necessary to advance or get licensed, but there may not be a significant boost in pay.

In the case of the following 15 highest paying master's degrees, you have a good chance to earn six figures. Salaries may vary based on position, years of experience, geographic location, and a variety of other factors. To determine the 15 top-paying master's degrees, subjects were ranked based on median pay and job outlook from both PayScale.com and the Bureau of Labor and Statistics (BLS). These rankings were averaged together to determine the overall rankings listed below. In case of a tie, the job with the highest median pay is listed first. A master's in business administration (MBA) was not included in these rankings.

Top 15 Master's Degrees worth the cost and in growing demand

Petroleum Engineering - The petroleum industry is one of the largest and most prominent in the United States today, and the companies involved are dependent on the services of petroleum engineers to explore, discover, and produce oil and gas to meet energy needs.

- Median Pay: $130,280

- Job Growth: 26%
- Possible Jobs: Petroleum geologist, production engineer, reservoir engineer

Nurse Anesthesia - Nurse anesthetists provide anesthesia and related care before and after medical procedures. They also provide pain management and emergency services. They are the sole anesthesia providers in nearly all rural hospitals, and the main provider of anesthesia to the men and women serving in the U.S. Armed Forces, according to the American Association of Nurse Anesthetists.

- Median Pay: $96,460
- Job Growth: 31%
- Possible Jobs: Nurse anesthetist

Physician Assistant Studies - Physician assistants are master's degree holders who support physicians, surgeons, and other healthcare professionals. These licensed professionals review medical histories, examine patients, and order diagnostic tests, with some also providing treatment. Most work in hospitals or physicians' offices, though some work in

Advisory services through Capital Advisory Group Advisory Services LLC and securities through United Planners Financial Services of America, a Limited Partnership. Member FINRA and SIPC. The Capital Advisory Group Advisory Services, LLC (CAG) and United Planners Financial Services are not affiliated.

outpatient care centers or educational organizations.

- Median Pay: $92,970
- Job Growth: 38%
- Possible Jobs: Physician assistant

Mathematics - Mathematics opens the doors to many promising career paths. Advanced mathematics is used to develop and understand mathematical principles, analyze data, and solve real-world problems in all disciplines.

- Median Pay: $101,360
- Job Growth: 23%
- Possible Jobs: Mathematician, software engineer, statistician

Political Science - Political Science focuses on the theory and practice of government and politics at the local, state, national, and international levels. Many job opportunities are available in both government and private businesses.

- Median Pay: $102,000
- Job Growth: 21%
- Possible Jobs: City manager, lobbyist, postsecondary teacher

Marketing - It's the job of the marketing professional to create, enhance, and manage brands. A career in marketing can take you in several different directions, from market research to contract negotiations.

- Median Pay: $123,220

- Job Growth: 12%
- Possible Jobs: Marketing manager, advertising/promotions manager, creative director

Healthcare Administration - Healthcare administrators direct the operation of hospitals, health systems, and other types of organizations. They have responsibility for facilities, services, programs, staff, budgets, and other management functions.

- Median Pay: $88,580
- Job Growth: 23%
- Possible Jobs: Healthcare administrator, executive director, chief nursing officer

Computer Science - Computer science is the science of using computers to solve problems in a variety of business, scientific, and social contexts. Computing drives innovation in the sciences, engineering, business, entertainment, and education.

- Median Pay: $102,190
- Job Growth: 15%

Advisory services through Capital Advisory Group Advisory Services LLC and securities through United Planners Financial Services of America, a Limited Partnership. Member FINRA and SIPC. The Capital Advisory Group Advisory Services, LLC (CAG) and United Planners Financial Services are not affiliated.

- Possible Jobs: Computer and information research scientist, software developer

Physical Therapy - Physical therapists help patients with injuries or illnesses develop mobility or reduce pain. This type of therapy can help patients recover without surgery and reduce the need for prescription medication. Some physical therapists work in hospitals, but many work in private offices or home care arrangements. All states require licensure for physical therapists.

- Median Pay: $81,030
- Job Growth: 36%
- Possible Jobs: Physical therapist

Information Systems - Information systems applies computer information to the work environment and management. The need to manage, support, and protect massive amounts of information has made the ever-changing information technology field one of the fastest-growing employment categories.

- Median Pay: $120,950
- Job Growth: 15%
- Possible Jobs: Information Technology (IT) manager, software engineer, systems analyst

Finance - Finance deals with matters related to money and the markets. The opportunities with a finance degree span several areas, including corporate and international financial management, personal financial planning, and investment services.

- Median Pay: $112,700,

Advisory services through Capital Advisory Group Advisory Services LLC and securities through United Planners Financial Services of America, a Limited Partnership. Member FINRA and SIPC. The Capital Advisory Group Advisory Services, LLC (CAG) and United Planners Financial Services are not affiliated.

- Job Growth: 8.9%
- Possible Jobs: Finance director, finance manager, financial analyst

Occupational Therapy - Occupational therapists help people of all ages participate in the things they want and need to do through the therapeutic use of everyday activities. There are six core practice areas of the profession: 1) Children and Youth, 2) Health and Wellness (Life Design), 3) Mental Health, 4) Work and Industry, 5) Rehabilitation, Participation, and Disability, and 6) Productive Aging.

- Median Pay: $75,400
- Job Growth: 29%
- Possible Jobs: Occupational therapist

Civil Engineering - Civil engineers design, review, and maintain public works, including roads, water systems, and other city structures. They split their time between offices and project sites, serving in both planning and supervisory roles. Those who do not work in private engineering or construction firms often work directly with federal, state, or local governments.

- Median Pay: $80,770
- Job Growth: 20%
- Possible Jobs: Civil engineer, structural engineer, project manager

Economics - Economics is the study of how people choose to use resources. Opportunities for economists range from positions in the business world in banking, insurance, investment and communications firms to those in academic settings, government agencies, trade associations, and consulting organizations.

- Median Pay: $91,860
- Job Growth: 14%
- Possible Jobs: Economist, data analyst, financial analyst

International Relations - International relations deals with political, economic, and cultural relations throughout the global community. Whether working for the U.S. government, an international organization, or a non-profit, there are a variety of career options in the field of international relations.

- Median Pay: $89,990
- Job Growth: 19%
- Possible Jobs: Intelligence analyst, research associate, foundation program officer

Section II

What Majors Offer the Greatest Challenges After Graduation and How to Minimize Your College Costs

"Don't pick a job that pays little while expecting to be rich. Make sure your desired lifestyle matches the lifestyle normally created by that profession."

—Brett Machtig

"The best way to predict the future is to create it."

—Abraham Lincoln

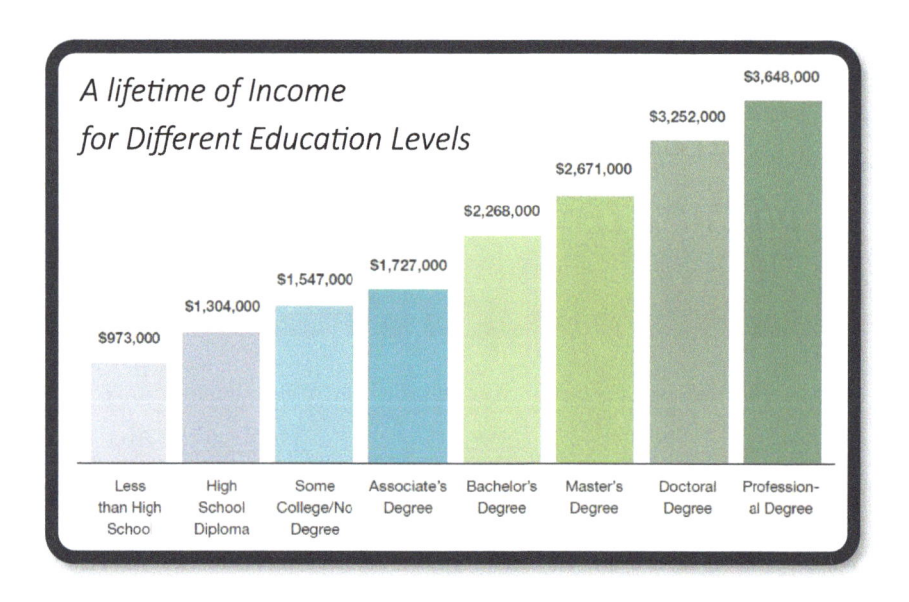

A lifetime of Income for Different Education Levels

Education Level	Lifetime Income
Less than High School	$973,000
High School Diploma	$1,304,000
Some College/No Degree	$1,547,000
Associate's Degree	$1,727,000
Bachelor's Degree	$2,268,000
Master's Degree	$2,671,000
Doctoral Degree	$3,252,000
Professional Degree	$3,648,000

"At the end of the day we are accountable to ourselves - our success is the result of what we do."

—Catherine Pulsifer

2.1 Which College Majors have the Lowest Median Earnings?

Based on the Georgetown center's recent data, from "What's It Worth: The Economic Value of College Majors," published in 2015, these are some of the lowest-paying majors an undergrad can pursue. The dollar figures, which are rounded, represent median earnings per year for workers age 25 to 59.

Of course, it's extremely important to note that our economy needs both teachers and engineers. We need social workers just as we need accountants.

It's easy to obsess over what major could make you the most money, but it's more important to find something that you enjoy and where you could excel in the field.

"Unemployment is capitalism's way of getting you to plant a garden."

—Olson Scott Card

"A day of worry is more exhausting than a week of work."

—John Lubbock

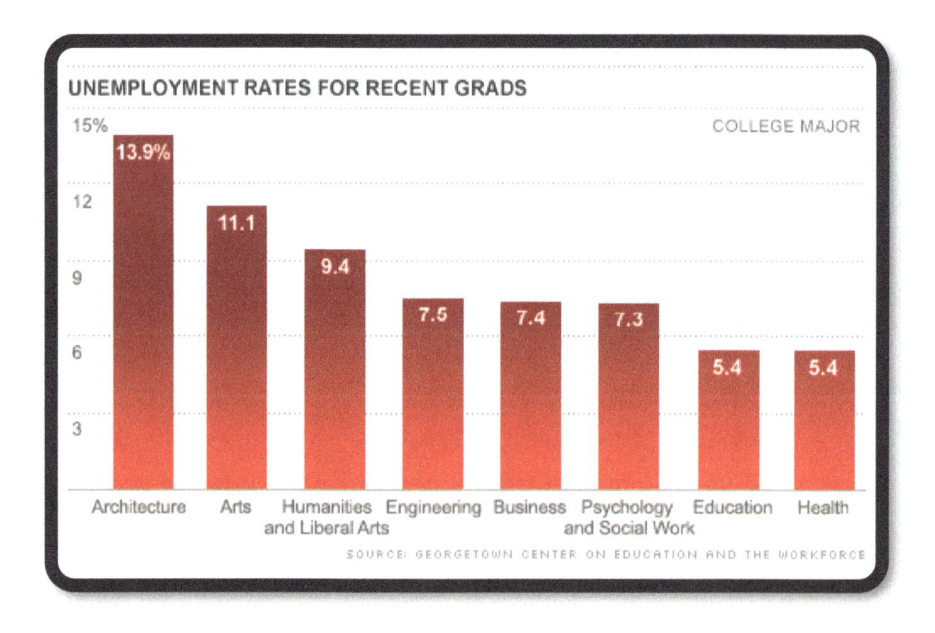

UNEMPLOYMENT RATES FOR RECENT GRADS
COLLEGE MAJOR

Major	Rate
Architecture	13.9%
Arts	11.1
Humanities and Liberal Arts	9.4
Engineering	7.5
Business	7.4
Psychology and Social Work	7.3
Education	5.4
Health	5.4

SOURCE: GEORGETOWN CENTER ON EDUCATION AND THE WORKFORCE

"The hardest work in the world is being out of work."

—Whitney Young, Jr.

2.2 Which College Majors have the Highest Unemployment?

While a degree is still an advantage in today's job market, the right major can make the difference between being happily employed and woefully underemployed. Some majors are clearly failing. Millions of Americans are underemployed, according to a new report from PayScale.

Not using their education and training is the primary reason why respondents consider themselves underemployed. In the survey, 79% of men and 72% of women say they are underemployed because of their education and training going to waste.

People who can't find full-time work in the field they studied often end up taking part-time work, or working in jobs unrelated to their field of study. The danger of underemployment is that if you're not using the skills you learned and want to develop, those skills will atrophy, leaving you less able to compete for the jobs you actually want.

Additionally, underemployed workers begin to disengage from their jobs, resulting in sub-par performance, further damaging future job prospects. In general, you're more likely to feel underemployed if you have a lower level of education (no higher than an associate's degree, GED, or high school diploma). However, a bachelor's degree isn't necessarily your ticket to professional bliss. Let's look at the 15 worst college majors for today's job market, according to PayScale.

Have you wondered if a particular college degree is worth it? Before you decide that the price tag is too high, be sure to look at what the statistics show. If you are concerned about saving for college, check with a financial advisor to discuss a college savings strategy right for you.

"Seven out of ten Americans are one paycheck away from being homeless."

—Pras Michel

"Although homelessness can happen to anyone, it just wasn't expected."

—Linda Lewis

"It is in our hands to create a better world for all that live in it."

—Nelson Mandella

"We make a living about what we get, we make a life by what we give."

—Winston Churchill

Advisory services through Capital Advisory Group Advisory Services LLC and securities through United Planners Financial Services of America, a Limited Partnership. Member FINRA and SIPC. The Capital Advisory Group Advisory Services, LLC (CAG) and United Planners Financial Services are not affiliated.

Here are the college majors who have the highest unemployment (UE) or underemployment:

Major	UE Rate	Education Reasons	Due to Part-time Work
Paralegal	50.9%	86.7%	13.3%
Health Sciences	50.9%	77.1%	22.9%
Exercise Science	51.8%	65.6%	34.4%
Animal Science	51.1%	83.7%	16.3%
Creative Writing	51.1%	76.2%	23.8%
Human Development & Family Studies	51.5%	75.0%	25.0%
Education	51.8%	77.7%	22.3%
Health Care Admin.	51.8%	83.3%	16.7%
Studio Art	52.0%	69.0%	32.2%
Radio/Television & Film Production	52.6%	68.4%	31.6%
Project Management	52.8%	91.5%	8.5%
Criminal Justice	53.0%	87.4%	12.8%
Illustration	54.7%	74.5%	25.5%
Human Services (HS)	55.6%	82.2%	17.8%
Physical Ed Teaching	56.4%	79.1%	20.9%

Advisory services through Capital Advisory Group Advisory Services LLC and securities through United Planners Financial Services of America, a Limited Partnership. Member FINRA and SIPC. The Capital Advisory Group Advisory Services, LLC (CAG) and United Planners Financial Services are not affiliated.

It's weird how you seem to get bigger every year...
COLLEGE TUITION

2.3 How Can You Most Effectively Reduce the Cost of College?

Here are thirteen of the big money wasters in college, and how students might consider whittling the costs of their education.

Tuition - The average tuition and fees for full-time students at public, in-state, two-year colleges is $3,131, less than half the cost of four-year, in-state, public colleges—which average $8,655, according to the College Board. However, high school students who take Advanced Placement classes for college credits and apply for scholarships can shave their tuition costs, and students who take their general education at the community college can save over $11,000 in tuition.

At minimum, students might consider taking a summer session or two for general education classes. By applying all three of these approaches, students may be able to significantly cut their college costs.

Rent - While you may still be reeling from the sticker shock of tuition, according to the College Board, room and board costs are actually the highest cost of college.

At your average public, in-state, four-year college, room and board runs $9,205 per year. Since housing may account for more than 50% of your college budget, cut that in half and you might be able to reduce your overall expenses by 25%. The best way to do that is to bunk up and share space instead of paying for the luxury of having your own room. Learning to live in close quarters with others for four years may be a sacrifice, but it is one with a high payoff.

Food - Dinner out on campus can easily cost $15 to $20 a person and a fast food lunch on campus isn't cheap, either. But one simple gadget can change that figure: I believe every college student should be issued a crock-pot as they exit the dorms after freshman year. Students can throw some meat, veggies and a pack of spices in the morning before class and come home to not only eat their meal, but freeze four to five "leftover" dinners. Cooking at home can reduce a price per meal from $10 or more at Chipotle to $1.50 to $2 per meal, and a student can save $200 a month in food costs as a result. This translates into about $9,600 in savings over their four years in college.

School Supplies - Sure, the campus bookstore is convenient, but most college students can't afford to sacrifice convenience for afford-ability. Large chain stores such as Staples, Target and Wal-Mart have school supplies at deeply discounted prices, especially during sales. Stocking up on college-ruled spiral notebooks for 25 cents a-piece—instead of ten times the price at the bookstore—can help their dollars go farther.

Textbooks - Selling textbooks back to the bookstore can be a waste of money. Students today have quite a few other

SLUGBOOKS
compare textbook prices

Advisory services through Capital Advisory Group Advisory Services LLC and securities through United Planners Financial Services of America, a Limited Partnership. Member FINRA and SIPC. The Capital Advisory Group Advisory Services, LLC (CAG) and United Planners Financial Services are not affiliated.

resources to buy discounted books (and sell them after the semester is over): Craigslist, Amazon, and sites like Slugbooks.com, which markets exclusively to students and tracks which editions professors currently use.

Another option is not to buy textbooks at all. If the option is available, you can rent books from the student library for the quarter or semester. If your library doesn't do that, check them out for a two-to three-hour span when you are studying. Some colleges, such as the University of California, have an inter-library loan program where you can borrow books from other campuses.

Goods and Services - Students who don't maximize their benefits with corporate student discount programs waste money. Banks may have no-fee student checking accounts. Retailers like Amazon offer discounts and free shipping for students. Discounts are everywhere, since retailers want college student dollars! The key, of course, is not to overdo it. Make sure you don't inadvertently spend more while trying to maximize your savings.

Beer - Recent research from the Social Science Research Council reports that college students spend 16% of their time going to class and studying, while 51% is spent socializing. The remaining 33% of their time is spent eating, sleeping and other routine activities. Since socializing often involves spending, consider that you don't have to attend every single social event for your fraternity or sorority. When you do go out with friends, make it a half-price happy hour.

Entertainment - Sure, your college student wants to go out. But you (and she) can maximize the student deals with free on-campus events. Your college may also have deeply-discounted recreation such as a gym and recreation center. There are free concerts, festivals and countless campus events. Take advantage of "college night" promotions by local busi-

Advisory services through Capital Advisory Group Advisory Services LLC and securities through United Planners Financial Services of America, a Limited Partnership. Member FINRA and SIPC. The Capital Advisory Group Advisory Services, LLC (CAG) and United Planners Financial Services are not affiliated.

nesses for drink and food specials as well as entertainment.

Spring Break - Despite the plethora of ads for spring break events, these are a luxury rather than a necessity. If you are paying for travel, skip Cabo and opt for a trip that will enhance your learning, give back, offer leadership skills and future resume building activities. Consider going with an on-campus club to learn leadership skills in Washington, D.C. or experience another culture with a guided trip to China or Peru. Wherever you go, maximize your student benefits with travel deals from STAtravel.com and travelzoo.com.

Not graduating - When you enter college, You may never think that you might not graduate, but many students who attend college never walk across the stage or receive their diplomas. Before applying to schools, check out their graduation rates here. The University of Utah has a four-year graduation rate of 20.8% while Marquette, a private school, comes in at 61% (with a five-year rate of over 80%). Though a private school may be more expensive, it may be worth it if you walk away with a full-fledged degree to show for your efforts.

That second senior year - The math isn't hard. It costs you about 25% more to graduate in five years versus four. Many majors like CPA programs require five years. Find out what your school does to help students graduate in four years instead of five or six. For example, the University of California, Santa Barbara keeps students on track to get out in four years by tracking students' "minimum cumulative progress"—in other words, making sure they have the correct amount of units each quarter so they're on track to graduate on time.

Not capitalizing on leadership opportunities and internships - In today's tough job market for recent grads, many employers are considering "entry level" as having two to three years of experience. Students who put in extra effort by participating in leadership positions on campus gain valuable skills that translate into the experience many employers look for. Though many students don't find their paths until later in their college years, and the club or organization may not quite line up with their future career paths, the skills will. Creating a budget for your campus club, public speaking and managing volunteers are all transferable skills to the business world.

Campus-sponsored student internships are a great way for students to gain experience in the workforce and often land jobs after college. Students who don't take advantage of these are missing opportunities.

Skipping recruiting fairs - According to Jobvite.com, 40% of new hires came from referrals, and on-campus recruiting is similar. Your school is the mutual friend your future employer knows, respects and trusts. Since employers recruit on campus to get the cream of the crop before everyone else does, this is one of the greatest benefits your school offers. Don't miss it.

Advisory services through Capital Advisory Group Advisory Services LLC and securities through United Planners Financial Services of America, a Limited Partnership. Member FINRA and SIPC. The Capital Advisory Group Advisory Services, LLC (CAG) and United Planners Financial Services are not affiliated.

Savvy students can have the best of both worlds—a great college experience and graduating with the least possible amount of student loan debt. By minimizing expenses and maximizing the value of what their university offers, they will also graduate with some serious financial acumen.

Advisory services through Capital Advisory Group Advisory Services LLC and securities through United Planners Financial Services of America, a Limited Partnership. Member FINRA and SIPC. The Capital Advisory Group Advisory Services, LLC (CAG) and United Planners Financial Services are not affiliated.

Advisory services through Capital Advisory Group Advisory Services LLC and securities through United Planners Financial Services of America, a Limited Partnership. Member FINRA and SIPC. The Capital Advisory Group Advisory Services, LLC (CAG) and United Planners Financial Services are not affiliated.

"Fifty years ago, great schools like the University of California and the City University of New York - as well as many state colleges - were tuition free. Today college is unaffordable for many working class families. For the sake of our economy and millions of Americans, we must make higher education more affordable."

—Bernie Sanders

"The only easy day was yesterday."

—U.S. Navy Seals

2.4 Can the Military Help you Reduce the Cost of Higher Education?

Enlisting in the military is not only an opportunity to serve your country, but there are several ways the military helps pay for college as an added bonus. If you join the Army, Navy, Air Force, Coast Guard, or Marines, here are the types of education assistance you can receive.

Learn about the programs available to you whether you took loans out prior to joining the military, during, or after. Understand there are strict eligibility requirements in order to receive financial assistance in obtaining your degree.

Here are some of the ways that the military pays for college.

Can the Military Offer Tuition Assistance? - Reserve military members and those on active duty may be eligible for tuition assistance, which means that the military pays up to 100% of your tuition. The eligibility requirements vary by branch and the total cannot exceed $4,500 per fiscal year.

This is not a loan, but it is a benefit of military service that is paid directly to your school to cover tuition and fees. This can help you to obtain a degree with little to no cost, depending on where you choose to go to school.

Tuition Assistance "Top-Up" Program - This program is an added benefit designed to supplement the tuition assistance from the military with GI Bill benefits. In order to be eligible for the Top-Up benefit, you must be approved for federal Tuition Assistance by a military department and also be eligible for GI Bill benefits. Tuition Assistance will pay for up to 75% of the cost and the Top-Up will pay the remainder.

The GI Bill - With the GI Bill, you can get up to 4 years of education benefits if you're a service member or a veteran. These benefits can be used to attend college, career schools, training programs, or licensing and testing programs. There are two separate GI Bills that are used in these ways, which are the Post-9/11 GI Bill and the Montgomery GI Bill.

The Post-9/11 GI Bill will give you paid tuition and fees in addition to a stipend for housing and books if you've served at least 90 days of active duty since September 10, 2001. These benefits are based on how long you served in active duty and can be transferred to your spouse or family member. People who have survived a military member's passing after September 10, 2001 may be eligible for the Fry Scholarship, which carries the same benefits.

Benefits and Eligibility for the Post-9/11 GI Bill

- The Post-9/11 GI Bill provides up to 3 years of education benefits. If your release from active duty was before January 1, 2013, then you must use the benefits within 15 years. If your discharge date was on or after January 1, 2013, the time limitation has been removed.

There are higher education programs that participate in the Yellow Ribbon Program that may make additional funds available to you without a charge to what you're entitled to with the GI Bill. You may also receive payments for a monthly housing allowance, annual books and supplies stipend, and a one-time rural benefit payment. If you're attending a private or foreign school, then tuition and fees are capped at the national maximum rate.

The Montgomery GI Bill extends educational benefits to any active duty member of the military who served for at least two years of active duty. This also extends to veterans of any

---

Advisory services through Capital Advisory Group Advisory Services LLC and securities through United Planners Financial Services of America, a Limited Partnership. Member FINRA and SIPC. The Capital Advisory Group Advisory Services, LLC (CAG) and United Planners Financial Services are not affiliated.

branch of the military. You receive up to $1,857 each month for educational expenses, as long as you're enrolled full-time. You cannot transfer these benefits. If you're in the Selected Reserve, then you receive up to $368 per month in exchange for a 6-year obligation of service to the reserves.

The two programs under the Montgomery GI Bill are as follows:

- Montgomery GI Bill Active Duty (MGIB-AD) For active duty members who enroll and pay $100 per month for a year and are then entitled to receive a monthly education benefit once they have completed a minimum service obligation.

- Montgomery GI Bill Selected Reserve (MGIB-SR) For Reservists with a six-year obligation in the Selected Reserve who are actively drilling.

Student Loan Repayment - If you're currently enrolled in the military, then the government may repay your student loans for you. Your eligibility depends on the military branch you're enlisted in, but your loans must be in good standing no matter what. The military may pay off some or all of your student loan debt through this program.

Active Duty Health Professions Student Loan Repayment Program
- Health professionals who are also on active duty can qualify for $40,000 per year toward your student loan debt for up to 3 years if you're serving in the dental, medical, allied health, nursing, or veterinary corps while on active duty. You can also be eligible for up to $50,000 in total loan forgiveness over 3 years if you're in the reserves for those professions.

Air Force College Student Loan Repayment Program
- You can get up to $10,000 of your student loan balance forgiven if you sign up for the Air Force College Stu-

dent Loan Repayment Program.

What Loans Qualify for Active Duty Health Professions Student Loan Repayment?

- Stafford loans
- Grad PLUS loans
- Consolidation loans
- Perkins loans
- Health professions student loans
- Private student loans

What Loans Qualify for Air Force Student Loan Repayment?

- Stafford loans
- Consolidation loans
- Parent PLUS loans
- Grad PLUS loans
- Perkins loans
- Auxiliary Loan Assistance for Students (ALAS loans)
- Federally Insured Student Loans

Advisory services through Capital Advisory Group Advisory Services LLC and securities through United Planners Financial Services of America, a Limited Partnership. Member FINRA and SIPC. The Capital Advisory Group Advisory Services, LLC (CAG) and United Planners Financial Services are not affiliated.

Advisory services through Capital Advisory Group Advisory Services LLC and securities through United Planners Financial Services of America, a Limited Partnership. Member FINRA and SIPC. The Capital Advisory Group Advisory Services, LLC (CAG) and United Planners Financial Services are not affiliated.

Section III
Keys to Success in Higher Education Before, During & After

Preparing for College

STEP 1: Prepare Yourself Academically

STEP 2: Become a Well-Rounded Student

STEP 3: Impress for Success

STEP 4: Set Smart Goals

STEP 5: Assemble Your College Prep Team

STEP 6: Get Ready to Take Standardized Admissions Tests — Conquering the SAT and ACT

STEP 7: Make Your College Preparation Checklist

3.1 How Can I Best Prepare for Getting into College?

Here are some tips to get you ready for college.

Get to know your counselor - The first step when getting ready for college is meeting with your high school counselor in your freshman year. This person will be supporting you through the next four years. They will ask you about your career plans and goals. Draft a plan of realistic choices that you feel confident doing. But be aware that your career plans can change in the course of study, so do not fully concentrate on a specific path. Your plans should be more fluid in these early stages.

Study your college degree requirements - Many colleges first focus on standard subjects, such as history, math, literature, and science. After that, an emphasis is placed on higher technical degrees with more specific subjects, depending on the student's goals.

Work with your counselor to create a four-year school schedule - Define which school courses you should take and pass while keeping in mind the specific degree that you are going to pursue. Again, you're preparing for college from day one, but nothing is set in stone. This schedule can be adjusted over time.

Take part in extracurricular activities - Colleges value people who actively participated in extracurricular activities while planning for college. Therefore, it is important to find the activity that suits you best. One option is to apply for pre-college summer programs. They can also choose more focused programs to learn everything from entrepreneurship in the residential business program to how to get into competitive gaming with the e-sports summer program.

There are also unique day programs like the coding academy, cooking school, and sports programs like tennis, golf, and more for prospective collegiate athletes.

Apply for internships - This is an optional step but it can be very helpful if you get such an opportunity. Internships are glimpses into possible career paths and maybe even your own professional future. As you walk away from your internship, you get a better understanding of industry realities as well as your own interest. As a result, you will have a better idea of what college program you would like to apply for.

Practice your note taking skills when preparing for college - In a college, the number of students attending a lecture can be four times greater than in a high school classroom. Therefore, it would be wise to adjust your listening and note taking skills as early as possible, as the professor will talk quickly and will not usually repeat lessons. Many college students use their smartphones to record the lectures, but such activity can drain the battery of a smartphone very quickly or require hours of transcribing, so being able to take notes during a lecture is valuable. See Oxfordlearning.com for more information and tools.

Develop writing skills and take every writing as-

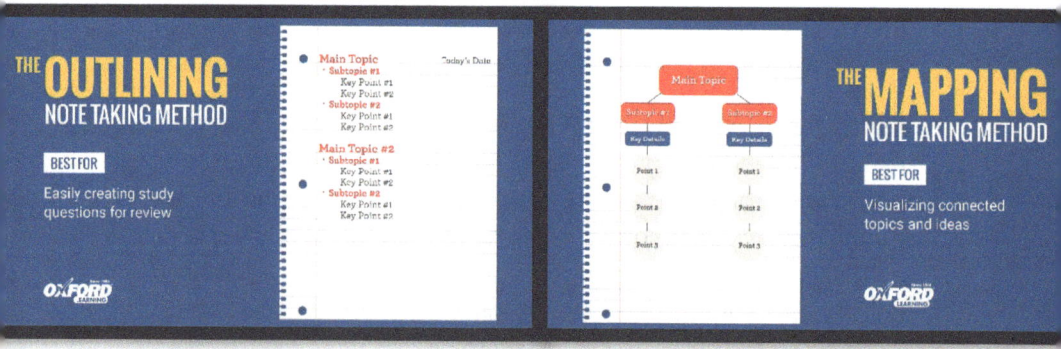

Advisory services through Capital Advisory Group Advisory Services LLC and securities through United Planners Financial Services of America, a Limited Partnership. Member FINRA and SIPC. The Capital Advisory Group Advisory Services, LLC (CAG) and United Planners Financial Services are not affiliated.

signment seriously - Term papers can teach you how to do research and use the research tools, such as library and proper internet resources. If your writing and researching skills are top notch, you can look at every writing assignment as a guaranteed A. Consider reading Essential Writing Skills for College and Beyond by C.M. Gill to get a jump on your writing skills.

Develop time management skills - Keep a computer file where you record how you are using your time. Try to dedicate specific amounts of time to study only, for example, 30-40 minutes, and then gradually increase those amounts so you end up with 60-90 minutes. This will also help you determine timelines for coursework. If you've tracked your time and know how long it takes to complete a certain assignment, you will know how much time you need to allot for similar work. This will not only help to improve your grades, but also prepare you for the heavier course load and more in depth work you will be doing once in your college of choice.

Develop speaking skills - Speak up in class even if it's something you're not totally comfortable with. Make notes about what you want to say before you raise your hand in order to overcome reluctance to speak up in class.

Start researching colleges - Prepare for college by learning about its requirements and prerequisites. If the college is far away from where you live, you should also plan your residential needs. Are you planning to rent an apartment with your friends or reside on campus? How much will it cost? You should also think about the cost of your studies. Colleges and universities typically define their tuition fees based on the amount of credits that you are planning to take.

Finally, you should plan your costs for learning materials. Unlike high school where books are provided to you as part of tuition, each college professor requires you to get specific textbooks and other necessary materials. The cost of books may

Advisory services through Capital Advisory Group Advisory Services LLC and securities through United Planners Financial Services of America, a Limited Partnership. Member FINRA and SIPC. The Capital Advisory Group Advisory Services, LLC (CAG) and United Planners Financial Services are not affiliated.

appear to be higher than you expected, but you can purchase used books from upperclassmen as well as get them for free from your friends or siblings.

Start preparing for tests - Many high schools require that you take tests such as PSAT/ACT/SAT either in your junior or senior year, and most colleges accept at least one of them as a requirement. This is one of the most important moments to consider when getting ready for college, even if your school is test optional because most scholarships require it. Remember, if you don't score well, you can usually retake these tests after a wait period to improve your score.

Visit college campuses of your top choices in your junior year - Learn how to get around the buildings, parking areas, any housing placements, etc. Some colleges offer tours around their premises, so take advantage of such tours. Start applying to colleges of your choice early in your senior year. Avoid colleges that do not meet your goals and experiences. Most colleges have application deadlines, so make sure that you have everything ready. This is the time to prove on paper to them why you wish to attend the college, what activities you have done, etc.

Planning for College Is All About Preparation

Now you have a better understanding of how to get ready for college and what you need to do before moving onto college from high school.

Advisory services through Capital Advisory Group Advisory Services LLC and securities through United Planners Financial Services of America, a Limited Partnership. Member FINRA and SIPC. The Capital Advisory Group Advisory Services, LLC (CAG) and United Planners Financial Services are not affiliated.

Advisory services through Capital Advisory Group Advisory Services LLC and securities through United Planners Financial Services of America, a Limited Partnership. Member FINRA and SIPC. The Capital Advisory Group Advisory Services, LLC (CAG) and United Planners Financial Services are not affiliated.

"The beautiful thing about learning is no one can take it from you."

—B.B. King

"Develop a passion for learning. If you do, you will never cease to grow."

—Anthony D'Angelo

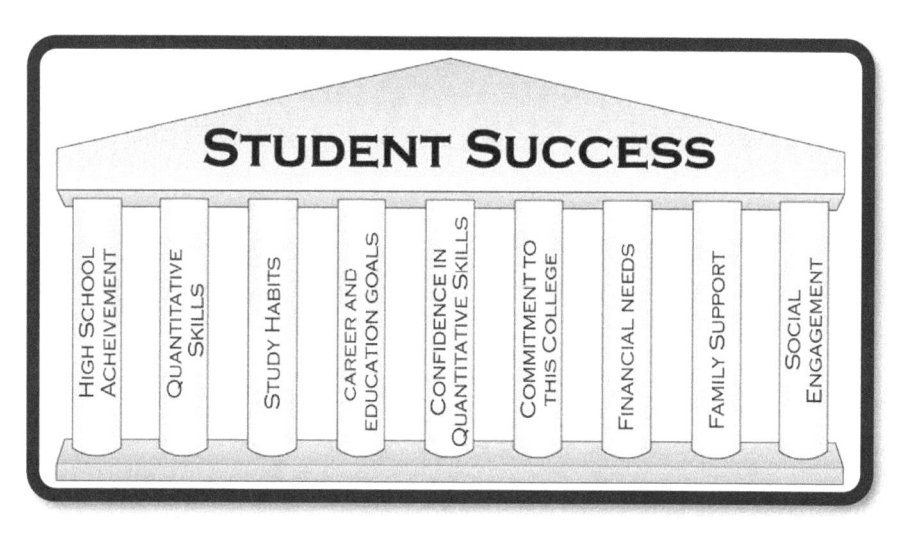

STUDENT SUCCESS

Pillars: High School Achievement | Quantitative Skills | Study Habits | Career and Education Goals | Confidence in Quantitative Skills | Commitment to This College | Financial Needs | Family Support | Social Engagement

"Grind while they sleep. Learn while they party. Live like they dream."

—Grant Cardone

"Do, or do not. There is no 'try.'"

—Yoda

3.2 What are the Keys for Success While Attending College?

For years college feels like an endpoint, the focus of so much of our students' energies. But it turns out to be just a beginning. Here are our keys for success while attending college.

Stick to your Own Definition of Success in College - Students who did best in college were not motivated by outside factors like jobs, or grades, but rather a genuine desire to learn.

Take One Small Class, Every Semester - Students who took one small class, defined as less than 16 students, had a higher level of engagement and actually worked harder, according to Professor Richard Light of the Harvard Graduate School of Education. Students who qualify for an "honors program" as a benefit, will be in smaller classes compared to the typical class-size. They also tend to have the best professors and more success-related classmates. Another study showed that students who took a small freshman seminar (thus had an early experience in a small class setting) were less likely to drop out of school.

Take Advantage of College partner Programs - Both of my daughters received two years of college credits while attending high school. This prepared them for college work demands, receiving both a high school diploma and an associate degree by age 18. College partner programs save time and money.

Engage with Faculty, Early and Often - Every study seemed to confirm that students who engaged with faculty, in venues outside of the classroom, had better educational outcomes. The studies concluded that for most students, more contact with faculty was always better.

"Informal student-faculty interaction activities—being a guest in a professor's home, working on a research project with a faculty member, talking with instructors outside of class, and serving on committees with faculty—are positively correlated with student learning and development."

Don't Just Look to Get Requirements Completed - It is tempting freshman year to look at the list of graduation requirements and to try to knock off a substantial portion of them freshman year, because when sophomore year begins, these students have little idea of what subject matter genuinely interests them.

"When talking with freshmen, I stress this point especially heavily. I urge them not to just choose a series of large, introductory courses during freshmen year. "

If it is an Option, Live on Campus Freshman Year - Every school is different and not all students are offered on-campus housing their first year or any year. But multiple studies showed that living in freshman housing increased social engagement. Students living on campus were more likely to be members of study groups and get involved in extracurricular activities, both markers for success.

"...living on campus had a direct, positive effect on learning outcomes, and educational aspirations had the greatest indirect effects on learning and intellectual development. In fact, living on campus had the greatest total effect (i.e., the combination of direct and indirect effects) on learning outcomes of any institutional characteristic. "

Pick the Right Friends - Students should think carefully in choosing their friends because no influence seems to be as forceful as peer group pressure. A student's peer group, ac-

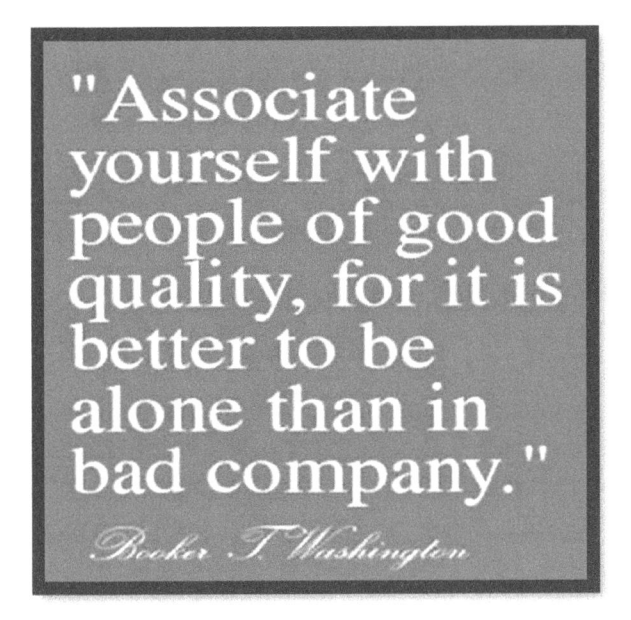

> "Associate yourself with people of good quality, for it is better to be alone than in bad company."
> — *Booker T. Washington*

cording to one study was, "'the single most potent source of influence,' affecting virtually every aspect of development—cognitive, affective, psychological, and behavioral."

"Peer interactions are particularly important with regard to social integration because students are more likely to stay in school when they feel comfortable and connected to other students with similar interests and aspirations. ... In addition, institutions with higher levels of student social interaction also have higher levels of student educational aspirations."

This is not High School, Work in Groups - In many high schools, individual work is stressed, but this is not high school. Students who seek out study groups and connect with their peers over academic content have greater academic success and satisfaction during their four years.

"Not only do students who work in small study groups outside of class commit more time to their coursework, feel more challenged by their work, and express a much higher level of personal interest in it—they are also much less likely to hesitate

to seek help. The critical point is that the relationships are not merely social. They are organized to accomplish some work—a substantive exploration that students describe as "stretching" themselves. And almost without exception, students who feel they have not yet found themselves, or fully hit their stride, report that they have not developed such relationships."

Parents Still Matter and Kids Need Encouragement - Even as kids move on with their lives, it appears parental influence is still very relevant. College can be a daunting and far more challenging experience than high school, requiring a great deal more self-direction. Some kids stumble their first year and can become demoralized. Research shows they are aided by a reminder that their parents' confidence in them is undimmed and support unreserved.

"Aspirations and family support foreshadow student success. ... On balance, it appears that students perform better and are more likely to succeed when their families affirm their students' choices and encourage them to stay the course; this is especially important for under-served populations."

The Effects of Success Linger Long After College - A 2014 Gallup-Purdue University study of college graduates showed that it is a few simple things that increase the odds of turning a successful college experience into satisfying work life. Every freshman should know that the positive effects of constructive relationships with professors, meaningful work experience and extracurricular activities and in-depth academic work, can last a lifetime.

"If graduates recalled having a professor who cared about them as a person, made them excited about learning, and encouraged them to pursue their dreams, their odds of being engaged at work more than doubled, as did their odds of thriving in all aspects of their well-being. And if graduates had an internship or job in college where they were able to apply what they were *learning in the classroom, were actively involved in extracurricular activities and organizations, and worked on projects that took a semester or more to complete, their odds of being engaged at work doubled as well."*

Financial Aid - Choosing a college is one hurdle, but figuring out how to pay for it is equally important. Helping match students to college scholarships for nearly two decades, **Scholarships.com** is a free source of wide-ranging information for more than 3.7 million local, state, and national college scholarships and grants. By answering questions relating to academics, skills, interests, and abilities, you'll be matched with a variety of funding opportunities. You can access all this through their website.

Another, newer resource is the **YesU** app. This app walks you through the financial aid process step by step: how to complete the FAFSA, decipher financial-aid terms and jargon, and receive notifications of approaching deadlines via push, SMS, and email. Plus, YesU offers secure document storage and access to advisors that can answer the inevitable questions which come up along the way.

Test Prep - Need to improve your reading comprehension? The free **Vocabulary for SAT** app on Google Play includes definitions and examples of 4,000 SAT-specific words, flashcards, and multiple tests for 800 high-frequency words. It also covers synonyms, antonyms, idioms, and idiomatic phrases. **ACT Prep Coach** and **ACT Prep for Dummies** on Apple are also highly rated apps.

To fine tune your math skills, check out the highly rated **Math Brain Booster** app on Google Play, or **Luminosity** on Apple. Work through a timed sequence of math problems, access different "boost modes," and track your progress through a personalized training option. Plus, you can pre-schedule sessions to keep on track with your progress.

Advisory services through Capital Advisory Group Advisory Services LLC and securities through United Planners Financial Services of America, a Limited Partnership. Member FINRA and SIPC. The Capital Advisory Group Advisory Services, LLC (CAG) and United Planners Financial Services are not affiliated.

The college search, admissions, and financial-aid processes can be daunting, even under the best of circumstances. However, if you do your research, stay ahead of the curve time-wise, and utilize the best available tools to cover all the necessary bases, you'll give yourself the best chance possible to get into (and pay for) the college of your choice. And once you are in college, consider the **College Planner** app to help manage the rigors of day-to-day college life, everything from class schedules to group projects, and exams.

Should I take a year off before starting college? - Many students choose to take a gap year before college, whether it is to get some work experience, volunteer, earn some money for their advanced education or travel the world and gain experiences that may help them during their degree. Some students are taking a gap year because they are undecided about their subject choice or career path and need some more time to ensure they are making the right long-term decisions.

While taking a gap year may be the right choice for some students, it could have negative ramifications for others. Before you take the year off, it is important to carefully weigh the gap year pros and cons of your decision and the effect it may have on your college application.

Pros Of Taking A Gap Year - Taking a gap year truly offers you a wealth of advantages, but only if you plan the year right. Check out how you could benefit from taking the year off before attending college:

- **It gives you time to think and figure out what you want -** High school can be a non-stop flurry of classes, tests, and homework too. There's barely any time to stop and think about what you really want to do. A gap year allows you to explore college majors and potential interests so you can identify your passion.

Advisory services through Capital Advisory Group Advisory Services LLC and securities through United Planners Financial Services of America, a Limited Partnership. Member FINRA and SIPC. The Capital Advisory Group Advisory Services, LLC (CAG) and United Planners Financial Services are not affiliated.

- **You learn responsibility at a different level -** Let's say you've always led a sheltered life with mom and dad always there for you. It can be difficult to suddenly take on a whole lot of responsibilities overnight. As a college student living away from home for the first time, the thought of having to manage finances, as well as university stresses and dorm life, can be overwhelming. Taking on a high school job during your gap year or even volunteering in another country will help you gain essential life-skills and learn responsibility on a different level.

- **You can submit a more impressive application -** Planning on applying for an architectural program? Spending your gap year exploring different architectural cultures and using your college application essay to emphasize how your experience influenced you is sure to impress any architectural college. It's the best way to ensure that you get into the college of your choice.

- **You can earn towards your education -** A college education is expensive. Most students graduate with debt. If you take up a job during your gap year, you may be able to earn some money to fund your education so you can graduate with minimal debt.

Cons of Taking a Gap Year:

- **It puts you a year behind -** Taking that year off will put you further back on the educational process and also a year behind your friends.

- **You take the risk of losing momentum -** Yes, taking a gap year can be a refreshing break from non-stop studying. However, many students find it difficult to get back into a schedule and regain their student momentum.

- **Gap years can be costly -** Many students want to travel around and explore during their gap year. But, this can be an expensive endeavor that will ultimately add to your student debt. Money spent is not money saved, after all.

- **Taking a gap year is not for everyone.** If you are planning on going this route, it is crucial to think long and hard about what you are going to do.

Advisory services through Capital Advisory Group Advisory Services LLC and securities through United Planners Financial Services of America, a Limited Partnership. Member FINRA and SIPC. The Capital Advisory Group Advisory Services, LLC (CAG) and United Planners Financial Services are not affiliated.

Advisory services through Capital Advisory Group Advisory Services LLC and securities through United Planners Financial Services of America, a Limited Partnership. Member FINRA and SIPC. The Capital Advisory Group Advisory Services, LLC (CAG) and United Planners Financial Services are not affiliated.

"The best preparation for tomorrow is doing your best today."

—*H. Jackson Brown, Jr.*

"Thorough preparation makes its own luck."

—*Joe Poyer*

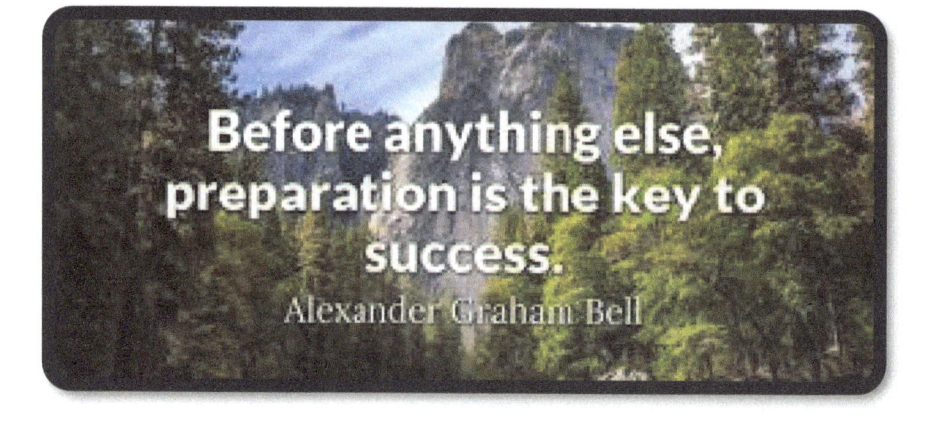

> **Before anything else, preparation is the key to success.**
> Alexander Graham Bell

"Striving for success without hard work is like trying to harvest where you haven't planted."

—*David Bly*

3.3 What are the Keys to Financial Success after College?

So you have worked hard for the last few years to get your degree. Now it is time prepare for the next stage in life, work. Here are some keys to make the next stage go well for you.

Go over the details of your student loans - Your student loans are one of the first things on your mind when you graduate college. Take the time to revisit the terms of your student loans and see what your interest rates are. More times than not, they are high and you may be able to get a better rate if you refinance. Your first step is to check the Federal Student Loan Website and see what you owe and the interest rate. Next, research banks that have the lowest student loan refinance rates. When all is said and done, you could potentially save a decent amount of money.

Pay your student loan payments on time - After you graduate from college, you have a six-month grace period before you need to begin making payments on your student loans. Start your financial journey on the right foot by following this money tip and make your payments on time every month. If you don't, you could wind up falling behind and it will be very difficult to catch up and get back on track.

Prioritize your financial goals - In general, there are four financial goals people work toward. Saving for retirement, an emergency fund, a large expense (home, new car) and repaying debt. Since you have just graduated, your timeline should look more like saving for an emergency fund, contributing to a retirement account and paying off your debt. Saving for the big ticket items can come later. Read chapter five of this book to help you plan better.

Don't wait for the perfect job - Your idea of the perfect job is not going to be waiting for you when you graduate. You want to get in the game and start networking and making connections where you can. Networking is a key part in succeeding at getting that job you ultimately want. So start talking with friends, family members, friends of friends, etc. Paid internships are another great way to help you get a foot in the door within your field. As a college graduate, you have a good chance of becoming a salaried employee within six months with a company you want to be a part of. Remember, it is easier to get a job if you have work experience.

Create a budget and stick to it - Creating a budget is an essential money tip and is crucial to your personal financial success. Even more so is sticking to it. The best way to keep track of your spending is to use a budgeting software or personal finance apps. You can use either to create a monthly budget, which makes it easier to track spending. When creating your budget, you want to make sure you are accounting for all your monthly expenses. Also, keep in mind that unexpected expenses are inevitable. You want to make sure you are stocking away money in an emergency fund.

Put the credit cards away - Give a college kid access to a credit card and they are likely to wind up in debt. Avoid this by only using a credit card when you absolutely have to and make sure that you pay it in full by the end of the month. Your ultimate goal is to stick to the budget you set for yourself and only use your debit card.

Avoid a car payment - If you can avoid having a car payment, do it. If you can, take public transportation while you save for a car. When you save up enough, check out Consumer Reports for their high rated vehicles and choose the least expensive one. Remember, you just want something you can pay in full and keep for the long run.

Advisory services through Capital Advisory Group Advisory Services LLC and securities through United Planners Financial Services of America, a Limited Partnership. Member FINRA and SIPC. The Capital Advisory Group Advisory Services, LLC (CAG) and United Planners Financial Services are not affiliated.

Choose your bank carefully - When choosing a bank to go with, we often choose the one that has the best promotion at the time. Take the time to research the best bank for you before you go ahead and start setting up features like bill pay. You want a bank that has a lot of ATM locations and does not hit you with fees for a low balance.

Move back in with your parents if you can - This money tip will save you money big time. Assuming your parents will not charge you rent, this is a no-brainer. You will have the opportunity to put that money towards your future housing plans, pay down any debt and start that emergency fund.

Get health insurance - When you are young, you may think health insurance is not necessary but accidents do happen as do illnesses. If you have access to health insurance through your work, take advantage of it. If you are under 26, you can look into getting on your parents health insurance as a dependent.

Set up alerts for your money - When you don't keep track of your checking balance, it is easy to go into the negative and get hit with overdraft fees. If you don't nip it in the bud, the

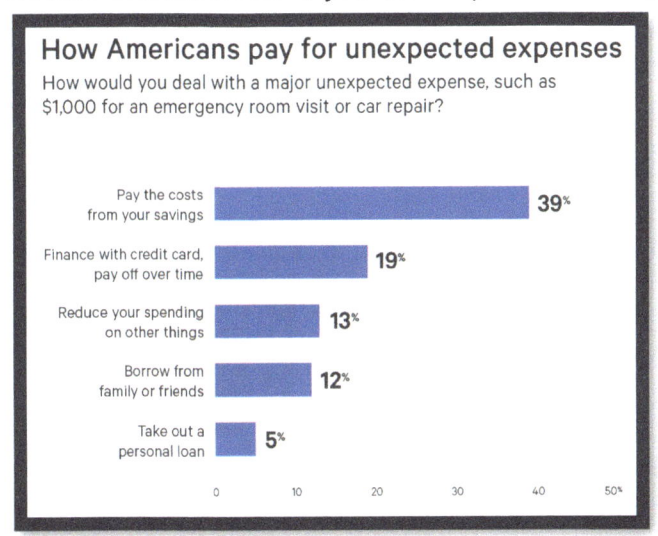

How Americans pay for unexpected expenses
How would you deal with a major unexpected expense, such as $1,000 for an emergency room visit or car repair?

Option	Percent
Pay the costs from your savings	39%
Finance with credit card, pay off over time	19%
Reduce your spending on other things	13%
Borrow from family or friends	12%
Take out a personal loan	5%

Advisory services through Capital Advisory Group Advisory Services LLC and securities through United Planners Financial Services of America, a Limited Partnership. Member FINRA and SIPC. The Capital Advisory Group Advisory Services, LLC (CAG) and United Planners Financial Services are not affiliated.

fees can really drain your money. Take the time to set up alerts on your phone for each bill you have. Set the alert up for five days prior to the due date. Also, go online and set up low balance alerts for your checking account.

If you don't have an emergency fund, start one today - Having an emergency fund for those unexpected expenses is crucial. Don't wait until you have a "real job." Any money you can put into this fund is worthwhile. The easiest way to get one going is to set up an automatic transfer to a savings account for each paycheck. Any extra money you receive like a raise or a bonus should be put into this account as well.

Invest in a retirement account - If you are lucky enough to land a job after graduating and your employer offers a 401k, start contributing to it. The maximum yearly investment into a retirement account is $6000 (up from $5500 in 2018) and if you can swing that, by all means do it. If your employer offers a contribution match, invest up to that amount and take the remainder and open your own Roth IRA.

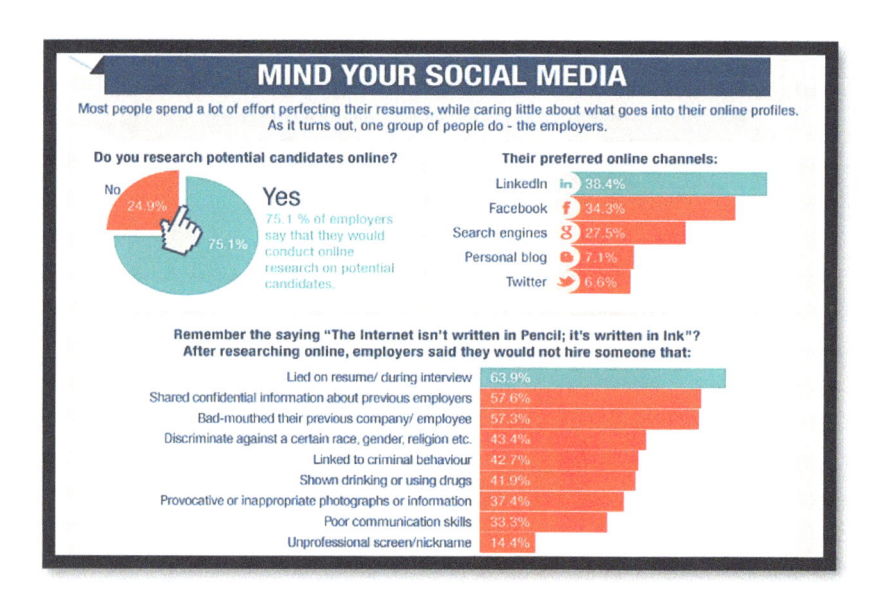

MIND YOUR SOCIAL MEDIA

Most people spend a lot of effort perfecting their resumes, while caring little about what goes into their online profiles. As it turns out, one group of people do - the employers.

Do you research potential candidates online?

No 24.9%
Yes 75.1%

75.1% of employers say that they would conduct online research on potential candidates.

Their preferred online channels:

Channel	%
LinkedIn	38.4%
Facebook	34.3%
Search engines	27.5%
Personal blog	7.1%
Twitter	6.6%

Remember the saying "The Internet isn't written in Pencil; it's written in Ink"?
After researching online, employers said they would not hire someone that:

Reason	%
Lied on resume/ during interview	63.9%
Shared confidential information about previous employers	57.6%
Bad-mouthed their previous company/ employee	57.3%
Discriminate against a certain race, gender, religion etc.	43.4%
Linked to criminal behaviour	42.7%
Shown drinking or using drugs	41.9%
Provocative or inappropriate photographs or information	37.4%
Poor communication skills	33.3%
Unprofessional screen/nickname	14.4%

Advisory services through Capital Advisory Group Advisory Services LLC and securities through United Planners Financial Services of America, a Limited Partnership. Member FINRA and SIPC. The Capital Advisory Group Advisory Services, LLC (CAG) and United Planners Financial Services are not affiliated.

Try to save money by cutting down on your largest expenses - This is one of the best money tips for recent college grads. Budgeting your money and cutting down where you can are essential to living your best life as you embark on your new financial journey. Go through your expenses and see where you can cut down on housing, food, commuting, etc. Look for roommates and eat at home as often as possible. If you can carpool or bike, do it.

Get a part-time job to earn extra money - Out of college you are young and energetic. This is the time to pick up some side jobs to boost your income. Today, there are so many different ways to make extra money. From babysitting to dog walking to becoming an Uber driver, it is up to you to get out there and make it happen. Surprisingly, students who work while attending school tend to do better in school than those who do not.

Start investing your money now- Investing money does not need to wait until you are making a six-figure income. Even investing a small amount like $20 will grow over time. As you add more money, you make money off of the compounding interest. Key takeaway is to start today; don't wait.

Track your money and investments - Even if you do not have much, this money tip is not one to skip over. It is important to get in the habit of tracking your net worth. Stay on top of your savings, account balances and investment performance. Seeing your savings grow along with your returns on investments will help keep you motivated to continue saving.

Choose your friends wisely - Stay away from people who encourage you to spend money foolishly. This goes for friends and anyone you date.

Advisory services through Capital Advisory Group Advisory Services LLC and securities through United Planners Financial Services of America, a Limited Partnership. Member FINRA and SIPC. The Capital Advisory Group Advisory Services, LLC (CAG) and United Planners Financial Services are not affiliated.

Clean up your social media profile - First impressions are important and potential employers will be looking at your social media accounts. Go through your photos and posts and make sure there is nothing questionable. If you don't have a LinkedIn profile set up, create one that highlights your skills. Be sure to check your grammar and spelling too.

Keep in touch with college friends and professors - Networking is an important skill to hone and with social media, it has become pretty easy. Years after you graduate, you could end up landing your dream job from an old college friend.

A great money tip: Keep your credit use low - Upon graduating college, most students are carrying a large student loan debt along with credit card debt. This can spell trouble if you are not diligent about making those payments on time each month. Not to mention you want your credit score to stay in good standing. If this is your situation, look into paying off your credit card debt first since that usually carries a higher interest rate than student loans.

Find frugal ways to have fun - Just because you are fresh out of college and money is tight, doesn't mean you can't enjoy life. There are tons of ways to still have fun and socialize without breaking your budget. Skip dinner and cocktails out and have friends over for dinner and a movie instead.

Further your education while you are young - Once you graduate college, you may or may not want to further your education. With that being said, one of the best investments you can make is in yourself and your lifetime earning power. The earlier you do this the better, and you will see the pay off over time. Even if you don't go after an advanced degree, pursuing certifications can also add to your earning power.

It's okay to splurge occasionally - As a recent grad, you are by default living frugally. It is okay, though, to splurge a

---

Advisory services through Capital Advisory Group Advisory Services LLC and securities through United Planners Financial Services of America, a Limited Partnership. Member FINRA and SIPC. The Capital Advisory Group Advisory Services, LLC (CAG) and United Planners Financial Services are not affiliated.

little on a purchase that will bring you joy. This is not a weekly or monthly thing. It is a once in a while thing and will help keep up your motivation to keep pursuing your financial goals.

Travel with a group to save money - It is possible to experience travel without breaking the bank. Get together a bunch of friends for a road trip and share hotel rooms. Set a budget for travel and stick to it.

Cancel unnecessary subscriptions and memberships - Go through your monthly bank statements and weed out any unnecessary subscriptions like streaming services and the gym. Try and work out at home and if your parents have a Netflix account for example, see if you can be included on it.

Come up with a down payment plan - One day down the line you will want to buy a house/condo and you will need the down payment for it. This may seem impossible, but it is doable. It is important to think out the next 5-10 years of your life and come up with a way to start saving for this.

Get your resume in order - Putting together a resume is hard when you are just graduating and you don't have much experience to add. The good news here is that you most likely do. Think about the skills your ideal employer would be looking for and see where you might have developed those skills. This could be from an on-campus job, volunteer work, an internship or work as a tutor. Emphasize any of these skills on your résumé.

Hire a financial planner - Even though you may not have much money or assets when you graduate, meeting with a financial planner is a smart move. They can help you figure out your student loans, investment choices and more. Financial literacy is something you want to familiarize yourself with from the beginning so that you start off your financial journey on the right foot.

Advisory services through Capital Advisory Group Advisory Services LLC and securities through United Planners Financial Services of America, a Limited Partnership. Member FINRA and SIPC. The Capital Advisory Group Advisory Services, LLC (CAG) and United Planners Financial Services are not affiliated.

Put these money tips into action - When you graduate college, you are starting a new financial life. The sooner you get a hold of your finances, the better off you will be down the road. Be very careful of how you spend your money, and when you are thinking about spending more than you should, envision the future. You may experience some setbacks on the job front, but keep your focus on your financial goals, and a successful financial future awaits you.

Advisory services through Capital Advisory Group Advisory Services LLC and securities through United Planners Financial Services of America, a Limited Partnership. Member FINRA and SIPC. The Capital Advisory Group Advisory Services, LLC (CAG) and United Planners Financial Services are not affiliated.

Advisory services through Capital Advisory Group Advisory Services LLC and securities through United Planners Financial Services of America, a Limited Partnership. Member FINRA and SIPC. The Capital Advisory Group Advisory Services, LLC (CAG) and United Planners Financial Services are not affiliated.

Section IV
Other Key Advice and Resources

"The computer was born to solve problems that did not exist before."

—Bill Gates

"Computing is not about computers any more. It is about living."

—Nicholas Negroponte

On-line College Resources

"Whether you want to uncover the secrets of the universe, or you just want to pursue a career in the 21'st century, basic computer [operation and] programming is an essential skill to learn."

—Stephen Hawking

4.1 How to Use On-line College Resources to Help Your Experience?

Online resources have made an entire revolution in education, not only because they are convenient and accessible, but also because they make the entire process of teaching and learning more interesting and memorable. There are free and paid online resources for college students and they usually complement one another quite well. Each student will prefer different resources according to their subjects of interest and learning style, but there are universally great tools that impress nearly every student who tries them.

In order to help college students locate the best online resources that will make their lives easier, we tailored a list of 13 most useful links that offer exactly what they need for achieving good grades.

Atrixware e-learning solutions blog- Atrixware.com is a company that has developed a great online learning management system that enables students to create great presentations easily. However, the really valuable resource is the blog section of this website, where you can read fresh information about the most popular and most useful e-learning tools.

Custom writing service NinjaEssays.com- NinjaEssays. com lists useful educative social media tools that will motivate you to learn new things each day by making the studying process easier and more fun. This is a very valuable resource that will help you advance your education and improve learning skills. With the usage of these tools, the entire classroom will be more effective and motivated.

NinjaEssays also provides:

- Essay Help Online
- Research Paper Help
- Dissertation Writing Services
- Buy Custom Essay
- Academic Writing Service
- Essay Writing
- Dissertation Writing
- Research Paper Writing
- Editing Service
- Proofreading Service
- Formatting

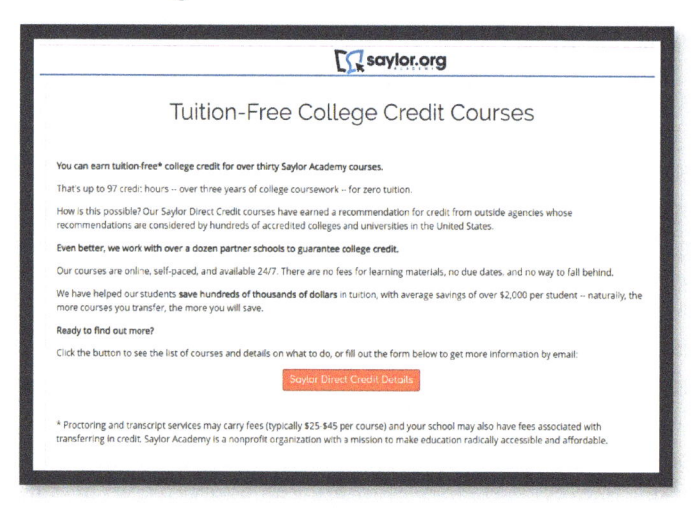

Tuition-Free College Credit Courses

You can earn tuition-free* college credit for over thirty Saylor Academy courses.

That's up to 97 credit hours -- over three years of college coursework - for zero tuition.

How is this possible? Our Saylor Direct Credit courses have earned a recommendation for credit from outside agencies whose recommendations are considered by hundreds of accredited colleges and universities in the United States.

Even better, we work with over a dozen partner schools to guarantee college credit.

Our courses are online, self-paced, and available 24/7. There are no fees for learning materials, no due dates, and no way to fall behind.

We have helped our students **save hundreds of thousands of dollars** in tuition, with average savings of over $2,000 per student -- naturally, the more courses you transfer, the more you will save.

Ready to find out more?

Click the button to see the list of courses and details on what to do, or fill out the form below to get more information by email:

Saylor Direct Credit Details

* Proctoring and transcript services may carry fees (typically $25-$45 per course) and your school may also have fees associated with transferring in credit. Saylor Academy is a nonprofit organization with a mission to make education radically accessible and affordable.

Saylor.org- The Saylor Foundation started with a very simple, honest, and strong idea: to make education free for everyone. If you are looking for free classes on all sorts of subjects, this is the place where you can find them.

Advisory services through Capital Advisory Group Advisory Services LLC and securities through United Planners Financial Services of America, a Limited Partnership. Member FINRA and SIPC. The Capital Advisory Group Advisory Services, LLC (CAG) and United Planners Financial Services are not affiliated.

StudyGuideZone.com - Although the website looks outdated, Study Guide Zone is a great place for free resources for any student who is looking for a way to improve the scores on a standardized test. The website offers study exams for SAT, ACT, and GED among many other tests.

GettingSmart.com - Getting Smart is one of the most passionate learning-focused communities on the web. The website will lead you to ways and resources that will increase your studying effectiveness.

CompassLearning.com - Compass Learning is a website that helps teachers understand the strengths, motivations, and needs of every student so they can personalize their approach to different types of learners. CompassLearning Odyssey is a product that assesses the needs and strengths of a student and then prescribes a learning path according to his/her individual characteristics.

KnowledgeNet.com - This is the website you should visit whenever you need useful sources that will help you understand the lectures of IT-related subjects.

Coursera.com - This is one of the most valuable learning resources on the web. Students can find free courses provided by prestigious universities. Almost all courses are offered, including humanities, computer science, business, mathematics, biology, and more. This website is necessary for all students who want to expand their knowledge on a subject or find information they will use for their school projects.

Alison.com - Alison.com is a website founded with a noble goal: to enable anyone to receive free education of high quality. All you need is a desire to learn new things, and this website will provide you with all necessary tools.

E-LearningCenter.com - This comprehensive website will provide you with learning resources relevant to the subjects of Web Development and IT. Although some of the content is accessible only through paid subscription, there are also free resources that can be enough for you to advance your knowledge in these subjects.

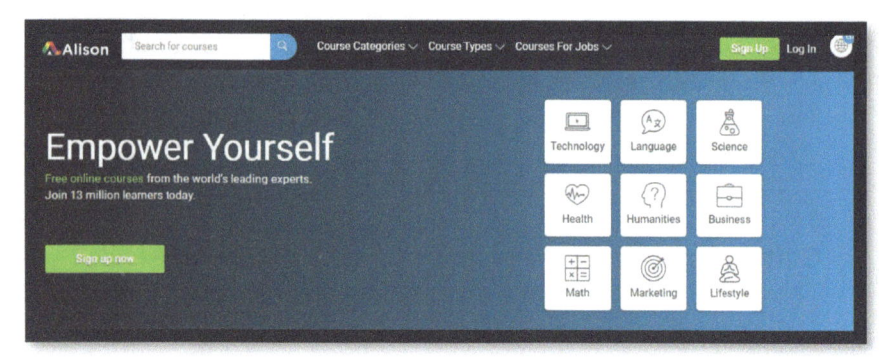

FindTutorials.com - This website collects useful tutorials from across the web, so you will find literally anything you need there. The best thing about FindTutorials.com is that the users vote on the quality of all offered tutorials, so you will know which links are worth clicking on.

CourseBuffet.com - This search engine will lead you to open courseware accessible from different websites. This will save you from going from one source to another without finding what you need.

Open Culture - The content offered on this website is not only useful for your school project, but your personal intellectual development as well. Open Culture delivers content from many different topics, from writing tips and literature characters to world history and wars.

One of the greatest benefits of the Internet technology is that now everyone has access to the information they need. The websites listed above can offer great help for all students who want to advance their knowledge or make the process of studying and writing papers easier.

Advisory services through Capital Advisory Group Advisory Services LLC and securities through United Planners Financial Services of America, a Limited Partnership. Member FINRA and SIPC. The Capital Advisory Group Advisory Services, LLC (CAG) and United Planners Financial Services are not affiliated.

Advisory services through Capital Advisory Group Advisory Services LLC and securities through United Planners Financial Services of America, a Limited Partnership. Member FINRA and SIPC. The Capital Advisory Group Advisory Services, LLC (CAG) and United Planners Financial Services are not affiliated.

"The internet is no longer a web that we connect to. Instead, it's a computerized, networked, and interconnected world that we live in. This is the future, and what we're calling the Internet of Things."

—Bruce Schneier

Best Apps for College Preparation

"The goal of the computer is to provide people with the means to extend people's minds and bodies. It is an exoskeleton that expands our human reach."

—Jean-Louis Gassee

"We are drowning in information but starved for knowledge."

—John Naisbitt

4.2 What are the Best Applications for Preparing for College?

So, it's time to start the college search, and you want to avoid becoming overwhelmed while simultaneously narrowing down your choice of schools, navigating the financial aid process, and preparing for the SAT or ACT. Fortunately, there's a number of apps available to help you prepare for college with the least amount of stress possible.

The College Search

When you're beginning your search, a comprehensive clearinghouse for information is The College Fair app. This free app allows you to research over 3,000 schools as well as search by location, major, or career. There is also a mobile mentor option to have your questions answered by college coaches.

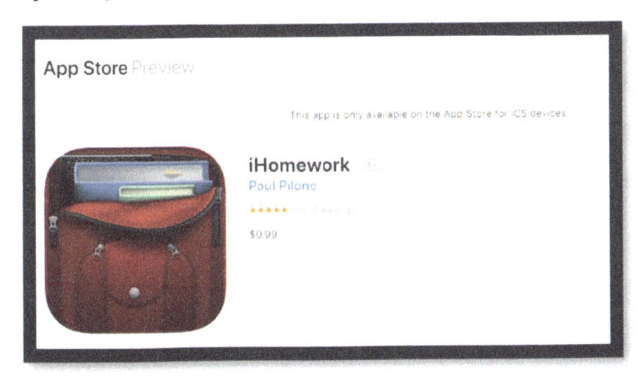

iHomework.com - This app is available on all Apple devices, so you can access it wherever you are.

The idea behind its concept is to make your life as a student easier. You can use iHomework to quickly enter important tasks, course information, and homework assignments.

CollegeHunch is a research app packed full of features. You can easily compile and compare data for multiple schools using the spreadsheet function. You can generate a spreadsheet with data for the schools you select in minutes rather than hours; view in app, export or print for easy reference. Streamline your research with advanced filtering, sorting, quick links and fast facts. Find stats on student demographics, test scores, admission requirements, tuition costs, and more. The app also has interactive guides for over 1,000 colleges and a calendar feature.

A college advice app, **CollegeGo** helps with the college-planning process. The app is particularly useful if you are just getting started and want to learn the basics. The game, video, and search features let you explore colleges and find scholarship and financial-aid data. You can use the app to help identify career opportunities or majors as well. If you have a College Board account, you can access your information from the app or online.

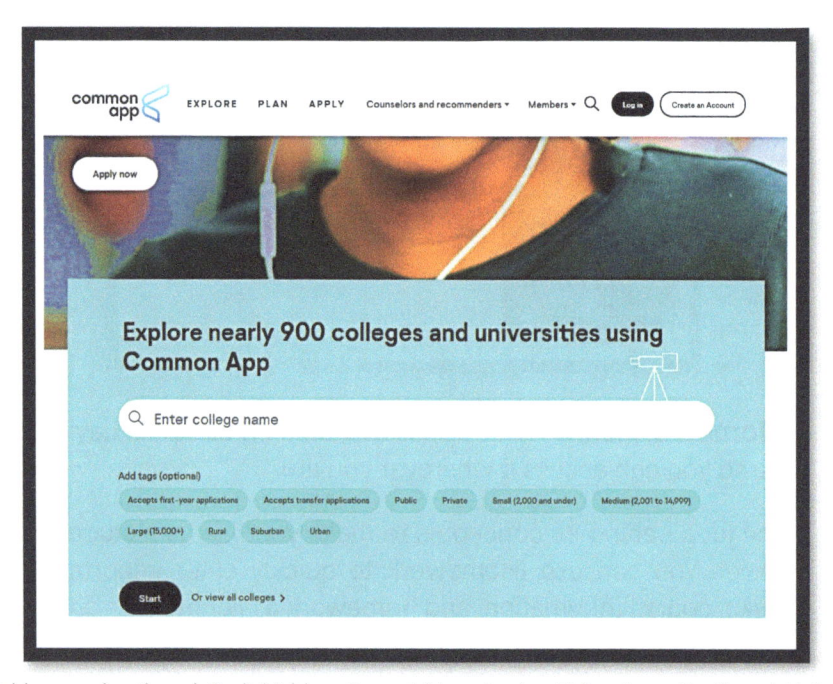

Advisory services through Capital Advisory Group Advisory Services LLC and securities through United Planners Financial Services of America, a Limited Partnership. Member FINRA and SIPC. The Capital Advisory Group Advisory Services, LLC (CAG) and United Planners Financial Services are not affiliated.

YouVisit offers visitors 360-degree and virtual-reality tours of over 600 colleges. Save time and resources by visiting college campuses from the convenience of your computer, phone or tablet. Not only can you see a campus from the outside, you can view the inside of advising offices, campus libraries, residential living areas, athletic complexes, and more.

Once you've narrowed down your choices, **The Common Application** allows you to complete one application online which can then be submitted to multiple schools. Over 700 colleges from Adelphi University to Zaytuna College accept this common app. As an added feature, your account dashboard allows you to manage all your applications and alerts you to upcoming deadlines. There is also a virtual counselor function and a separate set of materials for Spanish speakers. You can download the Common Application at iTunes and Google Play.

"The first step towards getting somewhere is to decide that you are not going to stay where you are."

—Anonymous

"Opportunities don't just happen, you create them."

—Anonymous

How to Successfully Change Your Career

- Assess your interests and skills
- Consider alternative careers
- Reach out for informational interviews
- Spend time job shadowing
- Volunteer in the field
- Take a class / upgrade your skills

the balance

"Choose a job you love and you will never have to work a day in your life."

—Confucius

"If you are not making mistakes, you are not doing anything."

—John Wooden

4.3 When Should You Consider Going Back to College to Learn a New Profession?

Making a career switch is no easy decision, especially when considering the change at 40 or older. You might be wondering which careers are really worth going back to school for at this stage in your career and if the time (and money) spent seeking a degree or certification is worth the payoff.

Luckily, there are several fields worth the mid-career return to school whether income, job security, happiness, or fulfillment at work is your focus for making the switch.

To help you get started, we've rounded up 17 careers across six fields with help from the Bureau of Labor Statistics that are absolutely worth the investment of returning to school.

Registered Nurse - With a stable and constant projected growth and a median salary of $70,000 per year, nursing is a secure career choice worth returning to school. To succeed in this field, expect to provide care, education, and support to patients with varying medical needs within hospitals, physicians' offices, and/or through home care.

Time in School: two to four years

Nursing students can shoot for an associate's degree in nursing (two years), a nursing-school specific diploma (time varies), or a Bachelor of Science degree in nursing (four years).

Medical Administrative Assistant - If you prefer to work in the medical field without direct contact with patients, then a career as a medical secretary may suit you well. The median salary of these professionals is around $34,610 per year. Medical secretaries do more than just set appointments. Often, this role also handles medical reports, billing, and creating medical charts. Successful candidates for this position will need a strong grasp on clerical skills as well as basic medical knowledge of terminology, technology, and procedures.

Time in School: Around two years

While entry-level positions may be offered to those with only a high-school diploma, taking specific training can help an aspiring medical administrative assistant land a position faster. Many community colleges and technical schools offer programs specific to medical administrative duties, where students learn the basics of administrative work, as well as the specific medical technology they will need to succeed in their roles.

Physical Therapist - Another fantastic option within the Healthcare field, physical therapists can earn a median salary of around $86,850 per year. A successful Physical Therapist will help patients manage pain and improve physical movement due to injuries, illnesses, and after procedures.

Time in School: Around seven years

To become a physical therapist, you will need to earn a doc-

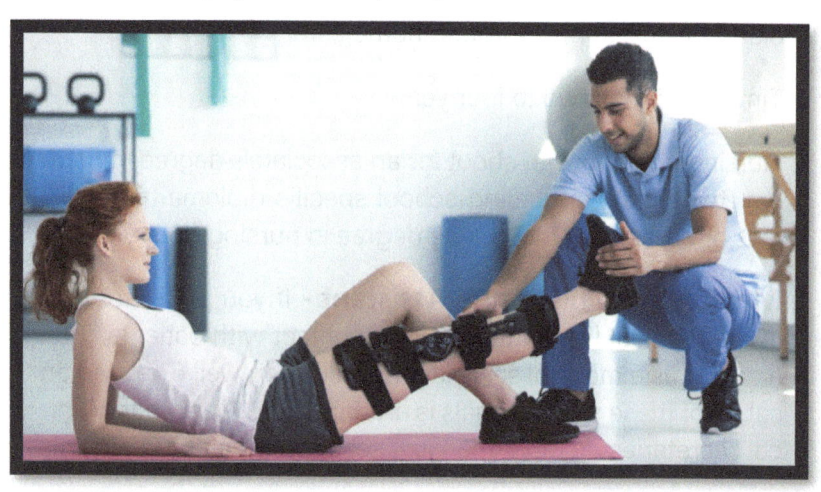

Advisory services through Capital Advisory Group Advisory Services LLC and securities through United Planners Financial Services of America, a Limited Partnership. Member FINRA and SIPC. The Capital Advisory Group Advisory Services, LLC (CAG) and United Planners Financial Services are not affiliated.

torate in physical therapy (three years) in addition to a Bachelor of Science Degree four4 years). If you're just starting fresh with no prior college education, many degree programs offer a 6-year degree program to complete all requirements from start to finish. While on the longer end of time from starting education to completion, the job satisfaction and salaries reported by America's physical therapists make this career well worth the wait.

Software Developer - The tech industry won't be slowing down anytime soon. In fact, as tech continues to take over the workforce, this career is a secure, safe, and even lucrative choice when considering a career switch. The median salary for a software developer is currently around $103,560 per year. To earn that salary, expect to be creating programs for devices such as computers, smartphones, tablets, and more!

Time in School: About four years

Successful software developers often earn a Bachelor of Science degree in either computer science or software engineering. If you have an associate's degree, you may be able to complete a Bachelor of Science degree program in as little as two years.

Web Developer - A web developer is just as it sounds—a professional who designs websites from start to finish for a median salary of around $67,990 per year. Web developers can work as part of a design or marketing agency, work as freelancers, or even start their own businesses creating websites for other businesses and professionals.

Time in School: two to four years

Web developers need to be well-versed in both coding and graphic design, as they often create both the back-end and the front-end of a website themselves. Due to this balance of skills, there are actually many routes one can take to jump-start a career in web development. An associate's degree or a four-year degree in web design is highly common in this field, but a mix of graphic design and coding for web courses can help start this career as well. It's not unusual for many web developers to be completely self-taught, which is definitely something to consider to save time and money.

Information Security Analyst - With a median salary of around $95,510 per year, information security analysts help protect the information and data of their business and organization clients. These professionals are often planning and creating strategies to combat cyber-security attacks with both businesses and consumers in mind.

Additionally, information security can be a highly lucrative career when working in conjunction with the U.S. military, where those with security clearances can earn at or well above the median salary.

Time in School: Around four years

Information security analysts typically earn a four-year Bachelor of Science degree in a tech-related field such as information assurance, computer science, and/or programming.

Accountant - Accountants (and auditors) work with financial reports, taxes, and records. Their job is to ensure all financial information, whether for a business, professional, or individual, is accurate and that taxes are paid properly and promptly. If you're considering a career as an accountant, expect to see a median salary of $69,350 per year.

Time in School: Around four to six years

Many auditors and accountants have a Bachelor of Science degree in accounting. Alternatively, there has been a shift in employers preferring those with a master's degree, either in accounting or a related field in business. A bachelor's degree

---

Advisory services through Capital Advisory Group Advisory Services LLC and securities through United Planners Financial Services of America, a Limited Partnership. Member FINRA and SIPC. The Capital Advisory Group Advisory Services, LLC (CAG) and United Planners Financial Services are not affiliated.

will set you back about four years, and a master's degree about two.

Financial Analyst - Unlike an accountant who focuses on the taxes and records side of a business, a financial consultant often deals with stocks and investments and guides both businesses and individuals in financial decisions. The median salary for a financial analyst is $84,300, or $40.53 per hour.

Time in School: About four years

Pursuing a career as a financial analyst creates a generous amount of freedom when choosing a degree field. Typically, a four-year degree in either economics, statistics, finance, or even mathematics can be suitable for this career path. Whichever path you may choose, a wide variety of fields are open to you as more often than not, all types of businesses need the expertise of a financial analyst.

Elementary School Teacher - A career in teaching can be a rewarding and secure choice, as elementary school teaching positions are at an average growth rate that is predicted to stay more or less the same in future years. While starting salaries may be low for new teachers, the median salary for elementary teaching positions is $57,160.

Time in School: At least four years

In addition to a bachelor's degree, elementary school teachers must also obtain a license or certification issued by the state in which they work. Expect a fair amount of continuing education to account for curriculum changes and new teaching materials over time.

Higher Education Professor - If you prefer to work with more mature pupils, a career in higher education can be just as rewarding as you work to help students succeed in their future careers. Additionally, the median salary for a career in higher education is considerable at $76,000 per year.

What's more, becoming a college professor can also allow you to work from anywhere as several colleges and universities offer online degree programs for their students.

Time in School: At least two to eight years post-grad

Most traditional four-year institutions require professors to have at least a master's, if not a doctoral degree. Pursuing a doctoral at age 40 might seem daunting, but if you've previously completed a bachelor's degree, you can easily expand this degree into a master's or even a doctoral degree in a major related to your previous field of study. Even if you don't want to spend quite that much time in school, you're still in luck—many private, state, and community colleges opt to hire higher education professors who've earned master's degrees with demonstrated expertise in their field.

Academic Success Counselor - If you desire a career in education but prefer to work outside of the classroom, then consider becoming an academic success counselor. These professionals provide guidance and support for students in higher education, helping them navigate the journey to completing their degrees. The median salary for school counselors (or academic success counselors) is $55,410.

Time in School: About four to six years

Most schools require counselors to have a master's degree as well as a certification or credential in school counseling. A good idea is to also specialize in career development, especially if you're considering becoming a counselor in higher education. If you have some previous education under your belt, like an associate's degree, the time to complete all schooling for a career as a school counselor can take as little as four years.

Market Research Analyst - With a growth rate of 26% and climbing, a career as a market research analyst is a secure choice for a career change. Even better, these professionals can work in a variety of fields, as several types of organizations often need the skills of a market research analyst to run their businesses. So just what does a market research analyst do? Typically, this position aims to study and predict trends among a target market for a specific business, helping to predict who to target for sales and how to sell to them. A career as a market research analyst earns a median salary of about $63,230 per year.

Time in School: Up to four years

These positions typically require a bachelor's degree in a field relating to market research. Additionally, strong analytical skills, as well as a tight grasp on mathematics, will help the aspiring market research analyst go far.

If you already have a bachelor's degree in a similar field, but feel the need to get more education under your belt, a master's degree in market research is always eye-catching to employers.

Search Engine Optimization Specialist - A relatively new career compared to the others in this roundup, search engine optimization specialists blend market research, web development, and advertising to succeed in their roles.

Simply put, they work closely with the algorithms of search engines like Google and Bing to bring traffic to their clients' websites, where the goal of that traffic can be anything from higher views and more social media engagement to increased sales. According to Payscale, the median salary for a search engine optimization specialist is around $55,530 per year, and the role boosts an impressive job satisfaction rate.

Time in School: Up to four years

Search engine optimization, or SEO, is a fast-paced and ever-changing aspect of internet marketing. As such, there aren't degree programs specific to the role, as the teachings could change in the blink of an eye. Instead, expect to seek a degree in fields such as business, digital marketing, and data analytics. If you're considering a career as an SEO specialist, be prepared for frequent continuing education in the form of industry-recognized digital marketing courses and certifications, such as those offered by Google and Hubspot.

Public Relations Specialist - Think you can cultivate and maintain a dynamic and positive public image for a business? That's exactly what the role of a public relations specialist entails. These professionals are responsible for handling announcements, press releases, and social media campaigns. Public relations specialists often earn a median income of around $59,300 per year.

Time in School: About four years

A career in public relations often requires a bachelor's degree in public relations, communications, business, or journalism. If you possess strong writing and communication skills, a career as a public relations specialist could be a great fit for you.

Project Manager - Those with exceptional organization and management skills would do well to consider a career as a project manager. These professionals manage several aspects of a business from internal communications to team members and, of course, projects. The median salary for a project manager is around $67,280 per year.

Time in School: Up to four years

Due to the flexibility of the position, those seeking a career in project management can pursue a degree in a wide variety of fields, such as business management, computer science, marketing, or even engineering, depending on the field you choose to work in.

Executive Administrative Assistant - An executive administrative assistant handles clerical tasks for their businesses on advanced levels. In addition to carrying out clerical tasks like filing and call routing (as an entry-level administrative assistant would), executive assistants often prepare critical re-

---

Advisory services through Capital Advisory Group Advisory Services LLC and securities through United Planners Financial Services of America, a Limited Partnership. Member FINRA and SIPC. The Capital Advisory Group Advisory Services, LLC (CAG) and United Planners Financial Services are not affiliated.

ports, documents, and oversee/train lower-level staff.

Time in School: Up to four years

Expect to earn a Bachelor of Science or a Bachelor of Arts degree in a business-related field. Your field of study will typically be determined by the type of business you choose. If you desire to work in the financial field, a financial-related business management degree can help prepare you for the high-level tasks expected of an executive administrative assistant.

Human Resources Manager - Another administrative role, human resource managers handle the employee side of a business. These professionals specialize in recruiting and hiring new employees for the business and often work with high-level executives on strategy.

Additionally, they act as a bridge between an employer and its employees while managing the relationships of employees as well.

The median salary for a human resources manager is about $110,120 per year.

Time in School: Up to four years

A bachelor's degree in human resources and strong interpersonal and communication skills are required for a career as a human resources manager. Additionally, employers often value varying types of previous work experience from administrative tasks and reporting to customer service and team management.

Advisory services through Capital Advisory Group Advisory Services LLC and securities through United Planners Financial Services of America, a Limited Partnership. Member FINRA and SIPC. The Capital Advisory Group Advisory Services, LLC (CAG) and United Planners Financial Services are not affiliated.

Final Words on Going Back to School Later In Life

While heading back to school in the middle of your career can seem daunting, you now have a clearer idea of what to expect when narrowing your selection to careers worthy of making the switch. The best part is, at 40 and older, you've already accumulated several years of valuable life and work experience, and can use this experience to guide you through the next chapter, or use it to help give you a boost in your new career.

Advisory services through Capital Advisory Group Advisory Services LLC and securities through United Planners Financial Services of America, a Limited Partnership. Member FINRA and SIPC. The Capital Advisory Group Advisory Services, LLC (CAG) and United Planners Financial Services are not affiliated.

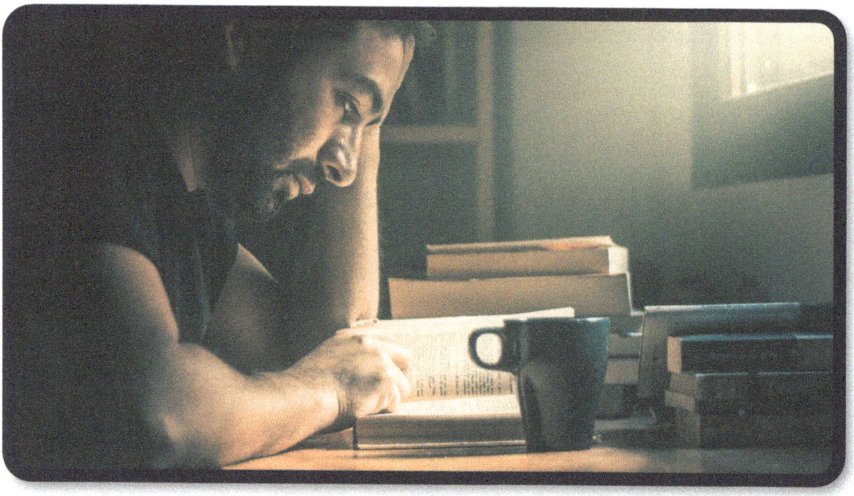

4.4 Greatest Tips for Going to School Later in Life

Advice for returning to school later in life: it's never too late to start a meaningful career. Today's colleges have students of all ages, from new high school graduates to professionals with decades of experience in nursing and other industries.

What unites them is a shared passion for a better life. We think that the right profession can be a calling, and sometimes it takes years to hear it. If you're among the many adults deciding to go back to school later in life, you're not alone, and you're not without support. Here are five helpful tips to make the transition back into student life a little easier.

Communicate with your loved ones - Deciding to go to college will require adjustments for you and for your family. If you're married with kids when you go back to school, the transition can be difficult for all of you, so from the very beginning you need to communicate clearly. What would earning your BS in Nursing mean to you and your family? What opportunities would arise by your becoming a certified medical assistant?

Even before you apply to college or technical programs, tell your kids, spouse, and friends why you want to become an accountant, nurse or dental lab technician, and explain what that will look like for your finances and time together. Setting clear and realistic short- and long-term expectations can alleviate a lot of the tensions that will arise when schedules change and clinical rotations absorb your emotional energy.

Make a schedule — and stick to it - As you communicate and set expectations, you need to make a plan for your

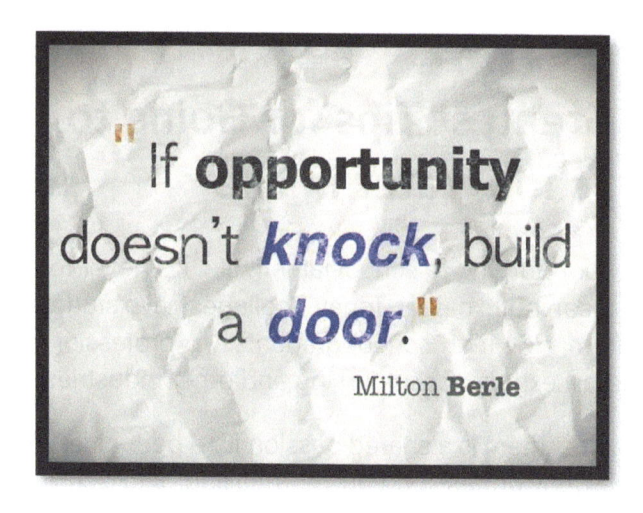

> "If **opportunity** doesn't *knock*, build a *door*."
>
> Milton **Berle**

time. Obviously, this will require some adjusting with each new term, but you should have a fairly rigid schedule outlining when you'll go to class, when you'll study, when you'll work, when you'll sleep, and when you'll spend time with family. It sounds like a lot, and it is, but remember that hundreds of thousands of adult students manage it all every year, and remember too that it's temporary.

You're not going to be a student and a parent and an employee at the same time, forever. For example, you can complete a medical assisting program in less than a year, or complete your BSN degree online in just three semesters. Once you finish, new opportunities will be opened to you for the rest of your career. Juggling everything won't be easy, but in the long run, it's worth it. Others choose attending night school or going on-line for classes in a more flexible format.

Don't stress the test - If you haven't been a student in a long time, going back to school and encountering exams and projects can feel especially daunting. That's natural, but remember what you heard over and over in high school: It's just a test. Grades and assessments matter, but exams are only designed to ensure you know the information you'll need for your nursing, medical assisting, or dental technician career.

Advisory services through Capital Advisory Group Advisory Services LLC and securities through United Planners Financial Services of America, a Limited Partnership. Member FINRA and SIPC. The Capital Advisory Group Advisory Services, LLC (CAG) and United Planners Financial Services are not affiliated.

At the end of the day, if you've retained that knowledge, you'll be fine, even if you haven't taken a test or written a report in years. And the less you stress, the better your mind will be at remembering that knowledge when it's time for finals.

Look into financial aid - Financial aid isn't just for young students. Anyone can qualify, so like everybody else you need to apply for the FAFSA and look into financial aid options as soon as you decide you're going back to school. College may not be the financial burden you and your family expected, but you'll never know unless you apply.

Remember to sleep - And just take care of yourself, overall. Major life changes entail stress, and if you're an adult adding school on top of all of your personal and professional responsibilities, it's easy to forget about your health in the process. Sufficient rest is essential to succeeding as a college student, whatever your age. You also need the same nutrition and aerobic exercise you're learning to recommend to future patients. Practice what you're taught until the day you graduate — and beyond.

> "Either run the day or the day runs you."
>
> *Jim Rohn*

Advisory services through Capital Advisory Group Advisory Services LLC and securities through United Planners Financial Services of America, a Limited Partnership. Member FINRA and SIPC. The Capital Advisory Group Advisory Services, LLC (CAG) and United Planners Financial Services are not affiliated.

"It is what you put into your college experience that makes you a success, not where you went to college."

—Brett Machtig

"My college is better that yours."

—Most College Graduates

4.5 How to Pick the Best College for You

The college search doesn't have to begin and end with the "Ivies" and the name brand schools. There are many schools out there to choose from -- some known and some less known, all worthy of your attention. Here's some advice for trying to find the school that works for you.

Start with who you are and why you are going. You need to examine yourself and your reasons for going to college before you start your search. Why, really, are you going? What are your abilities and strengths? What are your weaknesses? What do you want out of life — something tangible or intangible? Are you socially self-sufficient or do you need warm, familial support? Talk with your family, friends and high-school counselors as you ask these questions. The people who know you best can help you the most with these important issues.

Size matters: Your College does not have to be bigger than your high school. Most good liberal arts colleges have a population of fewer than 4,000 for a reason; college is a time to explore, and a smaller community is more conducive to internal exploration. It is not the number of people, but the people themselves and the kind of community in which you will learn that really matters. Many large universities have established "honors colleges" within the larger university for these same reasons.

A name-brand college will not guarantee your success. Think about the people in your life who are happy and successful and find out where (and if) they went to college. Ask the same about "famous" people.

You will likely find that success in life has less to do with the choice of college than with the experiences and opportunities encountered while in college, coupled with personal qualities and traits.

> ### More things to think about...
>
> - **A name brand college <u>does not</u> guarantee your success**
>   - Think about the people who are happy and successful in your life and ask where they went to college
>   - You will most likely find that success in life has a lot less to do with the choice of the college than with the experiences and opportunities you encountered while you were there. It truly is what you make of it!
>   - Employers and graduate schools look more at your outstanding skills and experience, and less at the college you attended.

Employers and graduate schools are looking for outstanding skills and experience, not college pedigree. As you search for colleges, ask about student outcomes; you will find many colleges that outperform the Ivies and "name brands," even though you may have never heard of them! Visit the National Survey of Student Engagement (NSSE) for help on sorting through the information and for great questions to ask when visiting and choosing a college.

You don't need to pick a major to pick a college. Very few high-school students have enough information or experience to choose a major. You need the variety and depth of

---

Advisory services through Capital Advisory Group Advisory Services LLC and securities through United Planners Financial Services of America, a Limited Partnership. Member FINRA and SIPC. The Capital Advisory Group Advisory Services, LLC (CAG) and United Planners Financial Services are not affiliated.

college coursework to determine your interest and aptitude. Most college students change their minds two or three times before they settle on a major, and they can still graduate in four years! Being undecided is a good thing and will leave you open to more academic experiences.

Don't be scared by the stories. If you only pay attention to the headlines, you might start to believe that no one is getting in anywhere! The truth is that the majority of the colleges and universities in this country admit more students than they reject. If you're worried about your chances of getting admitted -- and you're willing to investigate beyond the very narrow band of highly selective colleges -- you'll find that you have many options that will lead to a great fit for you. Ask your high-school counselor for additional advice and guidance as it applies to your school.

You can afford to go to college. If you make the assumption that you cannot afford college based on the "sticker price" of tuition, you will miss out. It is difficult to talk about money, but if you investigate all the options and ask for help and advice, you will find affordable choices. Online resources, as well as financial aid workshops sponsored by high schools in local communities, are widely available to get you started. College and university financial aid Web sites offer useful information and links as well. Investigate early and ask for help.

You don't have to go to college right away, and it's never too late. There is no such thing as the perfect time to start college. Some students benefit from a year off to work, study or travel, and these experiences allow them to be better, more engaged students. Some students choose to apply to college and gain admission and then defer their entrance, while others wait to apply until after they have had an alternative experience. Either way, admissions officers will be anxious

Advisory services through Capital Advisory Group Advisory Services LLC and securities through United Planners Financial Services of America, a Limited Partnership. Member FINRA and SIPC. The Capital Advisory Group Advisory Services, LLC (CAG) and United Planners Financial Services are not affiliated.

to learn about your experience during your time off, and they'll ask you to write about it as part of your admissions process. High-school and college admission counselors can provide resources for investigating alternatives that may be right for you. You could apply for an internship, study abroad, or participate in a community service project.

Many colleges have sister schools around the world. Below is a list of colleges outside the US.

#	College	Country	Size
	The 20 Best Colleges Outside the US		
1	University of Oxford	United Kingdom	20,664
2	University of Cambridge	United Kingdom	18,978
3	University of Edinburgh	United Kingdom	29,433
4	University of Toronto	Canada	73,370
5	Imperial College of London	United Kingdom	16,171
6	Technical University of Munich	Germany	40,472
7	University of Melbourne	Australia	47,385
8	National University of Singapore	Singapore	30,869
9	King's College	United Kingdom	26,057
10	LMU - Munich	Germany	34,519
11	London School of Economics	United Kingdom	10,570
12	Tsinghua University	China	38,783
13	Tel Aviv University	Israel	22,414
14	Kyoto University	Japan	22,566
15	Nanyang Technical University	Singapore	25,088
16	Australian National University	Australia	17,359
17	Paris Science et Lettres -PSL	France	21,298
18	Hong Kong University of Science and Technology	Hong Kong	10,125
19	Seoul University	South Korea	26,182
20	University of Hong Kong	China	18,260

Advisory services through Capital Advisory Group Advisory Services LLC and securities through United Planners Financial Services of America, a Limited Partnership. Member FINRA and SIPC. The Capital Advisory Group Advisory Services, LLC (CAG) and United Planners Financial Services are not affiliated.

The most important factor in choosing a college is fit.
Choosing a college because your friends are going there or because of where it ranks on a list does not take into account who you are and who you will become. College is a match to be made, not a prize to be won.

Finding a good fit requires time and thoughtfulness. Visiting college Web sites and learning about what events take place, who visits as guest speakers, and how to get in touch with current students and faculty is a good way to supplement a campus visit -- or to decide if you want to spend the time and money on a visit. Check a school's Web site to find the admissions officer assigned to your region of the country.

Send them an e-mail to ask about getting in touch with students from your area or identifying a few with interests similar to yours. When you visit, try to build in time to sit in on classes, eat in the dining hall and hang around in the student center or other high-traffic areas. That will help you imagine yourself as part of the community. Talk to a few students and ask if they would make the same college choice if they had to do it again. Go back to the first item in this list as you consider the information you've collected about the colleges. You will have great options!

Advisory services through Capital Advisory Group Advisory Services LLC and securities through United Planners Financial Services of America, a Limited Partnership. Member FINRA and SIPC. The Capital Advisory Group Advisory Services, LLC (CAG) and United Planners Financial Services are not affiliated.

"The more that you read, the more things you will know. The more that you learn, the more places you will go."

—Dr. Seuss

"When I think of all the books still left for me to read, I am certain of further happiness."

—Jules Renard

"Reading is the skill that makes all other learning possible."

—Barack Obama

"Reading to the mind is like exercise to the body."

—Richard Steele

4.6 Best Books on Where to Get Help

How to Prepare and Succeed in College

The Graduate Survival Guide: 5 Mistakes You Can't Afford To Make In College by Anthony O'Neal, who is on a mission to help EVERY high school graduate succeed in college and beyond. The Graduate Survival Guide is the ultimate manual for students, identifying five mistakes to avoid making in college. These mistakes can lead to years of pain and expensive life lessons. As Anthony tells students, "The caliber of your future will be determined by the choices you make today." This is a must-have book for every high school senior!

A Twenty-Something's Guide to Financial Freedom, by Josh Gronholz, Brett Machtig, and Henry H. Parker PhD. The main goal of this book is to teach you one of the most important secrets in life: how to let money make money for you. Although money is inanimate, it can breed like a living person. It can reproduce itself one time, 10 times, 100 times, 1000 times, a million times, and more.

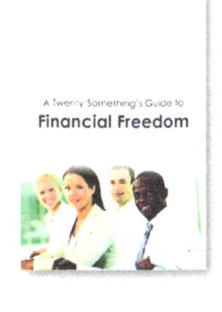

How to Win at College, by Cal Newport is still one of the best primers for college success I've ever read - especially when it comes to things beyond your grades. It's a

161

short read (I read it in about four hours), split into 75 "tips" that each takes up 1-4 pages.

"I read this book as a freshman, and it's one of the biggest reasons I was so focused on success in college; the book provides a great foundation for becoming a remarkable student and doesn't weigh you down with idle words. Countless teachers, counselors, bloggers, and other people will probably tell you to 'follow your passion' - but passion alone isn't going to land you your dream job. Plus, most of us don't even know what our 'passion' even is! That's why this book is such a breath of fresh air; Cal Newport counters this 'Passion Hypothesis' with what he calls the Craftsman Mindset, which focuses on getting really good at something. Not only will this help you build the career capital you'll need to get hired, but it'll also often lead to true enjoyment in your work."

How to Become a Straight-A Student, by Cal Newport. Whereas How to Win at College is a general, tip-based overview on ways you can become successful in college, this book gets its hands dirty by giving you an in-depth, well thought-out method for pulling epic grades in all of your classes. The book is based around that fact that there are many college students who get straight A's, yet don't study for more than a couple hours a day and still have plenty of other things going on in their lives. It lays out effective strategies for note-taking, quizzing yourself, writing papers, and more. If you want to be like one of the aforementioned students, get this book.

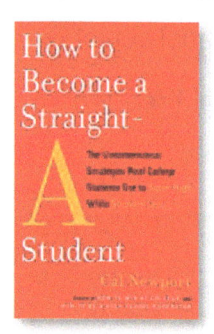

Brain Rules, By John Medina. If you know how the brain works, you'll be better equipped to manage your own and understand the ones contained inside the heads

---

Advisory services through Capital Advisory Group Advisory Services LLC and securities through United Planners Financial Services of America, a Limited Partnership. Member FINRA and SIPC. The Capital Advisory Group Advisory Services, LLC (CAG) and United Planners Financial Services are not affiliated.

of the people you know and meet. In Brain Rules, John Medina expertly shows us how the brain does things, and lays out 12 rules that form a basis for using that pile of mush more effectively. It's not just an excellent brain book, it's an excellent business book and an excellent college success book as well.

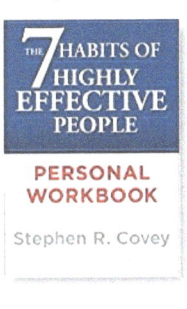

The 7 Habits of Highly Effective People, By Stephen Covey. I honestly think this book changed my life. The habits Covey describes here seem obvious at first, but you'll probably notice that you aren't following all of them. I know I wasn't. Take Habit 5 - Seek First to Understand, Then to be understood - how many of us actually do that? Before reading this book, I would always think very selfishly in my conversations. Whenever I'd listen to someone else speak, I'd listen - but I'd also be actively formulating my (usually self-serving) response and looking for the perfect moment to throw it in.

The Total Money Makeover: A Proven Plan for Financial Fitness, by Dave Ramsey. Okay, folks, do you want to turn those fat and flabby expenses into a well-toned budget? Do you want to transform your sad and skinny little bank account into a bulked-up cash machine? Then get with the program, people. There's one sure way to whip your finances into shape, and that's with The Total Money Makeover. It's the simplest, most straight-forward game plan for completely making over your money habits. And it's based on results, not pie-in-the-sky fantasies.

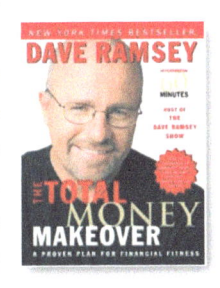

Where Financial Peace gave you the solid saving and investing principles, this book puts those principles into practice. You'll be exercising your financial strength every day and quickly freeing yourself of worry, stress, and debt. And that's a beautiful feeling.

Designing Your Life: How to Build a Well-Lived, Joyful Life by Bill Burnett and Dave Evans. At last, a book that shows you how to build - design - a life you can thrive in at any age or stage. Designers create worlds and solve problems using design thinking. Look around your office or home—at the tablet or smartphone you may be holding or the chair you are sitting in. Everything in our lives was designed by someone. And every design starts with a problem that a designer or team of designers seeks to solve.

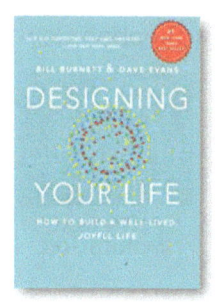

In this book, Bill Burnett and Dave Evans show us how design thinking can help us create lives that are both meaningful and fulfilling, regardless of whom or where we are, what we do or have done for a living, or how young or old we are. The same design thinking responsible for amazing technology, products, and spaces can be used to design and build your career and your life, a life of fulfillment and joy, constantly creative and productive, one that always holds the possibility of surprise.

Selecting the Best School

Find the Best Colleges for You! by U.S. News and World Report. The 2021 edition of U.S. News' famous best colleges guidebook is the indispensable navigator for high school students and their families seeking comprehensive advice on how to research their college choices, draw up a smart shortlist of schools, put together a slam-dunk application, and find the money to pay the bills.

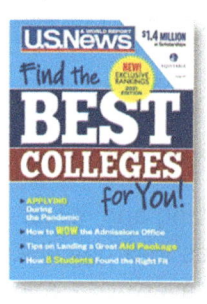

Advisory services through Capital Advisory Group Advisory Services LLC and securities through United Planners Financial Services of America, a Limited Partnership. Member FINRA and SIPC. The Capital Advisory Group Advisory Services, LLC (CAG) and United Planners Financial Services are not affiliated.

Fiske Guide to Colleges 2021 by Edward Fiske. "The best college guide you can buy."—USA Today. Every college and university has a story, and no one tells those stories like former New York Times education editor Edward B. Fiske. That's why, for more than 35 years, the Fiske Guide to Colleges has been the leading guide to 320+ four-year schools, including quotes from real students and information you won't find on college websites. Fully updated and expanded every year, Fiske is the most authoritative source of information for college-bound students and their parents. Helpful, honest, and straightforward, the Fiske Guide to Colleges delivers an insider's look at what it's really like to be a student at the "best and most interesting" schools in the United States, plus Canada, Great Britain, and Ireland, so you can find the best fits for you.

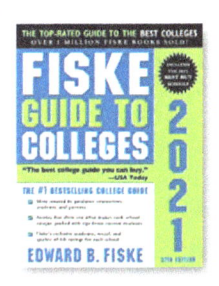

In addition to detailed and candid stories on each school, you will find:

- A self-quiz to help you understand what you are really looking for in a college
- Lists of strong programs and popular majors at each college
- "Overlap" listings to help you expand your options
- Indexes that break down schools by state, price, and average debt
- Exclusive academic, social, and quality-of-life ratings
- All the basics, including financial aid stats, SAT/ACT scores, and acceptance rates
- Plus a special section highlighting the public and private Best Buy schools—colleges that provide the best educational value

---

Advisory services through Capital Advisory Group Advisory Services LLC and securities through United Planners Financial Services of America, a Limited Partnership. Member FINRA and SIPC. The Capital Advisory Group Advisory Services, LLC (CAG) and United Planners Financial Services are not affiliated.

The Best 386 Colleges, 2021 Edition: In-Depth Profiles & Ranking Lists to Help Find the Right College For You (College Admissions Guides) by The Princeton Review. A revised and updated edition of the hottest college guidebook, a perennial favorite of the national media! NO ONE KNOWS COLLEGES LIKE THE PRINCETON REVIEW! The Princeton Review's college rankings started in 1992 with surveys from 30,000 students.

Over 25 years and more than a million student surveys later, we stand by our claim that there is no single "best" college, only the best college for you ... and that this is the book that will help you find it!

College Essays and ACT/SAT Preparation Courses

College Essay Essentials: A Step-by-Step Guide to Writing a Successful College Admissions Essay by Ethan Sawyer. Writing an amazing college admission essay is easier than you think! So you're a high school senior given the task of writing a 650-word personal statement for your college application. Do you tell the story of your life, or a story from your life? Do you choose a single moment? If so, which one? The options seem endless.

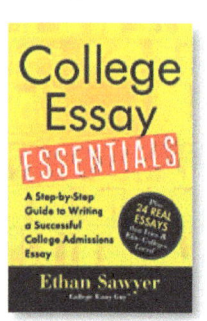

Lucky for you, they're not. College counselor Ethan Sawyer (aka The College Essay Guy) will show you that there are only four (really, four!) types of college admission essays. And all you have to do to figure out which type is best for you is answer two simple questions:

- Have you experienced significant challenges in your life?
- Do you know what you want to be or do in the future?

Advisory services through Capital Advisory Group Advisory Services LLC and securities through United Planners Financial Services of America, a Limited Partnership. Member FINRA and SIPC. The Capital Advisory Group Advisory Services, LLC (CAG) and United Planners Financial Services are not affiliated.

With these questions providing the building blocks for your essay, Sawyer guides you through the rest of the process, from choosing a structure to revising your essay, and answers the big questions that have probably been keeping you up at night: How do I brag in a way that doesn't sound like bragging? And how do I make my essay, like, deep? Packed with tips, tricks, exercises, and sample essays from real students who got into their dream schools, College Essay Essentials is the only college essay guide to make this complicated process logical, simple, and (dare we say it?) a little bit fun.

The Official ACT Prep Guide 2020-2021, (Book + 6 Practice Tests + Bonus Online Content) by ACT. The only guide from the makers of the ACT exam, packed with 6 genuine, full-length practice tests and 400 additional questions online. This new edition includes:

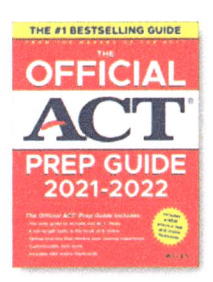

- The only book with 6 official practice tests written by the makers of the ACT

- Full of advice and suggestions to increase your studying speed

- Detailed explanations for every answer in the book

- Includes 400 flashcards online

The Official ACT Prep Guide 2020-2021 is the only guide from the makers of the exam and includes actual ACT test forms taken from past ACT exams. This updated edition includes 6 actual ACT tests (all with an optional writing test) to help you practice at your own pace and discover areas where you may need more work. The Official ACT Prep Guide 2020-2021 provides detailed explanations for every answer and practical tips on how to boost your score on the English, math, reading, science, and optional writing tests.

You'll also get access to special online bonus content developed with the test taking experience in mind where you can practice with 400 additional test questions that can be organized, filtered, and tracked for performance. Take a closer look at test day, learn what to expect, and get familiar with the test-taking strategies that are right for you. The Official ACT Prep Guide 2020-2021 is your definitive guide to getting ready for the ACT and feeling confident and comfortable on test day!

Official SAT Study Guide 2020 Edition by The College Board. Review every skill and question type needed for SAT success - now with eight total practice tests.

The 2020 edition of The Official SAT Study Guide doubles the number of official SAT(R) practice tests to eight - all of them created by the test maker. As part of the College Board's commitment to transparency, all practice tests are available on the College Board's website, but The Official SAT Study Guide is the only place to find them in print along with over 250 pages of additional instruction, guidance, and test information.

With updated guidance and practice problems that reflect the most recent information, this new edition takes the best-selling SAT guide and makes it even more relevant and useful. Be ready for the SAT with strategies and up-to-date information straight from the exam writers.

The Official SAT Study Guide will help students get ready for the SAT with:

- 8 official SAT practice tests, written in the exact same process and by the same team of authors as the actual exam

- detailed descriptions of the math and evidenced based reading and writing sections

- targeted practice questions for each SAT question type

- guidance on the new optional essay, including practice essay questions with sample responses

- seamless integration with Official SAT Practice on Khan Academy

College Financial Aid Assistance

Debt-Free U - If you're going to college - especially in the U.S. - you need to read this book. I may have graduated with no debt, but the average college graduate these days is coming out of school with around $30,000 of it. Having that amount of debt will limit your options when it comes to jobs, where you can live, etc. This is not how it should be. This is not how it has to be. Debt-Free U will show you how you can go to college and avoid debt - even if your family isn't loaded.

The Ultimate Scholarship Book 2021: Billions of Dollars in Scholarships, Grants and Prizes by Gen Tanabe and Kelly Tanabe. Information on 1.5 million scholarships, grants, and prizes is easily accessible in this revised directory with more than 300 new listings that feature awards indexed by career goal, major, academics, public service, talent, athletics, religion, ethnicity, and more.

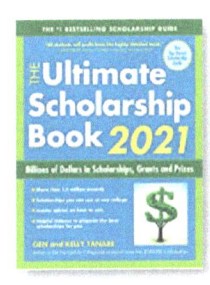

Advisory services through Capital Advisory Group Advisory Services LLC and securities through United Planners Financial Services of America, a Limited Partnership. Member FINRA and SIPC. The Capital Advisory Group Advisory Services, LLC (CAG) and United Planners Financial Services are not affiliated.

Each entry contains all the necessary information for students and parents to complete the application process, including eligibility requirements, how to obtain an application, how to get more information about each award, sponsor website listings, award amounts, and key deadlines.

With scholarships for high school, college, graduate, and adult students, this guide also includes tips on how to conduct the most effective search, how to write a winning application, and how to avoid scams.

LAUNCH: How to Get Your Kids Through College Debt-Free and Into Jobs They Love Afterward by Jeannie Burlowski, Stacy Ennis, and Kim Foster. You'd love to get your kids through college debt-free— but your kids aren't getting any scholarships, you haven't saved for college, and you make too much to get government financial aid. Is there still hope? Yes, but you'll need someone to guide you.

In LAUNCH, academic strategist Jeannie Burlowski lays out clear, step-by-step strategies that empower parents to get their kids through high quality, best-fit colleges debt-free— and then directly into jobs they love afterward.

Confessions of a Scholarship Winner: The Secrets That Helped Me Win $500,000 in Free Money for College - How You Can Too! by Kristina Ellis. How ANY student— including YOU!—can win scholarships and earn free money for college! On the first day of high school, Kristina Ellis' mom (a single, working mother who lost her husband to cancer) informed her that she could not financially support her after graduation. Kristina would need to find her own way to pay for college.

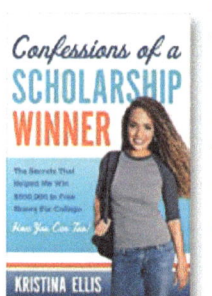

Advisory services through Capital Advisory Group Advisory Services LLC and securities through United Planners Financial Services of America, a Limited Partnership. Member FINRA and SIPC. The Capital Advisory Group Advisory Services, LLC (CAG) and United Planners Financial Services are not affiliated.

As an average student with less-than-impressive test scores, Kristina realized she would have to sell herself to scholarship committees if she wanted to stand out. That's when she devised the plan that led to her receiving over $500,000 in scholarships—enough to pay for her full education at a top-20 university, all the way through her doctoral degree, and make her dreams come true.

How she made it happen—and how you can too!—is the focus of this book. In Confessions of a Scholarship Winner, Kristina shares not just her little-known secrets for scholarship success, but her incredibly inspiring story.

Together, you'll explore how to:

- Find the best scholarships for you
- Uncover the secrets behind paying for college
- Make a great impression in a scholarship interview
- Overcome the personal obstacles that stand in your way
- Craft a strategy that highlights your strengths, no matter your challenges or your financial status

You don't have to be a star athlete, a top student, or a recognized leader to live your dreams! Here are the tools you need to catch a vision for your future and make your dreams a reality!

Advisory services through Capital Advisory Group Advisory Services LLC and securities through United Planners Financial Services of America, a Limited Partnership. Member FINRA and SIPC. The Capital Advisory Group Advisory Services, LLC (CAG) and United Planners Financial Services are not affiliated.

Colleges Who Offer Debt-Free College Educations

- United States Service Academies
- College of the Ozarks
- Deep Springs College
- Alice Lloyd College
- Berea College
- Curtis Institute of Music
- Barclay College
- Webb Institute

4.7 Colleges Who Offer Debt-Free College Educations

College of the Ozarks - With Christian values, dedication to responsibilities, and financial assistance, College of the Ozarks is one of the best regional colleges in the Midwest. From accounting to culinary arts, College of the Ozarks offers a wide array of rigorous, bachelor's degree programs for different fields of study.

College of the Ozarks provides free tuition for the 1,400 students that attend each year. Funded by generous donations, College of the Ozarks is able to offer students a full ride to their rigorous program. However, students must work at least 15 hours every week and two 40-hour workweeks through their campus jobs to be eligible for the free tuition at College of the Ozarks.

Deep Springs College - Deep Springs College is a school located at California's High Desert and is a cattle ranch and alfalfa farm. This male-only school offers a two-year education in liberal arts. With about 15 students admitted each year, Deep Springs College is an intimate institution that provides high quality education.

Every attendee at Deep Springs College receives a full financial reward, which is about $50,000 annually, plus free room and board; however, the trade-off is that students must work at least 20 hours per week on the ranch at Deep Springs College.

Alice Lloyd College - Located in Pippa Passes, KY, Alice Lloyd College is a recognized, private school that specializes in the liberal arts. This four-year college presents a wide variety of programs to obtain a bachelor's degree in science, arts and other specialties. With several minors, such as accounting and social science, students at Alice Lloyd College can further their education.

With a normal tuition of $7,000, Alice Lloyd College offers free

Advisory services through Capital Advisory Group Advisory Services LLC and securities through United Planners Financial Services of America, a Limited Partnership. Member FINRA and SIPC. The Capital Advisory Group Advisory Services, LLC (CAG) and United Planners Financial Services are not affiliated.

tuition to a certain group of students. Students must work at least 10 hours per week to obtain free tuition at Alice Lloyd College. If students would also like the perks of free room and board, they must work at least 15 hours a week to receive free tuition and boarding. From 550 jobs, Alice Lloyd College gives selected students, with more work experience and personal preferences, these jobs to allow them to attain free tuition.

Berea College - Founded by abolitionists and reformers in the 1800s, Berea College is a diverse and cultural learning institution that stands strong in their faith-based school. With a better opportunity for higher and stress-free learning, Berea College provides students with their Labor Program to obtain free tuition.

A necessary amount of at least 10 hours of work per week is required from students to receive free tuition at Berea College. From over 140 departments, students can decide which area they'd like to work in for extra pay and free tuition. Berea College is able to provide students with full tuition coverage up to $24,500 each year along with a $4,000 Labor Grant. Ranging from $3.80 to $6.25, Berea College presents a certain hourly rate depending on the job so that students can learn the values of being in the workforce and gain extra cash for room,

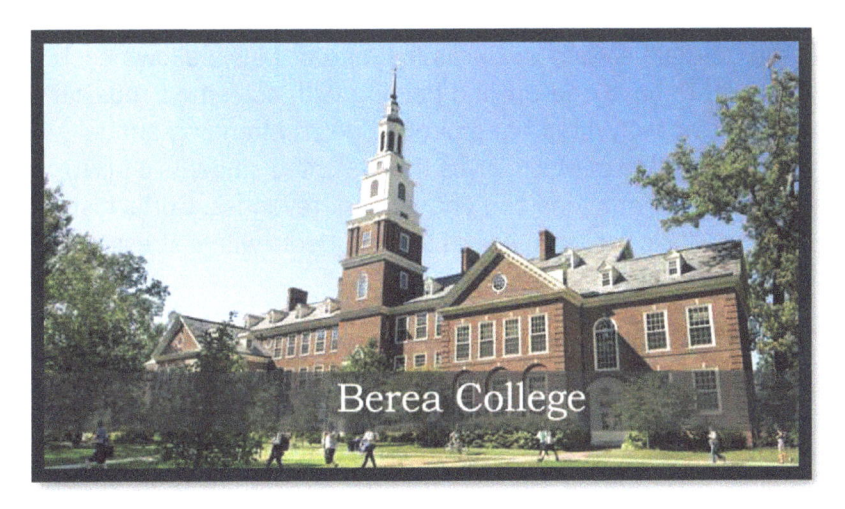

Berea College

Advisory services through Capital Advisory Group Advisory Services LLC and securities through United Planners Financial Services of America, a Limited Partnership. Member FINRA and SIPC. The Capital Advisory Group Advisory Services, LLC (CAG) and United Planners Financial Services are not affiliated.

school books, and boarding. From a very large endowment, Berea College makes it possible for students to receive free tuition and higher education at their school.

Curtis Institute of Music - As one of the most eminent performance arts schools in the U.S. next to Julliard, Curtis Institute of Music presents a hands-on approach to learning and provides students with a concert loaded schedule every year. At Curtis Institute of Music, only 165 students enroll each year to this prestigious school.

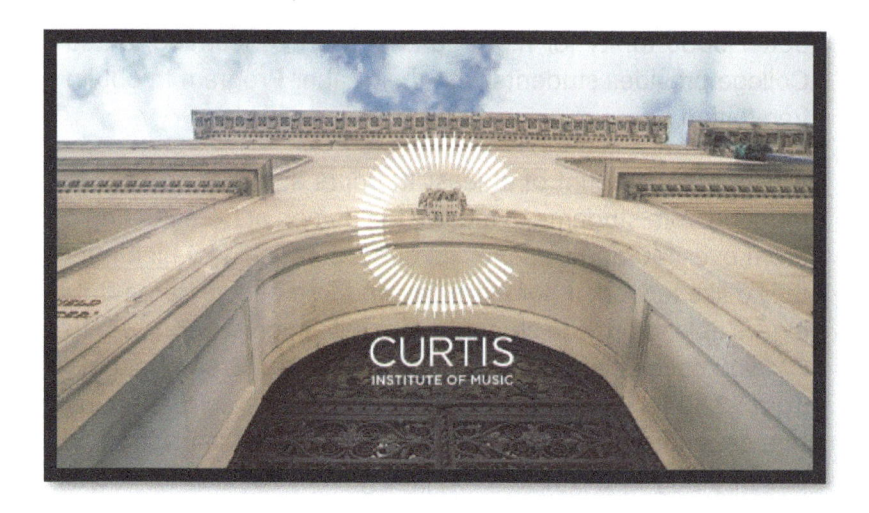

The intimate setting of Curtis Institute of Music allows each student to have one-on-one training with esteemed, musical professionals. With a handful of students attending annually, Curtis Institute of Music gives their talented students a full tuition. From donations and endowment revenues, Curtis Institute of Music is able to award their students with a stress-free gift of a lifetime.

Barclay College - As a Christian centered environment, Barclay College prepares students for a life of serving and leading the Christian life style. Offering degree programs from Youth Ministry to Christian Elementary Education, Barclay College dedicates their learning institution to Christian values and beliefs.

With a full scholarship awarded to every admitted student, Barclay College presents a free, high quality education in any Christian related fields. However, to receive the free tuition, students must live on the Barclay College campus.

United States Service Academies - United States service academies (West Point Military Academy, Anapolis Naval Academy, Coast Guard Academy, Merchant Marine Academy, and US Air Force Academy) all offer top-notch educations with selective admissions.

The catch of course is that you have a guaranteed job awaiting you following graduation – service time in a branch of the

Advisory services through Capital Advisory Group Advisory Services LLC and securities through United Planners Financial Services of America, a Limited Partnership. Member FINRA and SIPC. The Capital Advisory Group Advisory Services, LLC (CAG) and United Planners Financial Services are not affiliated.

United State military. All five academies have brutal selection processes, with only 8-15% of applicants being selected. Minimum terms of duty are usually five years active and three years reserve. The military also offers ROTC scholarships to colleges throughout the US with the same active and reserve duty requirements upon completion.

Webb Institute - Webb Institute is a highly accredited school that specializes in marine engineering and naval constructions. With around 80 undergraduates each year, Webb Institute has a job placement of 100 percent for their graduated students.

Webb Institute is the only marine engineering and naval architecture school that offers a full, four-year scholarship for their students, which is possible due to generous donations from numerous sources.

As the trend of free tuition becomes popular among noted colleges every year, education is now an obtainable opportunity and a dream come true for many academically driven people.

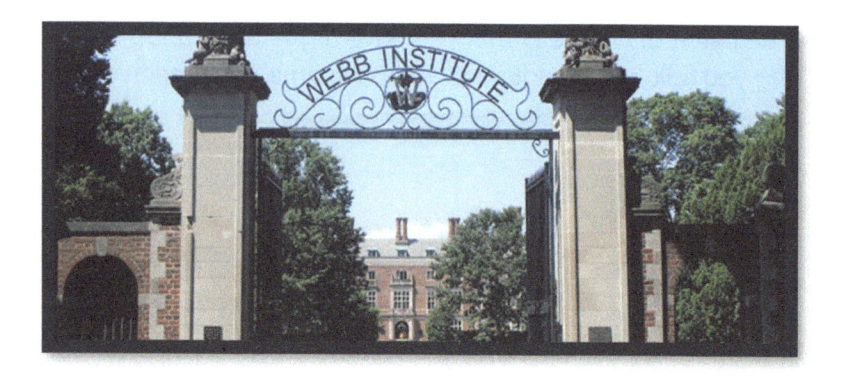

Advisory services through Capital Advisory Group Advisory Services LLC and securities through United Planners Financial Services of America, a Limited Partnership. Member FINRA and SIPC. The Capital Advisory Group Advisory Services, LLC (CAG) and United Planners Financial Services are not affiliated.

Conclusion

This is a "how-to" so you can get the most from higher education and to do it without saddling yourself with loads of debt after school. It is about getting a job you can embrace that can support your ideal lifestyle. It is about making you in demand and relevant in today's economy. Take control of the situation. You will be glad you did.

Less than 10% of all books, are read to the end. You are one who sees a task to the finish line and it will drive you to success.

Now go through and make a list of five things you are going to do in this book. Maybe it's reading one of the recommended books, finding a student mentor, shadowing a professional in your chosen field, writing a personal plan or selecting a career in the identified high-demand areas. Whatever you decide to do, let us know by emailing bmachtig@machtig.net.

Enjoy the journey!

Sincerely,

Jonathan Quinn Machtig and Brett Machtig

Section V

Bonus Material:

Excerpts from *Your Guide to Financial Freedom*

YOUR GUIDE TO FINANCIAL *Freedom*

Grow it.
Keep it.
Protect it.

BRETT MACHTIG

author of *Wealth in a Decade* and *The Corporate Guide to Profit and Wealth*

5.1 Your Guide to Financial Freedom: *How to Plan*

No matter the primary reason for reading this book, your first step is to create a financial plan. You need to know where you are. Right now. Today. Throughout the book you'll see steps labeled ACTION ITEM. These are key steps you should consider when working through your own financial plan. Keep an eye out for these and work your way through them deliberately and carefully.

Consider reading this book to the end without taking every action step. Then, go through it again to answer the questions and action items throughout the book. In the back is a handy financial checklist* so no financial stone is left unturned.

Know Where You Are - Before you become a client of any wealth management firm, it's important to determine exactly where you are financially.

A reputable financial advisor will analyze your income, spending, cash flow, tax situation, debt structure, savings, retirement plans, insurance coverage, planned purchases and asset structure. This data can be secured through a personal interview, investment statements, debt balances and tax returns.

With this information in hand, your financial professional can assess where you have been in the past, financially. Together you can come up with some best estimates for how these aspects will change in the future

*Some features of the book are not included in this excerpt. The complete book can be purchased through Amazon.com search word: Brett Machtig

While you may already know where you stand financially, the vast majority of people do not truly know their position. Simply working through this initial step is often an eye-opening experience, showing why a person is not as happy or secure about their finances as they would hope.

The majority of your work will most likely be on one or more of these lessons:

- Planning
- Cash flow
- Diversification
- Risk management
- Investment strategy
- Tax issues
- Estate planning
- Where to get help

Following are a few examples of people who once thought their situation was hopeless, but when focused on the creation of a plan to address one of the lessons above, discovered that they too could be financially free.

Jan was a stressed real estate broker in Panama City, FL, who had trouble sleeping. She began our interview thinking she might need a little help, but felt she had things generally under control. Upon completing the plan, she realized she was in very poor financial shape – the root cause of her stress and sleep troubles.

She realized if she did not act very quickly, she would run out of money within 18 to 24 months.

Advisory services through Capital Advisory Group Advisory Services LLC and securities through United Planners Financial Services of America, a Limited Partnership. Member FINRA and SIPC. The Capital Advisory Group Advisory Services, LLC (CAG) and United Planners Financial Services are not affiliated.

Together we focused on selling her real estate holdings which were consuming her liquid assets. Some of her real estate needed to be sold at a loss, and the equity that was left was added to her cash, paid off overwhelming debt, and reduced her overall expenses.

Tom and Kim, a couple from southern Oregon, "tried" to save while one of them piled on debt to start up a business. They fought often, over – you guessed it – money. Our meeting showed them the importance of creating a plan to light the way toward recovery from their debt and then move forward as a team.

Upon the creation of his plan, Al, a senior manufacturing executive from Boston, MA, clearly saw he was getting further away from his goal of retirement.

With each increase in his income, he offset the surplus with an even larger increase in spending. The net result was mounting debt and diminished annual savings. He said he felt depressed about being a slave to his lifestyle.

We helped change the negative cash flow by using the plan to track increases and decreases of his cash flow.

Within 30 months, this high earner and higher spender paid off all debt, except for his home mortgage. Finally, he got off the debt cycle and was progressing to financial freedom.

Andrew and Therese, a retired couple from Bloomington, MN, realized after creating a plan that their investments were not growing, except when they added money to their account. We helped change their asset mix, investment strategy and set up performance measures so they knew whether their investments were on track or not.

Each of these situations was improved by creating a workable financial plan. Don't stop there. Set up a personal advisory

Advisory services through Capital Advisory Group Advisory Services LLC and securities through United Planners Financial Services of America, a Limited Partnership. Member FINRA and SIPC. The Capital Advisory Group Advisory Services, LLC (CAG) and United Planners Financial Services are not affiliated.

team with a trusted financial advisor, a knowledgeable insurance specialist, a sharp accountant, a seasoned attorney and, if you run a business, an experienced business mentor who understands how to succeed in your business. This group will work much like a board of directors to help make sure your plan will succeed.

By clearly defining where you are right now, your advisory team can help you address roadblocks and quickly correct your course anytime you move away from your intended goals. Put this in writing and revise it at least quarterly.

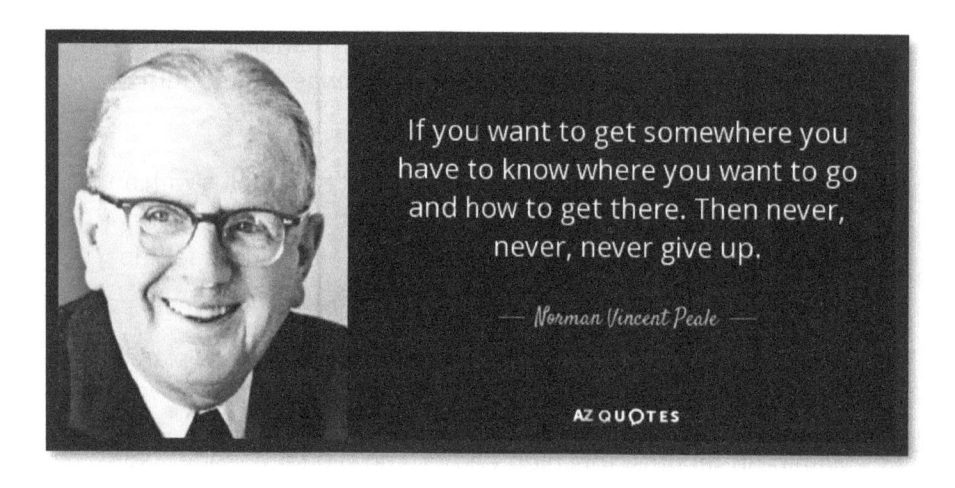

> If you want to get somewhere you have to know where you want to go and how to get there. Then never, never, never give up.
>
> — Norman Vincent Peale

The next step is to know where you want to go

- Planning a compelling future is a relatively new option. Just a few centuries ago, your life would have been pre-determined by your family and social status. If your family came from a long line of butchers, most likely, that would be your future as well. If your family farmed, that would most likely be your lot in life.

Conditions changed very slowly over the days, months, years, and generations.

Today, your actions can significantly change your socio-eco-

Advisory services through Capital Advisory Group Advisory Services LLC and securities through United Planners Financial Services of America, a Limited Partnership. Member FINRA and SIPC. The Capital Advisory Group Advisory Services, LLC (CAG) and United Planners Financial Services are not affiliated.

nomic future in a relatively short period of time.

Your past does not have to equal your future. Having a plan in place is the key to making this socio-economic change happen. Otherwise you will be carried by the inertia of the financial decisions of your past.

Once you know where you are now, the next step is to figure out where you want to go.

Write the story of your future life – as if it has already happened. Be sure to add in all the rich details to make this vision real for you.

Creating a plan and deciding where you want to go will give you "cause and control" over your future like no other action. It will help you keep your perspective in spite of minor set backs. Creating and then following a plan will help bring about happiness and peace because you'll be more in control of your destiny.

Put it all into the story of your future life. Keep the size manageable and the journal handy so you can work on it while you are between meetings, at the cabin, or before you go to bed at night. We suggest keeping your plan in a 5" X 8" journal found in most any bookstore.

Start out your plan with the end in mind and work backwards. First, you'll want to create a ten-year vision, then one for five years, one for three years, and finally a one-year vision.

10-Year Vision - Write the story of your life as you see it in 10 years– as if it has already happened. Add in all the details to make this story or vision real for you. Visualize an average day in your life exactly 10 years from now.

Ask yourself, "What milestones will show that I have reached my goal?" "Where do I want to be?" "What roadblocks did I have to overcome or bad habits did I need to break?" "What are the non-financial goals I want to achieve?"

Write your answers down to firmly set them in your mind.

Here are some more questions to ask yourself, but make up your own questions as well:

- When do I want to retire?
- When do I want to be debt-free?
- How will I pay for our kid's college?
- Do I want to move to a new home?
- What do I want to have, do, or be?
- How can I meet goals and enjoy the ride?

Non-financial keys to address in your vision:

- Who are you with? Who do you love, and who loves you? What positive people and things do you want to have in your life? What toxic or negative people, influences and environments need to be eliminated to make the ten-year vision compelling?

- How can you better serve others? Serving others is a critical key to being successful and feeling good about it. Ask yourself, "What groups need my help?" "What do I have to offer?" "How can I better serve my children, family or spouse?" "Who can I help or mentor?"

- Have you discovered your "Special Purpose?" If you love what you do and are very good at it, you probably have already discovered your "special purpose." But if you do not love what you do, find that one thing–and focus your energies on excelling in that specialization. Not only will you be

---

Advisory services through Capital Advisory Group Advisory Services LLC and securities through United Planners Financial Services of America, a Limited Partnership. Member FINRA and SIPC. The Capital Advisory Group Advisory Services, LLC (CAG) and United Planners Financial Services are not affiliated.

happier, you will be more successful.

- Does your spouse "buy" the plan? If you are married or have a partner, be sure the vision reflects both of your desires, directions and goals. Go to dinner or take a weekend trip and create compelling 10-year visions that excite both of you.

- Interview each other. Do not stifle the other's vision. Keep the discussion light and in the spirit of possibility. If your spouse truly isn't interested in planning, create the vision alone. Remember, the one who has the clearest vision will drive the family direction.

- Include all planned purchases and when you plan to make them. For example, let's say you are going to spend $15,000 to remodel your kitchen two years from now, replace your car three years from now, pay for four years of Susie's college beginning five years from now, and buy a cabin or second home in nine years. Put these planned expenses in your vision as well.

- Does your plan need alterations? Your 10-year vision may include staying in your current house until the kids leave or only replacing your cars every six years to build up your savings. It may even involve downsizing to live within your means, get out of debt and live a more stress-free life. You may be telling yourself, I don't want to live scrimping and pinching pennies. On the same note, ask yourself: do I want to be in the same place I am now ten years from now?

- If you plan to make more money, how will you do it? Include what you'll do to improve the economic value to your company. What training can you undertake? What skills need to be improved? What certifications should you get? When are you going to do these things? Who can mentor you?

Address all the areas that have sabotaged your plans in the past. If you had a bad business partner, write out the lessons you learned from the experience. If you spent too much and were in financial trouble, write down what you did wrong, so you do not repeat past mistakes. For example, if over spending was caused by remodeling your home, write down what you have learned, and what you can do to avoid repeating similar mistakes. If you have a friend or associate who has successfully handled the same problem, ask them how they overcame it and then model their behavior.

After you've crystallized your vision in writing of where you are now and created a compelling vision of where you want to be in 10 years, work backward from the 10 year vision, bridging the future back to your present situation.

Action Item: Write down your 10-year visions and include as many details as possible.

Five-Year Vision - Now, figure out what you need to do, be, or have in five years to be on track for your 10-year vision. Be as specific as you can. Remember, the clearer your future vision, the more likely it will happen and the more likely you'll know if you are off-track.

After adding up all future expenses and planned purchases, is there enough money going into savings? Are you realistic about your income increases? Does your past support your future view or make it seem unlikely?

In other words, if you spent more than you made over the last five years, what are you going to do differently so you can save this year? Remember, experience is important and mistakes are inevitable, but learn from these mistakes; do not repeat them.

As Tony Robbins said in one of his seminars, *Date with Destiny* (which we highly recommend), "When people do well they tend to party. When they do poorly, they tend to ponder." Pondering is good, but set up a personal policy so as not to continually repeat past mistakes. Write down exactly what you will change to avoid the same problems again, then run your solution by someone who has that problem solved.

Write down your five-year plan of where you need to be, what you need to do, and what you hope to have to ensure that your 10-year vision is real to you and feels achievable.

Do you feel good about your ten-and five-year future?

If you do not, go back and rework your 10-year vision until you feel GREAT about it and cannot wait to make it happen.

Action Item: Write down your five-year visions to make your five-year vision real to you.

Three-Year Vision - Once you create your five-year plan, do the same thing for a vision three years from now. Address income, expenses, career, education, savings, trips, lifestyle and any planned purchases to create a compelling, but realistic goal you can eagerly move toward.

Throughout this plan, you should ensure that your savings are going up and/or your debt is going down.

Doing so creates better and better cash flow. If you don't check and recheck your savings and debt management status, money will most likely continue to create stress, not freedom. It's so simple to understand, but much more difficult to live. Still, the reduction in stress created from operating true to your plan is priceless.

Spending more than you make creates a buildup of debt and/or a reduction of savings over time and a parallel increase in stress.

In our line of work we see far too many people depressed about life because they have no control over their spending and debt. I've seen some even turn to drugs or alcohol, effectively masking the pain, and doing nothing to address the underlying problem. Take control here, and you will be amazed at how it completely changes your overall attitude toward life.

If spending is a problem, a simple way to start the stress reduction process is to focus on your five largest bills and come up with specific ways you are willing to reduce them. If you're like most people, your largest bills might include your home mortgage, income taxes, autos, business expenses, debt, travel, child support, random purchases, home remodeling/repairs, dining out and insurance.

Most people, unless focused on reducing their largest bills, cut out the little pleasures that make life enjoyable, like going on a date with their spouse, having a cup of coffee at Starbucks, or belonging to a health club.

The results from cutting out the fun stuff usually are the same as going on a starvation diet; you don't lose weight and over the long run, you just get heavier (or in the case of money, more in debt). Instead, for each major expense, come up with at least five ways to reduce it. Then, as a couple, decide on realistic savings ideas you'll truly implement to save at least 10 percent of every income dollar.

Write down your three-year vision of where you need to be in order to be on track for your five-year plan.

Reread what you wrote for your five-and 10-year vision to see if they are all aligned and compelling so you are excited about your future.

Does your future require you to spend less? Put in milestones that do not cost a lot, but may give lots of happiness like learning to play the guitar, going with a church group to help the poor, writing a novel, or doing a bike trip down the Pacific Coast with a good friend.

Advisory services through Capital Advisory Group Advisory Services LLC and securities through United Planners Financial Services of America, a Limited Partnership. Member FINRA and SIPC. The Capital Advisory Group Advisory Services, LLC (CAG) and United Planners Financial Services are not affiliated.

Action Item: Write down your three-year visions to make your vision real to you.

Within One Year - Now, write a story of your "ideal scene" one year from now. Describe the milestones required to be on track. Depict how you will feel at that point, being on track towards your longer term plans. Does your list of one-year goals in the plan look familiar? If it resembles your New Year's Eve resolutions from years past, ask yourself what you are willing to do differently to make them really happen. Write down what you want, why you want it, and what you are willing to do to make it all happen.

Are you drifting away from your spouse? Come up with specific ways you can become closer. Have you addressed ways to improve your health? Come up with steps to eat better, exercise more or be more active.

These may seem unrelated to the topic of money, until you consider the costs of divorce and being too ill to enjoy your wealth.

Finally, figure out what five things you need to do right now in order to move towards your one-year ideal scene. If there are decisions you have been putting off, decide which path is best for you and your family.

Action Item: Write down your one-year vision, and contemplate what five things you can do right now to help you step towards your ultimate destination.

This will give you a direction to go so you can focus your efforts. Get the ball rolling by putting on your top five things list reading this book, and then doing all of the exercises, and committing them in writing to your journal. Now, keep the plan current by reviewing and revising your plan at least quarterly.

You're now on a three-month tracking program. It's not just

Advisory services through Capital Advisory Group Advisory Services LLC and securities through United Planners Financial Services of America, a Limited Partnership. Member FINRA and SIPC. The Capital Advisory Group Advisory Services, LLC (CAG) and United Planners Financial Services are not affiliated.

manageable, it is achievable! Write your refinements in your journal every 90 days. Then, once a year, buy a new journal and revise and update your plan.

Remember the acid test for wealth accumulation:

- Are you going in the direction of your goals?
- Are you on track? Are you saving?
- Are you paying off debt?

If the answer to any of these is, "No," consider getting help from a professional financial advisor.

Find Mentors - Do some leg-work to secure mentors who can help you avoid learning from the school of hard knocks.

Remember: only when a student is ready does the teacher appear. Be on the lookout for your next teacher. In some cases, mentors may even have the power to increase your income and help move your plan along.

Write down what your mentors suggest to you and ask them to review your plan to see if you missed any key steps. Ask

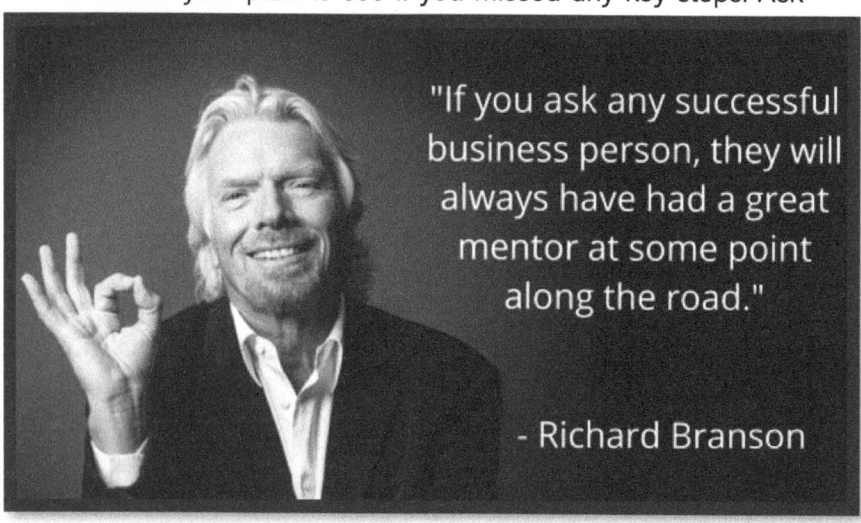

> "If you ask any successful business person, they will always have had a great mentor at some point along the road."
>
> - Richard Branson

Advisory services through Capital Advisory Group Advisory Services LLC and securities through United Planners Financial Services of America, a Limited Partnership. Member FINRA and SIPC. The Capital Advisory Group Advisory Services, LLC (CAG) and United Planners Financial Services are not affiliated.

permission to check in with them from time to time to keep on track. You will find most successful people want to help others, as long as you maintain responsibility for following the advice and producing the results.

Find mentors who have mastered a particular area in which you need improvement. If they haven't done it themselves, they might lead you in the wrong direction. Interview them. Ask them how they did it. Write down what you learn. Go over your revised plan with your mentors to make sure you heard them correctly. Then, do what they suggest. Let them know what worked. Also, let them know what didn't work, as they might know how you can get back on track.

Action Item: Find mentors who can help you get results. List several mentors in your journal and when you will ask them if they can help. Interview them. Write up your revised plan, then go over what you heard from the mentor, based on their feedback.

What Needs To Be In The Financial Plan?

To help you grow, keep and protect your money, so that you can live from its returns, several key terms need to be defined:

Net Income - What is your net income? Net income, is what you get to spend after taxes, after payroll deductions, after business expenses, and after alimony or child support, or after retirement contributions. It is your net paycheck.

You can improve net income by increasing your earned income. Ask yourself, "How can I improve my income by increasing my value to my company, to my co-workers, or to my customers?" Far too many people simply expect more money without adding any more value. This almost never works, except for an inflationary wage increase, or if it is early in a person's career.

Advisory services through Capital Advisory Group Advisory Services LLC and securities through United Planners Financial Services of America, a Limited Partnership. Member FINRA and SIPC. The Capital Advisory Group Advisory Services, LLC (CAG) and United Planners Financial Services are not affiliated.

> Financial planning is like navigation. If you know where you are and where you want to go, navigation isn't such a great problem. It's when you don't know the two points that it's difficult.
>
> — Venita VanCaspel

More likely, if you do not add more value, you should plan for an eventual pay cut. Why? Well, as the United States becomes a smaller player in the global economy, somewhere in this world, someone is willing to do what you do for less money. Write in your journal how you can do your job better for your clients and colleagues.

Your best defense against a pay cut is to continually strive to do your job better, or consider going into a more lucrative line of work. Educate yourself or interview someone already getting the financial results you want in your field, or outside of it.

Taxes - It is possible to reduce your taxes or payroll deductions. There are many ways of doing it, from starting a business to giving away the "junk" in your attic. In the chapter on tax planning we'll explore how to find a good accountant and where to look for the best deductions before the year is over.

List some ways you can reduce your taxes.

Payroll Deductions - Payroll deductions include many that you cannot change like FICA, FUTA, Medicare and withholdings. They also include deductions you can change, like your 401(k)s, 403(b)s and TSAs – your pre-tax retirement contributions.

Consider setting your 401(k) or retirement savings percent at least to the amount your employer matches.

For example, if your employer matches the first five percent, set your minimum 401(k) contribution to five percent. Anything above that depends on your cash flow and savings discipline.

If you tend to spend everything you get your hands on, max out your retirement contributions. If you are a good saver, however, consider diverting non-matched retirement contributions to debt reduction to improve your cash flow. Most families can reduce their spending by 25-50% by doing this.

Try to estimate what your net income will be for the next 10 years and outline your plan to increase your net income. If you don't know, guess. You are the only person who has to believe in the plan 100 percent for it to work. Be conservative on your income guesses and err on the side of under-estimating your income.

If you have been getting inflationary wage increases and believe they will continue, add an inflation increase to both income and expenses.

Here is a sample plan to show you how to create a plan for your income, debt-payoff, expenses and savings.

To illustrate, if Pete, an electrician, increased his debt by $25,000 over the year but his savings stayed the same, he has worsened his financial condition by spending $25,000 more than he makes. If your savings went up and/or debt went down, then you are spending less by that amount.

For example, 35-year-old Anne has $20,000 more in her checking account and $30,000 less debt over the course of a year. That means Anne spent $50,000 less than her net income of $100,000. This is good. Anne is saving 50 percent of her net income.

Advisory services through Capital Advisory Group Advisory Services LLC and securities through United Planners Financial Services of America, a Limited Partnership. Member FINRA and SIPC. The Capital Advisory Group Advisory Services, LLC (CAG) and United Planners Financial Services are not affiliated.

If you own rental property, track all the costs of continuing property ownership such as property taxes, repairs, insurance, rental fees, etc. Then, compare your rental income to your rental property expenses. Do not add in property appreciation for now.

Are you making any money?

What is your annual return?

To find this, divide the net property income, excluding property appreciation, by your net equity.

If you were to sell it and pay off your debts, how would this improve your cash flow and debt reduction? If you earn less than five percent on the investment property excluding appreciation, consider selling the property.

As in the earlier example, if you own a rental property that costs you more than you receive in income, sell it and use your equity to pay off debts. If there is no equity, consider selling it anyway to reduce your monthly outflow.

The biggest mistake we see in property ownership is not having the discipline to know when to buy and when to sell. For example, we only buy if we can net 10 percent positive cash flow excluding appreciation. We do not build in any appreciation into a "buy" decision.

We also will only buy at a discount to the true value of the property, so if we need to sell, we can without a loss.

If it does appreciate or rents drop so cash flow is five percent or less, we sell. Consider using these standards for all your investment real estate.

By using this example, you can create a financial plan for yourself. Upon creating this plan you will know where you are

---

Advisory services through Capital Advisory Group Advisory Services LLC and securities through United Planners Financial Services of America, a Limited Partnership. Member FINRA and SIPC. The Capital Advisory Group Advisory Services, LLC (CAG) and United Planners Financial Services are not affiliated.

and where you want to go! What else is necessary to stay on track? The answer lies where the rubber meets the road – living out the plan, reviewing your results, and making adjustments along the way to achieve your goals.

Monitor and Adjust To Stay on Track - It is simply not enough to create a great plan; you have to keep it current and updated. The plan must be taken out and reviewed at least quarterly. If you are off track, revise your actions toward what it takes to achieve your goals.

You're heading in the right direction if you see:

- Gross income increasing
- Net income increasing
- Expenses decreasing
- Debt balances decreasing
- Annual savings increasing
- Portfolio value increasing

You're moving away from your goals if you see:

- Debt increasing
- Debt payments increasing
- Savings decreasing
- Expenses increasing
- Net income decreasing
- Portfolio value decreasing

Advisory services through Capital Advisory Group Advisory Services LLC and securities through United Planners Financial Services of America, a Limited Partnership. Member FINRA and SIPC. The Capital Advisory Group Advisory Services, LLC (CAG) and United Planners Financial Services are not affiliated.

Don't expect perfection right away. Getting on track and staying there is a continually evolving process.

When a plane flies from New York to London, it is off track most of the flight as weather and winds change its course. With each change, the pilot and the airplane computers re-target the plane to its destination until it is ultimately reached in the end. Many of life's roadblocks, like weather and wind, exist to keep your plan from becoming a reality. Now that you have a plan, the rest of this book covers key investment issues, how you can stay on track, and reach your destination.

You can take a simple test and prove it to yourself.

Step 1 – Rate your financial stress from a low of 1 to a high of 10.

Step 2 – Create a financial plan and begin to follow it.

Step 3 – Retest your financial stress.

Financial success is that simple. The secret to stress reduction, relating to your finances, is having a plan and then following it. If you are still stressed, there is something in your plan that needs to be changed.

SUMMARY

1. Know where you are by taking a realistic snapshot of your financial situation. Establish where you are now financially by using the examples in this chapter as a guide.

2. Start with the end in mind. Create a compelling future 10 years out. Once that 10-year vision is clear, work backward to create a plan for five years, three years, and one year. Then, identify five things you need to do right now to be on track.

3. Test your financial stress before and after creating your plan. If it gives you a feeling of cause and control over your financ-

---

Advisory services through Capital Advisory Group Advisory Services LLC and securities through United Planners Financial Services of America, a Limited Partnership. Member FINRA and SIPC. The Capital Advisory Group Advisory Services, LLC (CAG) and United Planners Financial Services are not affiliated.

es, your stress level will drop. If not, refine your plan until you believe it will work.

4. Pull out your plan and check to see if you are on track at least quarterly. Adjust your course to stay or get on track.

5. Find mentors who have already achieved the goals you seek. Have them check the validity of your plan and point out shortfalls. Build an advisory team of your mentors, a trusted financial advisor, tax advisor, and attorney to serve as your "board of directors" to help you stay on track.

6. If you need help creating your plan, see an experienced financial advisor. Another option is to contact our office for a free spreadsheet to track your cash flow and create a plan.

Advisory services through Capital Advisory Group Advisory Services LLC and securities through United Planners Financial Services of America, a Limited Partnership. Member FINRA and SIPC. The Capital Advisory Group Advisory Services, LLC (CAG) and United Planners Financial Services are not affiliated.

> "It's not your **salary** that makes you **rich,** it's your **spending habits.**"
>
> — Charles A. Jaffe

5.2 Your Guide to Financial Freedom: *The Single Most Important Factor to Financial Success*

Have you ever wondered how rock stars or lottery winners or trust fund babies can lose it all, even though they have enough wealth to buy a small country? The answer lies in cash flow. Or better stated – the answer lies in the lack of cash flow.

THE IDEAL CASH FLOW - What is cash flow? It is the amount of money you have after paying all your bills and purchases.

If you spend more than you make, there are symptoms: you have no cash, a high level of financial stress, and lots of increasing debt. You are in a negative cash flow position; more money is going out than coming in.

If you spend less than you make, there are symptoms as well. You have savings, you are reducing debt, you have a positive financial outlook. This is a positive cash flow state – more money is coming in than going out.

Ideal cash flow is having enough non-retirement savings so you can live from your investment portfolio income within a reasonable time. For the purposes of this book, ideal minimum positive cash flow is at least 10 percent of funds that are free to use, save, or pay-off debt after paying all expenses and all purchases.

For the purposes of this chapter, savings does not include savings into your retirement accounts, since they do not impact your daily cash flow and have limited access without adverse tax consequences.

Without good cash flow, the chances of accumulating enough money to live off your investments are slim to none. That is why we put so much emphasis on this topic. Improving your cash flow should be your number one priority. It truly is that important to ensuring your financial freedom.

Some people learn its importance from a job loss, cash-draining investment choices, health problems, economic downturns, or needy adult kids. Many people, unfortunately, never learn its importance and continue to struggle financially.

As you read this chapter today, where are you in terms of cash flow?

Do you have GREAT cash flow? We define GREAT cash flow as saving 50 percent or more of every dollar you make in net income.

Do you have GOOD cash flow? We define GOOD cash flow as saving 10 to 50 percent of net income.

Do you have POOR cash flow? We define POOR cash flow as saving less than 10 percent of your net income.

If you're not happy with your cash flow, you can do something about it. Yes, it takes discipline and can involve some difficult choices, but in the long-term, getting a firm handle on cash flow is the best thing you can do for yourself and your family.

GREAT CASH FLOW – WHAT TO DO - If you are saving 50 percent or more of your net income – well done! Consider yourself amongst a small minority. You could stop here and skip on to the next chapter. However, with great cash flow already, I'm guessing you're driven to read on to improve things even more. Use that great cash flow to retire any remaining debt. Most likely you've already done so, but if not, this step will help you save even more down the road. Keep up the good work!

Action Item: Write in your journal which cash flow condition best describes your situation: GREAT, GOOD or POOR.

Pick the appropriate program from the following examples.

GOOD CASH FLOW - WHAT TO DO - If you are saving 10 to 50 percent of your net income, you may be well on your way to becoming wealthy. To make your position even better, use at least half of your monthly savings to clear up debts. This may seem obvious, but the following illustration will help drive home this point.

Suzy, the "Good Cash Flow" Example

Suzy, a 50-something flight attendant from Miami, FL, is doing very well in spite of going through a difficult divorce. She earns $80,000 per year from a combination of wages and alimony.

As a flight attendant, Suzy has learned the importance of having a backup plan. She has already been through many financial struggles, countless industry lay-offs, pay cuts and corporate restructurings, as well as a divorce from a pilot who had too much fun on his international layovers. She has been preparing for a rainy day for a long time. In fact, she saves 20 percent of every paycheck. "I can only count on myself," says Suzy. "So my financial future is in my own hands."

When we looked at Suzy's spending, her largest expense by far (like most Americans) was her debt payments. She owed $197,500 between her car, credit card, and condo mortgage. Her total payments were $2,360 per month or $28,320 per year, or about half of her monthly expenses.

Without this debt burden her other monthly and annual expenses would have been $3,000 per month or $36,000 per year.

According to her plan, Suzy will pay $20,000 extra per year toward her debt, on top of her car, credit card, and mortgage payments of $28,320. As a result, by paying a total of $48,320 per year, she will be debt-free in four and a half years and earning enough from her investments to cover her current expenses in six years.

As you can see, by using at least half of your free cash flow, you can begin to pay off your debt in a very short time. Use Suzy as an example. Write in your journal what you can do to pay off your consumer debt in no more than four years, and no more than 10 years for your mortgages. Paying off your debt will significantly increase your cash flow long term.

POOR CASH FLOW - WHAT TO DO - Are you saving less than 10 percent of your net income? Are you just keeping your head above water? Are you a slave to your lifestyle, increasing your debt, or just consuming your net pay every year?

How do you get the cash flow engine started? From the above example, it is easy to see the impact of getting out of debt. But, if you are just barely paying the bills, you need to add one more step. You need to spend less on each of your five largest bills and increase your income.

So, how do you do it? Make a date with your significant other to address the situation. Get a babysitter for the kids, a bottle of wine, and set aside the necessary time to truly look at where your extra spending is coming from. If you are divorced or single, sit down with a trusted advisor.

Are you eating out too often? Do you live in a home that is more than you can afford? Do you have expensive tastes in cars, clothes, or travel? You need to figure out what you need to change right now so you can save an ideal 20 percent.

Why 20 percent? That way you do not have to spend your whole life stressed out and working. Also, it will make 10 percent in actual savings much more likely, because unexpected purchases, repairs, etc., can waylay the best of plans.

Advisory services through Capital Advisory Group Advisory Services LLC and securities through United Planners Financial Services of America, a Limited Partnership. Member FINRA and SIPC. The Capital Advisory Group Advisory Services, LLC (CAG) and United Planners Financial Services are not affiliated.

Let's look at ways to increase your income and review the top expenses and some possible solutions to cut costs.

Increase Your Income - What ways can you add more value to your employer to deserve more compensation.

Here are some ways to increase your family's income:

- Have your spouse work
- Take on a part-time job
- Ask for a raise
- Set up a performance bonus
- Increase your output
- Move to a more prosperous area
- Do something else that pays more
- Get training, licensing, or a degree
- Go into sales or into a professional field where the pay is higher
- Be mentored by successful people who earn more than you working in the same field as you.

Action Item: Referring to your plan from the previous chapter, decide whether you want to increase your income, knowing at what cost it will be to you (time, more schooling, etc.). If you do, write down possible ways to increase family income.

Reduce Debt Expenses - Of all the expenses, debt paydown is the major key to improving cash flow for most families. Here are some ways to reduce debt expenses:

- Set up a plan to pay all non-mortgage debt in four years or less

Advisory services through Capital Advisory Group Advisory Services LLC and securities through United Planners Financial Services of America, a Limited Partnership. Member FINRA and SIPC. The Capital Advisory Group Advisory Services, LLC (CAG) and United Planners Financial Services are not affiliated.

- Negotiate lower interest rates and lock in low fixed rates (avoid adjustable rates)
- Sell assets to pay off debts
- Consider using retirement assets to pay off debt
- Stop buying "stuff" until debt-free
- Cut up your credit cards and use cash exclusively
- Minimize business expenses, until debts are paid off
- Sell toys, stuff, etc., to pay off debt
- Develop your own creative ways to pay off debts

Action Item: Choose three ways you are going to reduce debt, interest costs, or pay off your debt faster.

Reduce Vacation Expenses - Travel can be an expensive item for a family. Here are ways to keep costs down:

- Go on company-paid trips
- Go on tax-deductible trips with your church or to help others
- Shop for travel bargains online
- Set a budget and limit travel expenses
- Visit countries with favorable exchange rates
- Use frequent flyer miles

Action Item: Reduce vacation expenses by having a budget and a cost effective plan.

Reduce Business Expenses - In many cases, a business owner will spend money for the business when they would not spend that same money personally. Consider the following ways to reduce business expenses:

Advisory services through Capital Advisory Group Advisory Services LLC and securities through United Planners Financial Services of America, a Limited Partnership. Member FINRA and SIPC. The Capital Advisory Group Advisory Services, LLC (CAG) and United Planners Financial Services are not affiliated.

- Shut down or sell businesses consuming cash
- Save the first 20 percent of profit, then limit bills to the remaining 80 percent
- Clamp down on any unnecessary expenses
- Put systems in place to speed up cash payments into the business and make it hard to approve expenses
- Buy, instead of leasing, to avoid future payments
- Set a price ceiling for hotels, meals, etc.
- Use windfalls to pay off debt
- Provide incentives for cost-reduction ideas your company implements
- If business has limited potential, sell where possible, or shut it down and move on
- Buy used equipment instead new
- Bid out insurance, materials, and professional services regularly
- Look at each product line – make sure each adds to profit. If not, remove the bad lines
- Replace marginal employees quickly
- Promote, produce, and advertise out of low income emergencies instead of borrowing

Action Item: If applicable to you, identify business expenses you can cut now and other expenses you can drop over the next 12 months.

Reduce Insurance Expenses - Insurance can be a very high expense. Here are some ways to cut costs:

- Stay healthy: Work out, eat right, and get enough rest
- Bid out life, health, disability, auto, long-term care, and liability insurance regularly
- Create an insurance trust to reduce estate taxes
- Increase your deductibles to lower the policy cost as savings increase
- Have business pay for insurance, but know the tax consequences
- Maintain a good driving record
- Make fewer claims against your home and auto policies
- Don't smoke

Action Item: Write down your plan to reduce your insurance expenses

Reduce Child-Related Expenses - By teaching your children how to save, you will not only reduce your expenses now, but also you will make them feel self-sufficient and reduce your expenses in the future. Here are a few pointers:

- Pay for your children's needs, but have your children pay for their own wants
- Don't create a "welfare state" within the family by over-supporting or enabling a lifestyle your children cannot support
- Don't give children or teens credit cards
- Teach children to limit consumer spending to half of their income, while saving half
- Encourage kids to also save for college
- Give kids chores so they learn to be responsible

Advisory services through Capital Advisory Group Advisory Services LLC and securities through United Planners Financial Services of America, a Limited Partnership. Member FINRA and SIPC. The Capital Advisory Group Advisory Services, LLC (CAG) and United Planners Financial Services are not affiliated.

- Consider having kids take subsidized college classes while in high school to reduce college tuition expenses
- Put teens "in charge" of their expenses like insurance

Action Item: Identify and reduce unnecessary child-related expenses.

Reduce Home Expenses - One of the largest expense items is your home. Look at ways to reduce these expenses:

- Use cash flow to pay mortgage sooner
- Convert variable-rate loans to fixed-rate loans
- Rent instead of owning a home if you plan on moving within five years
- Move to a smaller home
- Bid out insurance costs regularly
- Get your lender's permission to cancel mortgage insurance once loan is below 80 percent market value.
- Do not borrow more than 80% of your home value
- Put off remodeling home
- Pay down mortgage with investments

Action Item: Write down how you plan to reduce your home expenses.

Reduce the Cost of "Toys" and Second Homes - It is amazing what we spend on grown-up toys – cabins, boats, motorcycles, airplanes, or RVs. Here are a few ways to make those grown-up playthings cost less:

- Sell your toy

- Buy a less expensive toy
- Buy fractional interest in a toy
- Buy with a partner or family
- Put a toy into a business
- Have friends with toys
- If it floats, flies or sits most of the time unused, rent and don't buy
- Add up the total cost; figure cost per use; determine whether to own versus rent
- Transfer carrying costs to users
- Use www.craigslist.com to get toys cheap

Action Item: Make a list of toys you don't need any more, and what you plan to do with them now.

Reduce Remodeling Expenses - Remodeling can send a savings plan out the window.

Here are some tips:

- Put off remodeling
- Check referrals of contractors before hiring
- Get multiple fixed bids for your remodeling projects
- Limit remodeling to projects that increase the resale value, like upgrading the bath, kitchen, or curb appeal
- Do not pay the full balance of a bill until work is completed to your satisfaction
- Hire an inspector to ensure work is done before paying final bill

Advisory services through Capital Advisory Group Advisory Services LLC and securities through United Planners Financial Services of America, a Limited Partnership. Member FINRA and SIPC. The Capital Advisory Group Advisory Services, LLC (CAG) and United Planners Financial Services are not affiliated.

- Buy materials from discount stores – Sam's Club, Costco, Amazon.com, ebay.com, directbuy.com, saveclub.com, craigslist.com

Action Item: Write down how you plan to reduce your remodeling expenses.

Reduce Investment Real Estate Expenses - Many investment property purchases do not make financial sense. Here are some ways to reduce your real estate expenses:

- Do not buy any real estate that cannot return 10 percent or more cash flow after all expenses, excluding appreciation
- If you cannot sell, lower your price, even sell at a loss if it still improves your overall monthly cash flow
- Transfer costs by selling as a "rent-to-own"
- Consider offering owner financing
- Rent property to contractor who can remodel in lieu of rent or for reduced rent
- Refinance variable mortgages to a fixed rate to prevent rate increases
- Sell a share of property to a partner
- Donate property to charity
- If the real estate pays less than 5 percent, consider selling it
- Transfer operating costs to renters
- Get lender to allow short sale. A short sale is where a lender agrees to sell real estate for less than the loan balance

Action Item: If applicable, evaluate your current real estate investments and identify places to save.

Advisory services through Capital Advisory Group Advisory Services LLC and securities through United Planners Financial Services of America, a Limited Partnership. Member FINRA and SIPC. The Capital Advisory Group Advisory Services, LLC (CAG) and United Planners Financial Services are not affiliated.

Reduce Unplanned Expenses - Unplanned expenses can make up a major source of expenses.

Here are some ways to minimize the costs:

- Carry fewer credit cards with lower limits
- Pay off credit cards monthly
- Limit access to spending by paying yourself and your spouse a weekly cash allowance
- Never buy groceries if hungry
- Set a maximum limit to spend without spousal approval
- Limit going where you spend—malls, QVC, eBay, Amazon.com, shopping vacations, or shoe stores
- Task the most responsible and frugal spouse in charge of the checkbook, limit money access of the free-spending spouse

Action Item: Look at your expenses for the past 3 months and identify areas of excessive unplanned spending.

Reduce Auto Expenses - Automobiles can represent status as well as mere transportation. Consider these suggestions to reduce your vehicle expenses:

- Consider less expensive vehicles
- Consider an extended warranty to minimize car maintenance costs
- Bid out insurance costs regularly
- Rent cars for high mileage trips
- Sell cars that aren't getting used
- Donate unused cars to charity

- Get a car with better gas mileage

- Move closer to work

- Keep your cars longer

- Find the best deal on-line to negotiate better pricing

Action Item: Write down how you plan to reduce your auto expenses.

Now, go through the various expense lists and pick at least three things you will do to reduce your spending so that you can save a minimum of 20 percent. Yes 20%, because from experience, it takes more than just a 10% identified reduction to actually get the results of a 10% actual spending reduction.

Remember what we said at the beginning of the chapter: poor cash flow is why most people never save. Do not put this difficult step off, or you will be in the same boat next year.

Why Most People Never Become Wealthy

This chapter will either be very easy or very hard for you. The pay-back for doing these exercises is life-changing, once you have done them long enough to build savings. Decide now that you will do what it takes to free up at least 10 percent of your net pay and use it to start eliminating your debt.

Use the ideas outlined in this chapter or make up your own plans to eliminate your debt through expense savings. Six months from now, you can expect to either be in the same place or you will begin to feel the freedom that a little cash flow can bring.

We have now covered what the single most important factor to financial success is: creating positive cash flow.

SUMMARY

1. Cash flow is the single most import factor as to whether you become financially free or become a slave to your lifestyle.

2. To change your cash flow, you must first analyze your income, taxes and spending.

3. Find out how much you currently save as a percent of your net income:

Your savings are GREAT if you are saving at least 50 percent of every dollar. Keep up the good work!

Your savings are GOOD if you are saving at least 10 to 50 percent of every net income dollar. Use your free cash flow to retire your debt in no more than four years. Every year you should retire 25 percent of your consumer debt and stop adding to the debt pile. Once your consumer debt is gone, use everything you were using to pay off debt, plus half of your free cash flow, to retire your mortgage in no more than 10 years. Before you know it, you'll have eliminated the average American family's largest expense – debt.

Your savings are POOR if you are saving less than 10 percent of your net income. You need to reduce your largest bills until you have a planned free cash flow of 20 percent. Then, follow the plan of GOOD savers for even less financial stress.

4. If getting started on reducing debt is overwhelming to you at this point in your life, be sure to connect with a trusted financial advisor who can guide you through the process. Do not let yourself be too overwhelmed.

Advisory services through Capital Advisory Group Advisory Services LLC and securities through United Planners Financial Services of America, a Limited Partnership. Member FINRA and SIPC. The Capital Advisory Group Advisory Services, LLC (CAG) and United Planners Financial Services are not affiliated.

Advisory services through Capital Advisory Group Advisory Services LLC and securities through United Planners Financial Services of America, a Limited Partnership. Member FINRA and SIPC. The Capital Advisory Group Advisory Services, LLC (CAG) and United Planners Financial Services are not affiliated.

Section VI

College Indexes

6.1 Top Rated Colleges in the US by Region - East

#	College	State
1	Harvard University	MA
2	Princeton University	NJ
3	United States Military Academy-West Point	NY
4	Columbia University	NY
5	Massachusetts Institute of Technology	MA
6	Yale University	CT
7	University of Pennsylvania	PA
8	John Hopkins University	MD
9	Brown University	RI
10	Dartmouth College	NH
11	United States Merchant Marine Academy	NY
12	Cornell University	NY
13	United States Coast Guard Academy	CT
14	Carnegie Mellon University	PA
15	New York University	NY

pub/priv	Size	Cost after Aid	ACT avg	Grad rate	Early Income
Private	20,823	$14,327	34	97%	$74,800
Private	5,422	$9,327	34	98%	$75,200
Public	4,389	$(13,806)	29	86%	$81,100
Private	26,665	$24,231	34	95%	$71,400
Private	4,530	$20,771	35	93%	$86,300
Private	12,402	$18,627	34	94%	$70,300
Private	20,578	$24,242	34	95%	$72,800
Private	16,171	$33,586	34	92%	$67,200
Private	9,391	$30,205	34	96%	$68,200
Private	6,247	$30,421	33	96%	$71,500
Public	1,025	$-	27	95%	$88,100
Private	22,319	$31,230	33	94%	$70,100
Public	1,069	$(12,423)	29	78%	$80,000
Private	13,430	$47,326	34	88%	$72,600
Public	44,466	$42,397	32	83%	$76,000

6.2 Top Rated Colleges in the US by Region - Midwest

#	College	State
1	United States Air Force Academy	CO
2	University of Chicago	IL
3	Northwestern University	IL
4	Washington University	MO
5	University of Notre Dame	IN
6	University of Michigan- Ann Arbor	MI
7	University of Illinois-Urbana	IL
8	University of Wisconsin-Madison	WI
9	Purdue University	IN
10	Michigan State	MI
11	University of Minnesota	MN
12	University of Iowa	IA
13	Ohio State University	OH
14	Iowa State University	IA
15	University of Minnesota- Duluth	MN

pub/priv	Size	Cost after Aid	ACT avg	Grad rate	Early Income
Public	6,512	$(13,806)	30	79%	$77,600
Private	13,833	$25,455	34	94%	$64,000
Private	17,951	$24,047	34	94%	$63,400
Private	13,401	$27,427	34	94%	$82,800
Private	12,104	$28,768	33	95%	$67,000
Public	42,982	$14,860	32	91%	$63,500
Public	44,916	$32,202	29	85%	$66,500
Public	39,154	$57,699	28	84%	$64,800
Private	40,451	$12,684	29	74%	$61,200
Private	44,789	$29,130	26	78%	$60,000
Public	61,120	$28,819	28	78%	$58,200
Public	28,945	$24,806	26	71%	$59,800
Public	54,372	$27,912	30	83%	$50,600
Public	28,294	$15,195	25	70%	$53,700
Public	61,120	$28,819	28	78%	$58,200

6.3 Top Rated Colleges in the US by Region - South

#	College	State
1	Duke University	NC
2	Vanderbilt University	TN
3	Emory University	GA
4	Georgetown University	DC
5	University of Virginia	VA
6	George Washington University	DC
7	University of North Carolina	NC
8	Wake forest	NC
9	Howard University	DC
10	University of Florida	FL
11	Clemson University	SC
12	Florida State University	FL
13	Louisiana State University	LA
14	Auburn University	AL
15	University of Alabama	AL

pub/priv	Size	Cost after Aid	ACT avg	Grad rate	Early Income
Private	15,309	$35,737	34	95%	$71,100
Private	12,006	$26,933	34	92%	$68,500
Private	12,735	$25,942	32	89%	$81,500
Private	16,279	$30,107	33	94%	$66,400
Public	23,116	$42,633	32	94%	$77,200
Private	23,488	$38,829	31	81%	$80,500
Public	35,419	$35,152	30	90%	$66,100
Private	7,591	$24,800	31	88%	$63,000
Private	8,447	$21,428	25	60%	$51,800
Public	46,642	$37,409	30	87%	$62,600
Private	20,195	$26,770	29	82%	$57,100
Public	38,520	$22,446	28	79%	$51,400
Public	25,826	$18,143	26	67%	$56,900
Private	24,594	$22,796	28	72%	$54,100
Public	16,575	$30,016	28	66%	$49,900

6.4 Top Rated Colleges in the US by Region - West

#	College	State
1	Stanford University	CA
2	California Institute of Technology	CA
3	Pomona College	CA
4	Rice University	TX
5	University of Southern California	CA
6	Harvey Mudd College	CA
7	Claremont McKenna College	CA
8	University of Texas	TX
9	University of Texas- Austin	TX
10	University of Washington	WA
11	Texas A&M	TX
12	University of California-Berkley	CA
13	University of California-LA	CA
14	University of Arizona	AZ
15	University of California-Long Beach	CA

pub/priv	Size	Cost after Aid	ACT avg	Grad rate	Early Income
Private	6,996	$13,361	33	94%	$79,000
Private	938	$24,245	35	93%	$84,100
Private	1,717	$15,859	33	97%	$63,800
Private	6,667	$20,237	34	93%	$71,000
Private	36,929	$30,232	32	92%	$68,500
Private	895	$33,000	34	93%	$91,400
Private	1,343	$26,933	32	93%	$64,500
Public	53,791	$32,488	28	80%	$68,600
Public	49,165	$27,728	30	80%	$68,600
Public	45,692	$38,159	30	84%	$65,800
Private	60,818	$43,848	28	79%	$65,600
Public	41,081	$15,859	33	63%	$70,700
Public	41,066	$15,859	32	63%	$70,700
Public	39,124		64	64%	$52,600
Public	5,460	$15,859	33	63%	$70,700

6.5 Top Hardest Colleges to Get Accepted in the US

#	College	Region
1	Massachusetts Institute of Technology	East
2	Harvard University	East
3	Princeton University	East
4	Columbia University	East
5	California Institute of Technology	West
6	Yale University	East
7	University of Chicago	Midwest
8	University of Pennsylvania	East
9	Stanford University	West
10	John Hopkins University	East
11	Northwestern University	Midwest
12	Duke University	South
13	Brown University	East
14	Pomona College	West
15	Vanderbilt University	South

State	Cost after Aid	ACT avg	Accept Rate	Grad rate
MA	$20,771.00	35	7%	93%
MA	$14,327.00	34	5%	97%
NJ	$9,327.00	34	6%	98%
NY	$24,231.00	34	5%	95%
CA	$24,245.00	35	5%	93%
CT	$18,627.00	34	6%	94%
IL	$25,455.00	34	6%	94%
PA	$24,242.00	34	6%	95%
CA	$13,361.00	33	4%	94%
MD	$33,586.00	34	7%	92%
IL	$24,047.00	34	8%	94%
NC	$35,737.00	34	8%	95%
RI	$30,205.00	34	8%	96%
CA	$15,859.00	33	9%	97%
TN	$26,933.00	34	9%	92%

#	College	Region
16	Rice University	West
17	Washington University	Midwest
18	Dartmouth College	East
19	Cornell University	East
20	University of Notre Dame	Midwest
21	Carnegie Mellon University	East
22	United States Air Force Academy	Midwest
23	Georgetown University	East
24	United States Military Academy-West Point	East
25	Harvey Mudd College	West
26	Emory University	South
27	University of Michigan- Ann Arbor	Midwest
28	University of Southern California	West
29	Tufts University	East
30	University of Virginia	East
31	Swarthmore College	East
32	Williams College	East

State	Cost after Aid	ACT avg	Accept Rate	Grad rate
TX	$20,237.00	34	9%	93%
MO	$27,427.00	34	10%	94%
NH	$30,421.00	33	10%	96%
NY	$31,230.00	33	11%	94%
IN	$28,768.00	33	16%	95%
PA	$47,326.00	34	13%	88%
CO	$(13,806.00)	30	8%	79%
DC	$30,107.00	33	14%	94%
NY	$(13,806.00)	29	12%	86%
CA	$33,000.00	34	14%	93%
GA	$25,942.00	32	16%	89%
MI	$14,860.00	32	15%	91%
CA	$30,232.00	32	15%	92%
MA	$26,280.00	33	15%	93%
VA	$42,633.00	32	16%	94%
PA	$20,511.00	33	9%	94%
MA	$22,667.00	33	13%	94%

#	College	Region
33	New York University	East
34	Bodoin College	East
35	Wake forest	South
36	Wellesly College	East
37	Boston University	East
38	Claremont McKenna College	West
39	University of North Carolina- Chapel Hill	South
40	United States Coast Guard Academy	East
41	George Washington University	East
42	University of California-Berkley	West
43	United States Merchant Marine Academy	East
44	Vassar College	East
45	United States Naval Academy	East
46	University of California-LA	West
47	Trinity College	East
48	University of Texas- Austin	West
49	University of Washington	West

State	Cost after Aid	ACT avg	Accept Rate	Grad rate
NY	$42,397.00	32	16%	83%
ME	$22,810.00	33	18%	95%
NC	$24,800.00	31	30%	88%
MA	$36,034.00	32	22%	92%
MA	$29,479.00	32	19%	87%
CA	$26,933.00	32	10%	93%
NC	$35,152.00	30	20%	90%
CT	$(12,423.00)	29	22%	78%
DC	$38,829.00	31	41%	81%
CA	$15,859.00	33	16%	63%
NY	$-	27	25%	95%
NY	$24,811.00	32	33%	91%
MD	$(13,806.00)	29	8%	88%
CA	$15,859.00	32	12%	63%
CT	$32,122.00	30	29%	85%
TX	$27,728.00	30	32%	80%
WA	$38,159.00	30	25%	84%

#	College	Region
50	University of Florida	South
51	University of Illinois-Urbana	Midwest
52	University of Texas	West
53	Purdue University	Midwest
54	Clemson University	South
55	Ohio State University	Midwest
56	Texas A&M	West
57	University of Massachusetts	East
58	University of Maryland	East
59	University of Wisconsin-Madison	Midwest
60	Penn State- Main Campus	East
61	University of Minnesota	Midwest
62	Rutgers, State University of New Jersey	East
63	Florida State University	South
64	Michigan State	Midwest
65	Auburn University	South
66	University of Alabama	South

State	Cost after Aid	ACT avg	Accept Rate	Grad rate
FL	$37,409.00	30	25%	87%
IL	$32,202.00	29	59%	85%
TX	$32,488.00	28	28%	80%
IN	$12,684.00	29	60%	74%
SC	$26,770.00	29	29%	82%
OH	$27,912.00	30	29%	83%
TX	$43,848.00	28	36%	79%
MA	$31,793.00	29	30%	82%
MD	$39,698.00	31	30%	79%
WI	$57,699.00	28	58%	84%
PA	$30,996.00	28	31%	86%
MN	$28,819.00	28	57%	78%
NJ	$28,482.00	28	83%	67%
FL	$22,446.00	28	33%	79%
MI	$29,130.00	26	23%	78%
AL	$22,796.00	28	80%	72%
AL	$30,016.00	28	83%	66%

#	College	Region
67	University of Iowa	Midwest
68	Louisiana State University	South
69	Howard University	East
70	Iowa State University	Midwest
71	University of Arizona	West

State	Cost after Aid	ACT avg	Accept Rate	Grad rate
IA	$24,806.00	26	83%	71%
LA	$18,143.00	26	72%	67%
DC	$21,428.00	25	36%	60%
IA	$15,195.00	25	92%	70%
AZ	$30,041.00	25	85%	64%

6.6 Top 50 Highest Mid-Career Paying Colleges

#	College	Region
1	Harvey Mudd College	West
2	Massachusetts Institute of Technology	East
3	United States Naval Academy	East
4	Princeton University	East
5	California Institute of Technology	West
6	Harvard University	East
7	Stanford University	West
8	Swarthmore College	East
9	Yale University	East
10	United States Air Force Academy	Midwest
11	University of Pennsylvania	East
12	Claremont McKenna College	West
13	United States Merchant Marine Academy	East
14	University of California-LA	West
15	University of Notre Dame	Midwest

State	Cost after Aid	ACT avg	Accept Rate	Grad rate	Median Income
CA	$33,000.00	34	14%	93%	$162,500
MA	$20,771.00	35	7%	93%	$158,100
MD	$(13,806.00)	29	8%	88%	$152,600
NJ	$9,327.00	34	6%	98%	$150,500
CA	$24,245.00	35	5%	93%	$150,300
MA	$14,327.00	34	5%	97%	$147,700
CA	$13,361.00	33	4%	94%	$147,100
PA	$20,511.00	33	9%	94%	$141,500
CT	$18,627.00	34	6%	94%	$141,400
CO	$(13,806.00)	30	8%	79%	$140,400
PA	$24,242.00	34	6%	95%	$138,500
CA	$26,933.00	32	10%	93%	$138,500
NY	$-	27	25%	95%	$138,500
CA	$15,859.00	32	12%	63%	$138,500
IN	$28,768.00	33	16%	95%	$136,900

#	College	Region
16	Duke University	South
17	Georgetown University	East
18	Rice University	West
19	Cornell University	East
20	Columbia University	East
21	University of Southern California	West
22	United States Military Academy-West Point	East
23	University of Virginia	East
24	Tufts University	East
25	New York University	East
26	George Washington University	East
27	Bodoin College	East
28	Williams College	East
29	University of California-Berkley	West
30	Wake forest	South
31	University of Chicago	Midwest
32	Vanderbilt University	South

State	Cost after Aid	ACT avg	Accept Rate	Grad rate	Median Income
NC	$35,737.00	34	8%	95%	$135,000
DC	$30,107.00	33	14%	94%	$134,500
TX	$20,237.00	34	9%	93%	$134,100
NY	$31,230.00	33	11%	94%	$133,100
NY	$24,231.00	34	5%	95%	$132,000
CA	$30,232.00	32	15%	92%	$126,300
NY	$(13,806.00)	29	12%	86%	$126,000
VA	$42,633.00	32	16%	94%	$125,200
MA	$26,280.00	33	15%	93%	$124,700
NY	$42,397.00	32	16%	83%	$124,700
DC	$38,829.00	31	41%	81%	$124,500
ME	$22,810.00	33	18%	95%	$124,400
MA	$22,667.00	33	13%	94%	$124,300
CA	$15,859.00	33	16%	63%	$124,000
NC	$24,800.00	31	30%	88%	$122,500
IL	$25,455.00	34	6%	94%	$122,400
TN	$26,933.00	34	9%	92%	$122,400

#	College	Region
33	Wellesly College	East
34	Pomona College	West
35	Boston University	East
36	Northwestern University	Midwest
37	Dartmouth College	East
38	United States Coast Guard Academy	East
39	University of Texas- Austin	West
40	Texas A&M	West
41	Washington University	Midwest
42	University of Illinois-Urbana	Midwest
43	John Hopkins University	East
44	Emory University	South
45	Trinity College	East
46	University of Washington	West
47	Rutgers, State University of New Jersey	East
48	Brown University	East
49	University of Michigan- Ann Arbor	Midwest
50	University of Maryland	East

State	Cost after Aid	ACT avg	Accept Rate	Grad rate	Median Income
MA	$36,034.00	32	22%	92%	$122,100
CA	$15,859.00	33	9%	97%	$121,300
MA	$29,479.00	32	19%	87%	$120,900
IL	$24,047.00	34	8%	94%	$120,300
NH	$30,421.00	33	10%	96%	$119,700
CT	$(12,423.00)	29	22%	78%	$119,000
TX	$27,728.00	30	32%	80%	$119,000
TX	$43,848.00	28	36%	79%	$119,000
MO	$27,427.00	34	10%	94%	$117,800
IL	$32,202.00	29	59%	85%	$117,800
MD	$33,586.00	34	7%	92%	$117,600
GA	$25,942.00	32	16%	89%	$116,900
CT	$32,122.00	30	29%	85%	$115,600
WA	$38,159.00	30	25%	84%	$115,500
NJ	$28,482.00	28	83%	67%	$115,200
RI	$30,205.00	34	8%	96%	$115,000
MI	$14,860.00	32	15%	91%	$111,500
MD	$39,698.00	31	30%	79%	$111,400

6.7 United States Colleges and Universities by State

Alaska
University of Alaska, www.alaska.edu, AK
Alaska Christian College, www.alaskacc.edu, AK
National Park Community College, www.npcc.edu, AK
University of Alaska Fairbanks, www.uaf.edu, AK

Alabama
Alabama A&M University, www.aamu.edu, AL
Athens State University, www.athens.edu, AL
Auburn University, www.auburn.edu, AL
Auburn University at Montgomery, www.aum.edu, AL
Birmingham-Southern College, www.bsc.edu, AL
Calhoun Community College, www.calhoun.edu, AL
Enterprise State Community College, www.escc.edu, AL
Faulkner State Community College, www.faulknerstate.edu, AL
Gadsden State Community College, www.gadsdenstate.edu, AL
Huntingdon College, www.huntingdon.edu, AL
Jacksonville State University, www.jsu.edu, AL
Lurleen B. Wallace Community College, www.lbwcc.edu, AL
University of Montevallo, www.montevallo.edu, AL
Northeast Alabama Community College, www.nacc.edu, AL
Northwest-Shoals Community College, www.nwscc.edu, AL
Oakwood University, www.oakwood.edu, AL
Samford University, www.samford.edu, AL
Southeastern Bible College, www.sebc.edu, AL
University of South Alabama, www.southalabama.edu, AL
Trenholm State Technical College, www.trenholmstate.edu, AL
Troy University, www.troy.edu, AL
Tuskegee University, www.tuskegee.edu, AL
University of Alabama, www.ua.edu, AL
University of Alabama at Birmingham, www.uab.edu, AL
University of Alabama in Huntsville, www.uah.edu, AL
University of North Alabama, www.una.edu, AL
Snead State Community College, www.snead.edu, AL

Arkansas
University of Arkansas – Fort Smith, www.uafs.edu, AR
Arkansas Northeastern College, www.anc.edu, AR
Arkansas State University, www.astate.edu, AR
Arkansas Tech University, www.atu.edu, AR
Central Baptist College, www.cbc.edu, AR
Harding University, www.harding.edu, AR
Hendrix College, www.hendrix.edu, AR
Henderson State University, www.hsu.edu, AR
John Brown University, www.jbu.edu, AR
Lyon College, www.lyon.edu, AR
Mid-South Community College, www.midsouthcc.edu, AR
North Arkansas College, www.northark.edu, AR
Northwest Arkansas Community College, www.nwacc.edu, AR
Northwest Technical Institute, www.nwti.edu, AR
Ouachita Baptist University, www.obu.edu, AR
University of the Ozarks, www.ozarks.edu, AR
Phillips Community College U of A, www.pccua.edu, AR
Pulaski Technical College, www.pulaskitech.edu, AR
Southern Arkansas University Magnolia, www.saumag.edu, AR
Southeast Arkansas College, www.seark.edu, AR

University of Arkansas Community College Batesville, www.uaccb.edu, AR
University of Arkansas at Little Rock, www.ualr.edu, AR
University of Arkansas - Medical Sciences, www.uams.edu, AR
University of Arkansas at Pine Bluff, www.uapb.edu, AR
University of Arkansas, www.uark.edu, AR
University of Central Arkansas, www.uca.edu, AR
Williams Baptist College, www.wbcoll.edu, AR

Arizona
University of Arizona, www.arizona.edu, AZ
Arizona State University, www.asu.edu, AZ
Arizona Western College, www.azwestern.edu, AZ
Bryan University, www.bryanuniversity.edu, AZ
Central Arizona College, www.centralaz.edu, AZ
Glendale Community College, www.gccaz.edu, AZ
Grand Canyon University, www.gcu.edu, AZ
Maricopa Community Colleges, www.maricopa.edu, AZ
Mesa Community College, www.mesacc.edu, AZ
Northern Arizona University, www.nau.edu, AZ
Northland Pioneer College, www.npc.edu, AZ
University of Phoenix, www.phoenix.edu, AZ
Phoenix College, www.phoenixcollege.edu, AZ
Pima Community College, www.pima.edu, AZ
Prescott College, www.prescott.edu, AZ
Rio Salado College, www.riosalado.edu, AZ
South Mountain Community College, www.southmountaincc.edu, AZ
University of Advancing Technology, www.uat.edu, AZ
Yavapai College, www.yc.edu, AZ

California
Academy of Arts University, www.academyart.edu, CA
Advance Computing Institute, www.advancedcomputinginstitute.edu, CA
Acupuncture & Integrative Medicine College, www.aimc.edu, CA
Alliant International University, www.alliant.edu, CA
Allied American University, www.allied.edu, CA
Anaheim University, www.anaheim.edu, CA
Angeles College, www.angelescollege.edu, CA
Antioch University Los Angeles, www.antiochla.edu, CA
Argosy University, www.argosy.edu, CA
Art Center College of Design, www.artcenter.edu, CA
The Art Institute, www.artinstitutes.edu, CA
Ashford University, www.ashford.edu, CA
ATI College, www.ati.edu, CA
Antelope Valley College, www.avc.edu, CA
Bakersfield College, www.bakersfieldcollege.edu, CA
Barstow Community College, www.barstow.edu, CA
Berkeley University of California, www.berkeley.edu, CA
Berkeley City College, www.berkeleycitycollege.edu, CA
Brandman University, www.brandman.edu, CA
Butte College, www.butte.edu, CA
Cabrillo College, www.cabrillo.edu, CA
California Institute of the Arts, www.calarts.edu, CA
California Baptist University, www.calbaptist.edu, CA
California Lutheran University, www.callutheran.edu, CA

California Miramar University, www.calmu.edu, CA
California Polytechnic State University, www.calpoly.edu, CA
California State University, www.calstate.edu, CA
California Institute of Technology, www.caltech.edu, CA
Canada College, www.canadacollege.edu, CA
College of the Canyons, www.canyons.edu, CA
California College of the Arts, www.cca.edu, CA
California Community Colleges, www.cccco.edu, CA
City College of San Francisco, www.ccsf.edu, CA
Cerritos College, www.cerritos.edu, CA
Cerro Coso Community College, www.cerrocoso.edu, CA
Claremont Graduate University, www.cgu.edu, CA
Chaffey College, www.chaffey.edu, CA
Chapman University, www.chapman.edu, CA
California Institute of Integral Studies, www.ciis.edu, CA
Citrus College, www.citruscollege.edu, CA
The Claremont Colleges, www.claremont.edu, CA
Claremont McKenna College, www.cmc.edu, CA
Copper Mountain College, www.cmccd.edu, CA
Cogswell Polytechnical College, www.cogswell.edu, CA
College of San Mateo, www.collegeofsanmateo.edu, CA
College of the Desert, www.collegeofthedesert.edu, CA
El Camino College Compton Center, www.compton.edu, CA
Contra Costa College, www.contracosta.edu, CA
College of the Sequoias, www.cos.edu, CA
Crafton Hills College, www.craftonhills.edu, CA
California State University Bakersfield, www.csub.edu, CA
California State University Channel Islands, www.csuci.edu, CA
California State University Dominguez Hills, www.csudh.edu,CA
California State University East Bay, www.csueastbay.edu, CA
California State University Fresno, www.fresnostate.edu, CA
California State University Long Beach, www.csulb.edu, CA
California State University Monterey Bay, www.csumb.edu, CA
California State University Northridge, www.csun.edu, CA
California State Polytechnic University Pomona, www.csupomona.edu, CA
California State University Sacramento, www.csus.edu, CA
California State University San Bernardino, www.csusb.edu, CA
California State University San Marcos, www.csusm.edu, CA
California State University Stanislaus, www.csustan.edu, CA
Cuesta College, www.cuesta.edu, CA
Cuyamaca College, www.cuyamaca.edu, CA
California Western School of Law San Diego, www.cwsl.edu,CA
Cypress College, www.cypresscollege.edu, CA
DeAnza College, www.deanza.edu, CA
San Joaquin Delta College, www.deltacollege.edu, CA
Dominican University of California, www.dominican.edu, CA
Dominican School of Philosophy & Theology, www.dspt.edu,CA
Diablo Valley College, www.dvc.edu, CA
East Los Angeles College, www.elac.edu, CA
El Camino College, www.elcamino.edu, CA
Expression College, www.expression.edu, CA
Foothill-De Anza Community College District, www.fhda.edu, CA
Fashion Institute of Design & Merchandising, www.fidm.edu, CA
Fielding Graduate University, www.fielding.edu, CA
Foothill College, www.foothill.edu, CA
Fresno Pacific University, www.fresno.edu, CA
Fresno City College, www.fresnocitycollege.edu, CA
Frederick Taylor University, www.ftu.edu, CA
Fullerton College, www.fullcoll.edu, CA
Fuller Theological Seminary, www.fuller.edu, CA
California State University Fullerton, www.fullerton.edu, CA
Gavilan College, www.gavilan.edu, CA
Golden Gate Baptist Theological Seminary, www.ggbts.edu, CA
Glendale Community College, www.glendale.edu, CA

Gnomon School of Visual Effects, www.gnomon.edu, CA
Columbia College, www.gocolumbia.edu, CA
Golden West College, www.goldenwestcollege.edu, CA
Grossmont College, www.grossmont.edu, CA
Allan Hancock College, www.hancockcollege.edu, CA
Hartnell College, www.hartnell.edu, CA
Henley-Putnam University, www.henley-putnam.edu, CA
Harvey Mudd College, www.hmc.edu, CA
Holy Names University, www.hnu.edu, CA
Humboldt State University, www.humboldt.edu, CA
Humphreys College, www.humphreys.edu, CA
Imperial Valley College, www.imperial.edu, CA
International Sports Sciences Assoc., www.issaonline.edu, CA
International Technological University, www.itu.edu, CA
Irvine Valley College, www.ivc.edu, CA
William Jessup University, www.jessup.edu, CA
John F. Kennedy University, www.jfku.edu, CA
Keck Graduate Institute, www.kgi.edu, CA
Mount Saint Mary's College, www.la.edu, CA
Los Angeles Community College District, www.laccd.edu, CA
Los Angeles City College, www.lacitycollege.edu, CA
Los Angeles Harbor College, www.lahc.edu, CA
Los Angeles Mission College, www.lamission.edu, CA
Laney College, www.laney.edu, CA
Los Angeles Southwest College, www.lasc.edu, CA
La Sierra University, www.lasierra.edu, CA
Las Positas College, www.laspositascollege.edu, CA
LA Trade-Tech Community College, www.lattc.edu, CA
Laurus College, www.lauruscollege.edu, CA
Los Angeles Valley College, www.lavc.edu, CA
University of La Verne, www.laverne.edu, CA
UCLA School of Law, www.ucla.edu, CA
Long Beach City College, www.lbcc.edu, CA
Life Chiropractic College West, www.lifewest.edu, CA
Loma Linda University, www.llu.edu, CA
Loyola Marymount University, www.lmu.edu, CA
Los Medanos College, www.losmedanos.edu, CA
Los Rios Community College District, www.losrios.edu, CA
Lake Tahoe Community College, www.ltcc.edu, CA
College of Marin, www.marin.edu, CA
Marymount California University, www.marymountcalifornia.edu, CA
The Master's College, www.masters.edu, CA
Merced Community College, www.mccd.edu, CA
Mills College, www.mills.edu, CA
MiraCosta College, www.miracosta.edu, CA
Modesto Junior College, www.mjc.edu, CA
Mount San Jacinto College, www.msjc.edu, CA
Mount San Antonio College, www.mtsac.edu, CA
Napa Valley College, www.napavalley.edu, CA
Notre Dame de Namur University, www.ndnu.edu, CA
New School of Architecture & Design, www.newschoolarch.edu, CA
Norco College, www.norcocollege.edu, CA
Naval Postgraduate School, www.nps.edu, CA
Ohlone College, www.ohlone.edu, CA
Orange Coast College, www.orangecoastcollege.edu, CA
Otis College of Art & Design, www.otis.edu, CA
Occidental College, www.oxy.edu, CA
University of the Pacific, www.pacific.edu, CA
Pacific College of Oriental Medicine, www.pacificcollege.edu, CA
Palomar College, www.palomar.edu, CA
Pasadena City College, www.pasadena.edu, CA
Pepperdine University, www.pepperdine.edu, CA
Peralta Community College District, www.peralta.edu, CA
Pierce College, www.piercecollege.edu, CA
Pitzer College, www.pitzer.edu, CA
Pacific Lutheran Theological Seminary, www.plts.edu, CA
Point Loma Nazarene University, www.pointloma.edu, CA

Pomona College, www.pomona.edu, CA
Porterville College, www.portervillecollege.edu, CA
Pacific School of Religion, www.psr.edu, CA
Riverside City College, www.rcc.edu, CA
Riverside Community College District, www.rccd.edu, CA
University of Redlands, www.redlands.edu, CA
College of the Redwoods, www.redwoods.edu, CA
Rio Hondo College, www.riohondo.edu, CA
Rosemead College, www.rosemeadcollege.edu, CA
Santa Ana College, www.sac.edu, CA
Saddleback College, www.saddleback.edu, CA
University of San Diego, www.sandiego.edu, CA
Santa Rosa Junior College, www.santarosa.edu, CA
Santa Barbara City College, www.sbcc.edu, CA
School of Continuing Education, www.sce.edu, CA
Scripps College, www.scrippscollege.edu, CA
Santa Clara University, www.scu.edu, CA
Southern California University of Health Sciences, www.scuhs.edu, CA
San Diego City College, www.sdcity.edu, CA
San Diego Mesa College, www.sdmesa.edu, CA
San Diego State University, www.sdsu.edu, CA
San Francisco State University, www.sfsu.edu, CA
Shasta College, www.shastacollege.edu, CA
The Institute of Buddhist Studies, www.shin-ibs.edu, CA
Sierra College, www.sierracollege.edu, CA
Simpson University, www.simpsonu.edu, CA
College of the Siskiyous, www.siskiyous.edu, CA
San Jose State University, www.sjsu.edu, CA
Starr King School for the Ministry, www.sksm.edu, CA
Skyline College, www.skylinecollege.edu, CA
Santa Monica College, www.smc.edu, CA
San Mateo County Community College, www.smccd.edu, CA
Soka University of America, www.soka.edu, CA
Solano Community College, www.solano.edu, CA
Sonoma State University, www.sonoma.edu, CA
Stanford University, www.stanford.edu, CA
Saint Mary's College, www.stmarys-ca.edu, CA
Taft College, www.taftcollege.edu, CA
Touro University California, www.tu.edu, CA
University of California Davis, www.ucdavis.edu, CA
University of California Hastings College of the Law, www.uchastings.edu, CA
University of California Irvine, www.uci.edu, CA
University of California Los Angeles, www.ucla.edu, CA
University of California Los Angeles Extension, www.uclaextension.edu, CA
University of California Merced, www.ucmerced.edu, CA
University of California, www.ucop.edu, CA
University of California Press, www.ucpress.edu, CA
University of California Riverside, www.ucr.edu, CA
University of California Santa Barbara, www.ucsb.edu, CA
University of California Santa Cruz, www.ucsc.edu, CA
University of California Santa Cruz Silicon Valley Extension, www.ucsc-extension.edu, CA
University of California San Diego, www.ucsd.edu, CA
University of California San Francisco, www.ucsf.edu, CA
University of California, www.universityofcalifornia.edu, CA
University of the Pacific, www.uop.edu, CA
University of Southern California, www.usc.edu, CA
University of San Francisco, www.usfca.edu, CA
San Bernardino Valley College, www.valleycollege.edu, CA
Ventura College, www.venturacollege.edu, CA
Victor Valley College, www.vvc.edu, CA
West Coast Baptist College, www.wcbc.edu, CA
Western University of Health Sciences, www.westernu.edu, CA
Westmont College, www.westmont.edu, CA
West Valley College, www.westvalley.edu, CA
West Hills Community College District, www.whccd.edu, CA
Whittier College, www.whittier.edu, CA

West Los Angeles College, www.wlac.edu, CA
Yuba Community College District, www.yccd.edu, CA
Yosemite Community College District, www.yosemite.edu, CA
Unitek College, www.unitekcollege.edu, CA
Vanguard University, www.vanguard.edu, CA
Southwestern College, www.swcc.edu, CA
Monterey Institute of International Studies, www.miis.edu, CA

Colorado
Adams State University, www.adams.edu, CO
Auraria Higher Education Center, www.ahec.edu, CO
Aims Community College, www.aims.edu, CO
Arapahoe Community College, www.arapahoe.edu, CO
Community College of Aurora, www.ccaurora.edu, CO
Community College of Denver, www.ccd.edu, CO
Colorado Heights University, www.chu.edu, CO
University of Colorado Boulder, www.colorado.edu, CO
Colorado College, www.coloradocollege.edu, CO
Colorado Mesa University, www.coloradomesa.edu, CO
Colorado State University, www.colostate.edu, CO
Colorado State University-Pueblo, www.colostate-pueblo.edu, CO
University of Denver, www.du.edu, CO
Fort Lewis College, www.fortlewis.edu, CO
Front Range Community College, www.frontrange.edu, CO
Jones International University, www.jiu.edu, CO
Colorado School of Mines, www.mines.edu, CO
Metro State University of Denver, www.msudenver.edu, CO
Naropa University, www.naropa.edu, CO
Pikes Peak Community College, www.ppcc.edu, CO
Pueblo Community College, www.pueblocc.edu, CO
Redstone College, www.redstone.edu, CO
Regis University, www.regis.edu, CO
University of the Rockies, www.rockies.edu, CO
Red Rocks Community College, www.rrcc.edu, CO
William Howard Taft University, www.taft.edu, CO
University Corporation for Atmospheric Research, www.ucar.edu, CO
University of Colorado - Colorado Springs, www.uccs.edu, CO
University of Colorado Denver, www.ucdenver.edu, CO
University of Northern Colorado, www.unco.edu, CO
University of Colorado, www.cu.edu, CO
Western State Colorado University, www.western.edu, CO

Connecticut
Albertus Magnus College, www.albertus.edu, CT
Asnuntuck Community College, www.asnuntuck.edu, CT
Connecticut College, www.conncoll.edu, CT
Eastern Connecticut State University, www.easternct.edu, CT
Fairfield University, www.fairfield.edu, CT
Goodwin College, www.goodwin.edu, CT
University of Hartford, www.hartford.edu, CT
Hartford Seminary, www.hartsem.edu, CT
University of New Haven, www.newhaven.edu, CT
Queens University of Charlotte, www.quinnipiac.edu, CT
Quinebaug Valley Community College, www.qvcc.edu, CT
Sacred Heart University, www.sacredheart.edu, CT
Southern Connecticut State University, www.southernct.edu, CT
Three Rivers Community College, www.threerivers.edu, CT
Trinity College, www.trincoll.edu, CT
Tunxis Community College, www.tunxis.edu, CT
University of Connecticut Health Center, www.uchc.edu, CT
University of Connecticut, www.uconn.edu, CT
University of Saint Joseph Connecticut, www.usj.edu, CT
Western Connecticut State University, www.wcsu.edu, CT
Wesleyan University, www.wesleyan.edu, CT

Yale University, www.yale.edu, CT

D.C., Washington
American University, www.american.edu, DC
Carnegie Institution for Science, www.carnegiescience.edu, DC
The Catholic University of America, www.cua.edu, DC
Gallaudet University, www.gallaudet.edu, DC
Georgetown University, www.georgetown.edu, DC
The George Washington University, www.gwu.edu, DC
Howard University, www.howard.edu, DC
Johns Hopkins School of Advanced International Studies, www.sais-jhu.edu, DC
University of California Washington Center, www.ucdc.edu, DC
University of the District of Columbia, www.udc.edu, DC

Delaware
Delaware State University, www.desu.edu, DE
Delaware Technical Community College, www.dtcc.edu, DE
Goldey-Beacom College, www.gbc.edu, DE
University of Delaware, www.udel.edu, DE
Wesley College, www.wesley.edu, DE
Wilmington University, www.wilmu.edu, DE

Florida
Carlos Albizu University, www.albizu.edu, FL
Acupuncture Massage College, www.amcollege.edu, FL
Atlantic Institute of Oriental Medicine, www.atom.edu, FL
Barry University, www.barry.edu, FL
Broward College, www.broward.edu, FL
College of Central Florida, www.cf.edu, FL
Chipola College, www.chipola.edu, FL
Bethune-Cookman University, www.cookman.edu, FL
Dade Medical College, www.dadmedical.edu, FL
Daytona State College, www.daytonastate.edu, FL
Eckerd College, www.eckerd.edu, FL
Edison State College, www.edison.edu, FL
Embry-Riddle Aeronautical University, www.erau.edu, FL
Everglades University, www.evergladesuniversity.edu, FL
Florida Atlantic University, www.fau.edu, FL
Florida Gulf Coast University, www.fgcu.edu, FL
Florida Institute of Technology, www.fit.edu, FL
Florida International University, www.fiu.edu, FL
Flagler College, www.flagler.edu, FL
Florida Southern College, www.flsouthern.edu, FL
Florida National University, www.fnu.edu, FL
Florida State College at Jacksonville, www.fscj.edu, FL
Florida State University, www.fsu.edu, FL
Gulf Coast State College, www.gulfcoast.edu, FL
Hillsborough Community College, www.hccfl.edu, FL
Jacksonville University, www.ju.edu, FL
Keiser University, www.keiseruniversity.edu, FL
Loraines Academy Inc., www.lorainesacademy.edu, FL
Lake Sumter State College, www.lssc.edu, FL
Lynn University, www.lynn.edu, FL
Millennia Atlantic University, www.maufl.edu, FL
Miami Dade College, www.mdc.edu, FL
University of Miami, www.miami.edu, FL
Miami International University of Art & Design, www.mymiu.edu, FL
New College of Florida, www.ncf.edu, FL
North Florida Community College, www.nfcc.edu, FL
Nova Southeastern University, www.nova.edu, FL
National University of Health Sciences, www.nuhs.edu, FL
Northwest Florida State College, www.nwfsc.edu, FL
Palm Beach State College, www.palmbeachstate.edu, FL
Palm Beach Atlantic University, www.pba.edu, FL
Pensacola State College, www.pensacolastate.edu, FL
Pasco-Hernando State College, www.phsc.edu, FL
Ringling College of Art & Design, www.ringling.edu, FL
Rollins College, www.rollins.edu, FL
Saint Leo University, www.saintleo.edu, FL
State College of Florida, www.scf.edu, FL
Seminole State College of Florida, www.seminolestate.edu, FL
Santa Fe College, www.sfcollege.edu, FL
South Florida State College, www.southflorida.edu, FL
Space Coast Health Institute, www.spacecoast.edu, FL
Saint Petersburg College, www.spcollege.edu, FL
Stetson University, www.stetson.edu, FL
Saint Thomas University, www.stu.edu, FL
Saint Vincent de Paul Regional Seminary, www.svdp.edu, FL
Traviss Career Center, www.traviss.edu, FL
University of Central Florida, www.ucf.edu, FL
University of Florida, www.ufl.edu, FL
University of North Florida, www.unf.edu, FL
University of South Florida, www.usf.edu, FL
University of South Florida Sarasota-Manatee, www.usfsm.edu,FL
University of South Florida Saint Petersburg, www.usfsp.edu,FL
University of Tampa, www.ut.edu, FL
University of West Florida, www.uwf.edu, FL
Valencia College, www.valenciacollege.edu, FL
Warner University, www.warner.edu, FL
Webber International University, www.webber.edu, FL

Georgia
Agnes Scott College, www.agnesscott.edu, GA
Albany Technical College, www.albanytech.edu, GA
Armstrong Atlantic State University, www.armstrong.edu, GA
Atlanta Technical College, www.atlantatech.edu, GA
Atlanta Metropolitan State College, www.atlm.edu, GA
Berry College, www.berry.edu, GA
Carver College, www.carver.edu, GA
Child Care Education Institute, www.cceionline.edu, GA
Central Georgia Technical College, www.centralgatech.edu, GA
Clayton State University, www.clayton.edu, GA
Columbus State University, www.columbusstate.edu, GA
Columbus Technical College, www.columbustech.edu, GA
Covenant College, www.covenant.edu, GA
Dalton State, www.daltonstate.edu, GA
Darton State College, www.darton.edu, GA
East Georgia State College, www.ega.edu, GA
Emory University, www.emory.edu, GA
Georgia Institute of Technology, www.gatech.edu, GA
Georgia College, www.gcsu.edu, GA
Georgia Southern University, www.georgiasouthern.edu, GA
Georgia Gwinnett College, www.ggc.edu, GA
Georgia Perimeter College, www.gpc.edu, GA
Georgia Regents University Augusta, www.gru.edu, GA
Georgia State University, www.gsu.edu, GA
Georgia South Western State University, www.gsw.edu, GA
Interactive College of Technology, www.ict.edu, GA
John Marshall Law School, www.johnmarshall.edu, GA
Kennesaw State University, www.kennesaw.edu, GA
Lanier Technical College, www.laniertech.edu, GA
Life University, www.life.edu, GA
Mercer University, www.mercer.edu, GA
Middle Georgia State College, www.mga.edu, GA
Morehouse College, www.morehouse.edu, GA
Morehouse School of Medicine, www.msm.edu, GA
North Georgia Technical College, www.northgatech.edu, GA
Oglethorpe University, www.oglethorpe.edu, GA
Okefenokee Technical College, www.okefenokeetech.edu, GA
Paine College, www.paine.edu, GA
Pfeiffer University, www.pfeiffer.edu, GA

Piedmont College, www.piedmont.edu, GA
Reinhardt University, www.reinhardt.edu, GA
Savannah State University, www.savannahstate.edu, GA
Savannah College of Art & Design, www.scad.edu, GA
Shorter University, www.shorter.edu, GA
Southeastern Technical College,
www.southeasterntech.edu,GA
Spelman College, www.spelman.edu, GA
Southern Polytechnic State University, www.spsu.edu, GA
Thomas University, www.thomasu.edu, GA
University of Georgia, www.uga.edu, GA
University of North Georgia, www.ung.edu, GA
University System of Georgia, www.usg.edu, GA
Valdosta State University, www.valdosta.edu, GA
University of West Georgia, www.westga.edu, GA
Wiregrass Georgia Technical College, www.wiregrass.edu, GA

Hawaii

Brigham Young University Hawaii, www.byuh.edu, HI
Chaminade University, www.chaminade.edu, HI
University of Hawaii at Manoa, www.hawaii.edu, HI
Mid-Pacific Institute, www.midpac.edu, HI

Iowa

AIB College of Business, www.aib.edu, IA
Central College, www.central.edu, IA
Coe College, www.coe.edu, IA
Cornell College, www.cornellcollege.edu, IA
Des Moines Area Community College, www.dmacc.edu, IA
Dordt College, www.dordt.edu, IA
Drake University, www.drake.edu, IA
Divine Word College, www.dwci.edu, IA
Eastern Iowa Community Colleges, www.eicc.edu, IA
Grinnell College, www.grinnell.edu, IA
Hawkeye Community College, www.hawkeyecollege.edu, IA
Iowa State University, www.iastate.edu, IA
Iowa Central Community College, www.iowacentral.edu, IA
Iowa Wesleyan College, www.iwc.edu, IA
Iowa Western Community College, www.iwcc.edu, IA
Kaplan University, www.kaplanuniversity.edu, IA
Kirkwood Community College, www.kirkwood.edu, IA
La' James College, www.lajames.edu, IA
Loras College, www.loras.edu, IA
Luther College, www.luther.edu, IA
Maharishi University of Management, www.mum.edu, IA
Northeast Iowa Community College, www.nicc.edu, IA
Palmer College of Chiropractic, www.palmer.edu, IA
Saint Ambrose University, www.sau.edu, IA
Simpson College, www.simpson.edu, IA
Southwestern Community College, www.swcciowa.edu, IA
University of Iowa, www.uiowa.edu, IA
Upper Iowa University, www.uiu.edu, IA
University of Northern Iowa, www.uni.edu, IA
Wartburg College, www.wartburg.edu, IA
Waldorf College, www.waldorf.edu, IA

Idaho

Boise State University, www.boisestate.edu, ID
Brigham Young University Idaho, www.byui.edu, ID
The College of Idaho, www.collegeofidaho.edu, ID
College of Southern Idaho, www.csi.edu, ID
Idaho State University, www.isu.edu, ID
University of Idaho, www.uidaho.edu, ID

Illinois

Augustana College, www.augustana.edu, IL
Aurora University, www.aurora.edu, IL
Benedictine University, www.ben.edu, IL
Bradley University, www.bradley.edu, IL
City Colleges of Chicago, www.ccc.edu, IL
The University of Chicago Booth School of Business, www.chicagobooth.edu, IL
College of Lake County, www.clcillinois.edu, IL
College of DuPage, www.cod.edu, IL
Columbia College Chicago, www.colum.edu, IL
Danville Area Community College, www.dacc.edu, IL
DePaul University, www.depaul.edu, IL
Dominican University, www.dom.edu, IL
Eastern Illinois University, www.eiu.edu, IL
Elmhurst College, www.elmhurst.edu, IL
Governors State, www.govst.edu, IL
Greenville College, www.greenville.edu, IL
The Hadley School for the Blind, www.hadley.edu, IL
Harper College, www.harpercollege.edu, IL
Heartland Community College, www.heartland.edu, IL
Illinois Central College, www.icc.edu, IL
Illinois College of Optometry, www.ico.edu, IL
Illinois Institute of Technology, www.iit.edu, IL
University of Illinois at Urbana-Champaign, www.illinois.edu, IL
Illinois State University, www.illinoisstate.edu, IL
Illinois Mathematics & Science Academy, www.imsa.edu, IL
Illinois Valley Community College, www.ivcc.edu, IL
Illinois Wesleyan University, www.iwu.edu, IL
John A. Logan College, www.jalc.edu, IL
Joliet Junior College, www.jjc.edu, IL
The John Marshall Law School, www.jmls.edu, IL
Judson University, www.judsonu.edu, IL
Kaskaskia College, www.kaskaskia.edu, IL
Kankakee Community College, www.kcc.edu, IL
IIT Chicago-Kent College of Law, www.iit.edu, IL
Kishwaukee College, www.kishwaukeecollege.edu, IL
Knox College, www.knox.edu, IL
Lake Forest College, www.lakeforest.edu, IL
Lakeview College of Nursing, www.lakeviewcol.edu, IL
Lewis & Clark Community College, www.lc.edu, IL
Lewis University, www.lewisu.edu, IL
Lincoln Land Community College, www.llcc.edu, IL
Loyola University Chicago, www.luc.edu, IL
Midwestern Career College, www.mccollege.edu, IL
McHenry County College, www.mchenry.edu, IL
McKendree University, www.mckendree.edu, IL
Midwestern University, www.midwestern.edu, IL
Monmouth College, www.monmouthcollege.edu, IL
Moraine Valley Community College, www.morainevalley.edu, IL
Morton College, www.morton.edu, IL
Northeastern Illinois University, www.neiu.edu, IL
Northern Illinois University, www.niu.edu, IL
National Louis University, www.nl.edu, IL
North Park University, www.northpark.edu, IL
Northwestern University, www.northwestern.edu, IL
Oakton Community College, www.oakton.edu, IL
Olivet Nazarene University, www.olivet.edu, IL
Chicago ORT Technical Institute, www.ortchicagotech.edu, IL
Parkland College, www.parkland.edu, IL
Prairie State College, www.prairiestate.edu, IL
Principia College, www.principiacollege.edu, IL
Resurrection University, www.resu.edu, IL
Robert Morris University Illinois, www.robertmorris.edu, IL
Rockford University, www.rockford.edu, IL
Rock Valley College, www.rockvalleycollege.edu, IL
Roosevelt University, www.roosevelt.edu, IL
Rosalind Franklin University, www.rosalindfranklin.edu, IL
Saint Anthony College of Nursing, www.sacn.edu, IL

School of the Art Institute of Chicago, www.saic.edu, IL
Saint Francis Medical Center College of Nursing, www.sfmccon.edu, IL
Shawnee Community College, www.shawneecc.edu, IL
Southeastern Illinois College, www.sic.edu, IL
Southern Illinois University, www.siu.edu, IL
Southern Illinois University Edwardsville, www.siue.edu, IL
Spoon River College, www.src.edu, IL
South Suburban College, www.ssc.edu, IL
University of Saint Francis, www.stfrancis.edu, IL
Southwestern Illinois College, www.swic.edu, IL
Saint Xavier University, www.scu.edu, IL
Trinity Christian College, www.trnty.edu, IL
University of Chicago, www.uchicago.edu, IL
University of Illinois at Chicago, www.uic.edu, IL
University of Illinois, www.uillinois.edu, IL
University of Illinois Springfield, www.uis.edu, IL
University of Illinois at Urbana-Champaign, www.illinois.edu, IL
Waubonsee Community College, www.waubonsee.edu, IL
Wheaton College, www.wheaton.edu, IL
Western Illinois University, www.wiu.edu, IL
Saint John's College, www.stjohnscollegespringfield.edu, Ill
Anabaptist Mennonite Biblical Seminary, www.ambs.edu, IN
Anderson University, www.anderson.edu, IN
Bethel College Indiana, www.bethelcollege.edu, IN
Brown Mackie College, www.brownmackie.edu, IN
Ball State University, www.bsu.edu, IN
Butler University, www.butler.edu, IN
DePauw University, www.depauw.edu, IN
Earlham College, www.earlham.edu, IN
University of Evansville, www.evansville.edu, IN
Goshen College, www.goshen.edu, IN
Grace College & Seminary, www.grace.edu, IN
Hanover College, www.hanover.edu, IN
Harrison College, www.harrison.edu, IN
Holy Cross College, www.hcc-nd.edu, IN
Indiana University, www.indiana.edu, IN
Indiana State University, www.indstate.edu, IN
Indiana Wesleyan University, www.indwes.edu, IN
Indiana University – Purdue University Fort Wayne, www.ipfw.edu, IN
Indiana University, www.iu.edu, IN
Indiana University Bloomington, www.iub.edu, IN
Indiana University East, www.iue.edu, IN
Indiana University Northwest, www.iun.edu, IN
Indiana University – Purdue University Indianapolis, www.iupui.edu, IN
Indiana University Southeast, www.ius.edu, IN
Indiana University South Bend, www.iusb.edu, IN
Ivy Tech Community College, www.ivytech.edu, IN
Manchester University, www.manchester.edu, IN
Marian University Indianapolis, www.marian.edu, IN
University of Notre Dame, www.nd.edu, IN
Oakland City University, www.oak.edu, IN
Purdue University North Central, www.pnc.edu, IN
Purdue University, www.purdue.edu, IN
Purdue University Calumet, www.purduecal.edu, IN
Rose-Hulman Institute of Technology, www.rose-hulman.edu, IN
Saint Mary's College, www.saintmarys.edu, IN
Trine University, www.trine.edu, IN
University of Indianapolis, www.uindy.edu, IN
University of Southern Indiana, www.usi.edu, IN
Valparaiso University, www.valpo.edu, IN
Wabash College, www.wabash.edu, IN

Kansas
Benedictine College, www.benedictine.edu, KS
Butler Community College, www.butlercc.edu, KS
Emporia State University, www.emporia.edu, KS
Fort Hays State University, www.fhsu.edu, KS
Flint Hills Technical College, www.fhtc.edu, KS
Fort Scott Community College, www.fortscott.edu, KS
Garden City Community College, www.gcccks.edu, KS
Hesston College, www.hesston.edu, KS
Highland Community College, www.highlandcc.edu, KS
Johnson County Community College, www.jccc.edu, KS
Kansas City Kansas Community College, www.kckcc.edu, KS
Kansas State University, www.k-state.edu, KS
The University of Kansas, www.ku.edu, KS
McPherson College, www.mcpherson.edu, KS
Neosho County Community College, www.neosho.edu, KS
Newman University, www.newmanu.edu, KS
Pittsburg State University, www.pittstate.edu, KS
Saint Paul School of Theology & Ministry, www.spst.edu, KS
Sterling College, www.sterling.edu, KS
University of Saint Mary, www.stmary.edu, KS
Washburn University, www.washburn.edu, KS
Washburn University School of Law, www.washburnlaw.edu, KS
Wichita State University, www.wichita.edu, KS

Kentucky
Asbury University, www.asbury.edu, KY
Bellarmine University, www.bellarmine.edu, KY
Berea College, www.berea.edu, KY
Centre College, www.centre.edu, KY
Eastern Kentucky University, www.eku.edu, KY
Frontier Nursing University, www.frontier.edu, KY
Georgetown College, www.georgetowncollege.edu, KY
Kentucky Community & Technical College System, www.kctcs.edu, KY
Kentucky Christian University, www.kcu.edu, KY
Kentucky State University, www.kysu.edu, KY
Lindsey Wilson College, www.lindsey.edu, KY
The University of Louisville, www.louisville.edu, KY
Midway College, www.midway.edu, KY
Morehead State University, www.moreheadstate.edu, KY
Murray State University, www.murraystate.edu, KY
Northern Kentucky University, www.nku.edu, KY
The Southern Baptist Theological Seminary, www.sbts.edu, KY
Saint Catharine College, www.sccky.edu, KY
Sullivan University, www.sullivan.edu, KY
University of the Cumberlands, www.ucumberlands.edu, KY
Western Kentucky University, www.wku.edu, KY

Louisiana
Bossier Parish Community College, www.bpcc.edu, LA
Centenary College of Louisiana, www.centenary.edu, LA
Louisiana Tech University, www.latech.edu, LA
Louisiana Culinary Institute, www.lci.edu, LA
University of Louisiana Lafayette, www.louisiana.edu, LA
Loyola University New Orleans, www.loyno.edu, LA
Louisiana State University, www.lsu.edu, LA
Louisiana State University – Eunice, www.lsue.edu, LA
LSU Health Sciences Center–New Orleans, www.lsuhsc.edu,LA
LSU Health Sciences Center – New Orleans, www.lsuhscshreveport.edu, LA
Louisiana State University System, www.lsusystem.edu, LA
Nicholls State University, www.nicholls.edu, LA
New Orleans Baptist Theological Seminary, www.nobts.edu, LA
Nunez Community College, www.nunez.edu, LA
Southeastern Louisiana University, www.southeastern.edu, LA
Southern University, www.subr.edu, LA

Tulane University, www.tulane.edu, LA
University of Louisiana at Monroe, www.ulm.edu, LA
University of New Orleans, www.uno.edu, LA
Xavier University of Louisiana, www.xula.edu, LA

Massachusetts
Amherst College, www.amherst.edu, MA
Assumption College, www.assumption.edu, MA
Babson College, www.babson.edu, MA
Boston College, www.bc.edu, MA
Bentley University, www.bentley.edu, MA
Berklee College of Music, www.berklee.edu, MA
Berkshire Community College, www.berkshirecc.edu, MA
The Boston Conservatory, www.bostonconservatory.edu, MA
Brandeis University, www.brandeis.edu, MA
Bridgewater State University, www.bridgew.edu, MA
Boston University, www.bu.edu, MA
Cambridge College, www.cambridgecollege.edu, MA
Clark University, www.clarku.edu, MA
Curry College, www.curry.edu, MA
Elms College, www.elms.edu, MA
Emerson College, www.emerson.edu, MA
Emmanuel College, www.emmanuel.edu, MA
Endicott College, www.endicott.edu, MA
Fitchburg State University, www.fitchburgstate.edu, MA
Framingham State University, www.framingham.edu, MA
Gordon Conwell Theological Seminary, www.gordonconwell.edu, MA
Gordon College, www.gordon.edu, MA
Hampshire College, www.hampshire.edu, MA
Harvard University, www.harvard.edu, MA
Harvard Business School, www.hbs.edu, MA
College of the Holy Cross, www.holycross.edu, MA
Lesley University, www.lesley.edu, MA
Massachusetts Maritime Academy, www.maritime.edu, MA
Massachusetts Department of Higher Education, www.mass.edu, MA
Massachusetts College of Art & Design, www.massart.edu, MA
MassBay Community College, www.massbay.edu, MA
Marine Biological Laboratory, www.mbl.edu, MA
Merrimack Education Center, www.mec.edu, MA
Merrimack College, www.merrimack.edu, MA
MGH Institute of Health Professions, www.mghihp.edu, MA
Milton Academy, www.milton.edu, MA
Massachusetts Institute of Technology, www.mit.edu, MA
Montserrat College of Art, www.montserrat.edu, MA
Mount Ida College, www.mountida.edu, MA
Mount Holyoke College, www.mtholyoke.edu, MA
Middlesex Community College, www.mxcc.edu, MA
Middlesex School, www.mxschool.edu, MA
North Bennet Street School, www.nbss.edu, MA
New England Law – Boston, www.nesl.edu, MA
Northeastern University, www.northeastern.edu, MA
Olin College of Engineering, www.olin.edu, MA
Salem State University, www.salemstate.edu, MA
Simmons College, www.simmons.edu, MA
Smith College, www.smith.edu, MA
Spa Tech Institute, www.spatech.edu, MA
Springfield College, www.springfieldcollege.edu, MA
Springfield Technical Community College, www.stcc.edu, MA
Suffolk University, www.suffolk.edu, MA
Boston Architectural College, www.the-bac.edu, MA
Tufts University, www.tufts.edu, MA
University of Massachusetts Amherst, www.umass.edu, MA
University of Massachusetts Dartmouth, www.umassd.edu, MA
University of Massachusetts Medical School, www.umassmed.edu, MA
University of Massachusetts, www.umassp.edu, MA
University of Massachusetts Boston, www.umb.edu, MA
University of Massachusetts Lowell, www.uml.edu, MA
Wellesley College, www.wellesley.edu, MA
Wheaton College, Norton, www.wheatoncollege.edu, MA
Wheelock College, www.wheelock.edu, MA
Williams College, www.williams.edu, MA
Western New England University, www.wne.edu, MA
Worcester State University, www.worcester.edu, MA
Worcester Polytechnic Institute, www.wpi.edu, MA

Maryland
Anne Arundel Community College, www.aacc.edu, MD
Baltimore City Community College, www.bccc.edu, MD
Bowie State University, www.bowiestate.edu, MD
Carroll Community College, www.carrollcc.edu, MD
The Community College of Baltimore County, www.ccbcmd.edu, MD
Chesapeake College, www.chesapeake.edu, MD
Coppin State University, www.coppin.edu, MD
College of Southern Maryland, www.csmd.edu, MD
Frederick Community College, www.frederick.edu, MD
Frostburg State University, www.frostburg.edu, MD
Garrett College, www.garrettcollege.edu, MD
Goucher College, www.goucher.edu, MD
Hagerstown Community College, www.hagerstownccc.edu, MD
Harford Community College, www.harford.edu, MD
Hood College, www.hood.edu, MD
Howard Community College, www.howardcc.edu, MD
Johns Hopkins Bloomberg School of Public Health, www.jhsph.edu, MD
Johns Hopkins University, www.jhu.edu, MD
Loyola University Maryland, www.loyola.edu, MD
Montgomery Blair High School, www.mbhs.edu, MD
McDaniel College, www.mcdaniel.edu, MD
Maryland Institute College of Art, www.mica.edu, MD
Montgomery College, www.montgomerycollege.edu, MD
Mount Saint Mary's University, www.msmary.edu, MD
Maryland University of Integrative Health, www.muih.edu, MD
Prince George's Community College, www.pgcc.edu, MD
Salisbury University, www.salisbury.edu, MD
Sojourner-Douglass College, www.sdc.edu, MD
Saint Mary's College of Maryland, www.smcm.edu, MD
Saint James School, www.stjames.edu, MD
Towson University, www.towson.edu, MD
University of Baltimore, www.ubalt.edu, MD
University of Maryland, www.umaryland.edu, MD
University of Maryland Baltimore County, www.umbc.edu, MD
University of Maryland, www.umd.edu, MD
University of Maryland University College, www.umuc.edu, MD
University System of Maryland, www.usmd.edu, MD
United States Naval Academy, www.usna.edu, MD
Washington College, www.washcoll.edu, MD
Wor-Wic Community College, www.worwic.edu, MD
Saint John's College, www.sjc.edu, MD

Maine
Bates College, www.bates.edu, ME
Bowdoin College, www.bowdoin.edu, ME
Central Maine Community College, www.cmcc.edu, ME
College of the Atlantic, www.coa.edu, ME
Colby College, www.colby.edu, ME
Husson University, www.husson.edu, ME
Maine Maritime Academy, www.mainemaritime.edu, ME
Northern Maine Community College, www.nmcc.edu, ME
Saint Joseph's College, www.sjcme.edu, ME
Southern Maine Community College, www.smccme.edu, ME
University of Maine, www.umaine.edu, ME

University of Maine Fort Kent, www.umfk.edu, ME
University of Maine at Presque Isle, www.umpi.edu, ME
University of New England, www.une.edu, ME
Unity College, www.unity.edu, ME
York County Community College, www.yccc.edu, ME
University of Main at Augusta, www.uma.edu, ME

Michigan
Adrian College, www.adrian.edu, MI
Albion College, www.albion.edu, MI
Alma College, www.alma.edu, MI
Alpena Community College, www.alpenacc.edu, MI
Andrews University, www.andrews.edu, MI
Aquinas College, www.aquinas.edu, MI
Baker College, www.baker.edu, MI
Bay College, www.baycollege.edu, MI
Calvin College, www.calvin.edu, MI
Central Michigan University, www.cmich.edu, MI
College for Creative Studies, www.collegeforcreativestudies.edu, MI
Cornerstone University, www.cornerstone.edu, MI
Davenport University, www.davenport.edu, MI
Delta College, www.delta.edu, MI
Douglas J. Aveda Institute, www.douglasj.edu, MI
Eastern Michigan University, www.emich.edu, MI
Ferris State University, www.ferris.edu, MI
Finlandia University, www.finlandia.edu, MI
Grand Rapids Community College, www.grcc.edu, MI
Grand Valley State University, www.gvsu.edu, MI
Henry Ford College, www.hfcc.edu, MI
Hillsdale College, www.hillsdale.edu, MI
Hope College, www.hope.edu, MI
Jackson College, www.jccmi.edu, MI
Kettering University, www.kettering.edu, MI
Kalamazoo Valley Community College, www.kvcc.edu, MI
Kalamazoo College, www.kzoo.edu, MI
Lake Michigan College, www.lakemichigancollege.edu, MI
Lansing Community College, www.lcc.edu, MI
Lake Superior State University, www.lssu.edu, MI
Lawrence Technological University, www.ltu.edu, MI
Macomb Community College, www.macomb.edu, MI
Marygrove College, www.marygrove.edu, MI
Monroe County Community College, www.monroeccc.edu, MI
Michigan State University, www.msu.edu, MI
Michigan Technological University, www.mtu.edu, MI
Northwestern Michigan College, www.nmc.edu, MI
Northern Michigan University, www.nmu.edu, MI
Oakland University, www.oakland.edu, MI
Oakland Community College, www.oaklandcc.edu, MI
Saginaw Chippewa Tribal College, www.sagchip.edu, MI
Saginaw Valley State University, www.svsu.edu, MI
University of Detroit Mercy, www.udmercy.edu, MI
University of Michigan-Flint, www.umflint.edu, MI
University of Michigan, www.umich.edu, MI
Wayne State, www.wayne.edu, MI
Washtenaw Community College, www.wccnet.edu, MI
Western Michigan University, www.wmich.edu, MI

Minnesota
Alexandria Technical & Community College, www.alextech.edu, MN
Anoka-Ramsey Community College, www.anokaramsey.edu, MN
Augsburg College, www.augsburg.edu, MN
Bemidji State University, www.bemidjistate.edu, MN
Bethel University, www.bethel.edu, MN
Carleton College, www.carleton.edu, MN
Century College, www.century.edu, MN
Central Lakes College, www.clcmn.edu, MN
Concordia College, www.cord.edu, MN
Crown College, www.crown.edu, MN
College of Saint Benedict, Saint John's University, www.csbsju.edu, MN
Concordia University Saint Paul, www.csp.edu, MN
The College of Saint Scholastica, www.css.edu, MN
Dakota County Technical College, www.dctc.edu, MN
Gustavus Adolphus College, www.gustavus.edu, MN
Globe University, www.globeuniversity.edu, MN
Hamline University, www.hamline.edu, MN
Inver Hills Community College, www.inverhills.edu, MN
Institute of Production & Recording, www.ipr.edu, MN
Leech Lake Tribal College, www.lltc.edu, MN
Luther Seminary, www.luthersem.edu, MN
Macalester College, www.macalester.edu, MN
McNally Smith College of Music, www.mcnallysmith.edu, MN
Mesabi Range College, www.mesabirange.edu, MN
Metropolitan State University, www.metrostate.edu, MN
Minnesota State University Moorhead, www.mnstate.edu, MN
Minnesota State University Mankato, www.mnsu.edu, MN
North Hennepin Community College, www.nhcc.edu, MN
Normandale Community College, www.normandale.edu, MN
Rasmussen College, www.rasmussen.edu, MN
Ridgewater College, www.ridgewater.edu, MN
Southwest Minnesota State University, www.smsu.edu, MN
Saint Mary's University of Minnesota, www.smumn.edu, MN
South Central College, www.southcentral.edu, MN
Saint Cloud State University, www.stcloudstate.edu, MN
Saint Olaf College, www.stolaf.edu, MN
University of Saint Thomas, www.stthomas.edu, MN
University of Minnesota, www.umn.edu, MN
United Theological Seminary of the Twin Cities, www.unitedseminary.edu, MN
University of Northwestern Saint Paul, www.unwsp.edu, MN
Walden University, www.waldenu.edu, MN
Winona State University, www.winona.edu, MN

Missouri
Assemblies of God Theological Seminary, www.agts.edu, MO
Aquinas Institute of Theology, www.ai.edu, MO
A.T. Still University, www.atsu.edu, MO
Avila University, www.avila.edu, MO
Columbia College, www.ccis.edu, MO
Central Methodist University, www.centralmethodist.edu, MO
Crowder College, www.crowder.edu, MO
Culver-Stockton College, www.culver.edu, MO
Drury University, www.drury.edu, MO
Evangel University, www.evangel.edu, MO
Fontbonne University, www.fontbonne.edu, MO
Hannibal-LaGrange, www.hlg.edu, MO
Harris-Stowe State University, www.hssu.edu, MO
Jefferson College, www.jeffco.edu, MO
Kansas City University of Medicine & Biosciences, www.kcumb.edu, MO
Lincoln University, www.lincolne.edu, MO
Lindenwood University, www.lindenwood.edu, MO
Linn State Technical College, www.linnstate.edu, MO
Maryville University, www.maryville.edu, MO
Metropolitan Community College, www.mcckc.edu, MO
Mineral Area College, www.mineralarea.edu, MO
Mizzou University of Missouri, www.missouri.edu, MO
Missouri State University, www.missouristate.edu, MO
Missouri Valley College, www.moval.edu, MO
Missouri Southern State University, www.mssu.edu, MO
Missouri University of Science & Technology, www.mst.edu, MO

North Central Missouri College, www.ncmissouri.edu, MO
Nazarene Theological Seminary, www.nts.edu, MO
Northwest Missouri State University, www.nwmissouri.edu, MO
Ozarks Technical Community College, www.otc.edu, MO
Park University, www.park.edu, MO
Rockhurst University, www.rockhurst.edu, MO
Southwest Baptist University, www.sbuniv.edu, MO
South Central Career Center, www.scccwp.edu, MO
Southeast Missouri State University, www.semo.edu, MO
Saint Louis University, www.slu.edu, MO
Saint Charles Community College, www.stchas.edu, MO
Saint Louis Community College, www.stlcc.edu, MO
Truman State University, www.truman.edu, MO
University of Central Missouri, www.ucmo.edu, MO
University of Missouri Kansas City, www.umkc.edu, MO
University of Missouri Saint Louis, www.umsl.edu, MO
University of Missouri System, www.umsystem.edu, MO
Webster University, www.webster.edu, MO
Westminster College, Missouri, www.westminster-mo.edu, MO
Washington University in Saint Louis, www.wustl.edu, MO

Mississippi
Alcorn State University, www.alcorn.edu, MS
Belhaven University, www.belhaven.edu, MS
Delta State University, www.deltastate.edu, MS
East Mississippi Community College, www.eastms.edu, MS
Jackson State University, www.jsums.edu, MS
Mississippi Gulf Coast Community College, www.mgccc.edu, MS
Mississippi State University, www.msstate.edu, MS
Northeast Mississippi Community College, www.nemcc.edu, MS
The University of Mississippi, www.olemiss.edu, MS
Pearl River Community College, www.prcc.edu, MS
Reformed Theological Seminary, www.rts.edu, MS
University of Mississippi Medical Center, www.umc.edu, MS
University of Southern Mississippi, www.usm.edu, MS
William Carey University, www.wmcarey.edu, MS
Itawamba Community College, www.iccms.edu, MS

Montana
Blackfeet Community College, www.bfcc.edu, MT
Carroll College, www.carroll.edu, MT
Fort Peck Community College, www.fpcc.edu, MT
Flathead Valley Community College, www.fvcc.edu, MT
Miles Community College, www.milescc.edu, MT
Montana State University, www.montana.edu, MT
Montana State University Billings, www.msubillings.edu, MT
Montana State University – Northern, www.msun.edu, MT
Montana Tech of the University of Montana, www.mtech.edu, MT
Montana University System, www.mus.edu, MT
Rocky Mountain College, www.rocky.edu, MT
University of Montana Helena College, www.umhelena.edu, MT
University of Montana, www.umt.edu, MT
University of Montana Western, www.umwestern.edu, MT

North Carolina
Asheville-Buncombe Technical Community College, www.abtech.edu, NC
Alamance Community College, www.alamancecc.edu, NC
Appalachian State University, www.appstate.edu, NC
Bladen Community College, www.bladencc.edu, NC
Body Therapy Institute, www.bti.edu, NC
Campbell University, www.campbell.edu, NC
Cape Fear Community College, www.cfcc.edu, NC
Charlotte School of Law, www.charlottelaw.edu, NC
Chowan University, www.chowan.edu, NC
Central Piedmont Community College, www.cpcc.edu, NC
Craven Community College, www.cravencc.edu, NC
Davidson College, www.davidson.edu, NC
Duke University, www.duke.edu, NC
Durham Technical Community College, www.durhamtech.edu, NC
Elizabeth City State University, www.ecsu.edu, NC
East Carolina University, www.ecu.edu, NC
Elon University, www.elon.edu, NC
Fayetteville Technical Community College, www.faytechcc.edu, NC
Forsyth Technical Community College, www.forsythtech.edu, NC
Gardner-Webb University, www.gardner-webb.edu, NC
Gaston College, www.gaston.edu, NC
Guilford Technical Community College, www.gtcc.edu, NC
Heritage Bible College, www.heritagebiblecollege.edu, NC
High Point University, www.highpoint.edu, NC
Isothermal Community College, www.isothermal.edu, NC
Lenoir Community College, www.lenoircc.edu, NC
Lees McRae College, www.lmc.edu, NC
Methodist University, www.methodist.edu, NC
The University of Mount Olive, www.umo.edu, NC
Montgomery Community College, www.montgomery.edu, NC
North Carolina Central University, www.nccu.edu, NC
North Carolina School of Science & Mathematics, www.ncssm.edu, NC
North Carolina State University, www.ncsu.edu, NC
North Carolina Wesleyan College, www.ncwc.edu, NC
New Life Theological Seminary, www.nlts.edu, NC
University of North Carolina, www.northcarolina.edu, NC
Piedmont Community College, www.piedmontcc.edu, NC
Pitt Community College, www.pittcc.edu, NC
Queens University of Charlotte, www.queens.edu, NC
Randolph Community College, www.randolph.edu, NC
Roanoke-Chowan Community College, www.roanokechowan.edu, NC
Salem College, www.salem.edu, NC
Sampson Community College, www.sampsoncc.edu, NC
Sandhills Community College, www.sandhills.edu, NC
Saint Andrews University, www.sapc.edu, NC
Southeastern Community College, www.sccnc.edu, NC
Southeastern Baptist Theological Seminary, www.sebts.edu, NC
Shaw University, www.shawu.edu, NC
Southwestern Community College, www.southwesterncc.edu, NC
South Piedmont Community College, www.spcc.edu, NC
Stanly Community College, www.stanly.edu, NC
Saint Augustine's University, www.st-aug.edu, NC
University of North Carolina at Chapel Hill, www.unc.edu, NC
University of North Carolina Asheville, www.unca.edu, NC
University of North Carolina Charlotte, www.uncc.edu, NC
University of North Carolina Greensboro, www.uncg.edu, NC
University of North Carolina Pembroke, www.uncp.edu, NC
University of North Carolina School of the Arts, www.uncsa.edu, NC
University of North Carolina Wilmington, www.uncw.edu, NC
Vance-Granville Community College, www.vgcc.edu, NC
Wake Technical Community College, www.waketech.edu, NC
Warren Wilson College, www.warren-wilson.edu, NC
Western Carolina University, www.wcu.edu, NC
Wake Forest University, www.wfu.edu, NC
Western Piedmont Community College, www.wpcc.edu, NC
Winston-Salem State University, www.wssu.edu, NC

North Dakota
Dakota College at Bottineau, www.dakotacollege.edu, ND
Mayville State University, www.mayvillestate.edu, ND
Minot State University, www.minotstateu.edu, ND
North Dakota State University, www.ndsu.edu, ND
North Dakota University System, www.ndus.edu, ND
Turtle Mountain Community College, www.tm.edu, ND
University of North Dakota, www.und.edu, ND
United Tribes Technical College, www.utcc.edu, ND
Valley City State University, www.vcsu.edu, ND
Williston State College, www.willistonstate.edu, ND

Nebraska
Bellevue University, www.bellevue.edu, NE
Bryan College of Health Sciences, www.bryanhealth.com NE
Creighton University, www.creighton.edu, NE
Chadron State College, www.csc.edu, NE
Concordia University Nebraska, www.cune.edu, NE
Joseph's College, www.josephscollege.edu, NE
Little Priest Tribal College, www.littlepriest.edu, NE
Mid-Plains Community College, www.mpcc.edu, NE
University of Nebraska, www.nebraska.edu, NE
Northeast Community College, www.northeast.edu, NE
Union College, www.ucollege.edu, NE
University of Nebraska at Kearney, www.unk.edu, NE
University of Nebraska at Lincoln, www.unl.edu, NE
University of Nebraska Medical Center, www.unmc.edu, NE
University of Nebraska Omaha, www.unomaha.edu, NE
Wayne State College, www.wsc.edu, NE

New Hampshire
Saint Anselm College, www.anselm.edu, NH
Antioch University New England, www.antiochne.edu, NH
Community College System of New Hampshire, www.ccsnh.edu, NH
Colby Sawyer College, www.colby-sawyer.edu, NH
Dartmouth College, www.dartmouth.edu, NH
Phillips Exeter Academy, www.exeter.edu, NH
Granite State College, www.granite.edu, NH
Keene State College, www.keene.edu, NH
Manchester Community College, www.mccnh.edu, NH
Mount Washington College, www.mountwashington.edu, NH
Nashua Community College, www.nashuacc.edu, NH
New England College, www.nec.edu, NH
NHTI Concord's Community College, www.nhti.edu, NH
Plymouth State University, www.plymouth.edu, NH
Rivier University, www.rivier.edu, NH
Southern New Hampshire University, www.snhu.edu, NH
University of New Hampshire, www.unh.edu, NH
White Mountains Community College, www.wmcc.edu, NH

New Jersey
Atlantic Cape Community College, www.atlantic.edu, NJ
Burlington County College, www.bcc.edu, NJ
Bergen Community College, www.bergen.edu, NJ
Brookdale Community College, www.brookdalecc.edu, NJ
Centenary College of New Jersey, www.centenarycollege.edu, NJ
Drew University, www.drew.edu, NJ
Eastwick College, www.eastwickcollege.edu, NJ
Fairleigh Dickinson University, www.fdu.edu, NJ
Felician College, www.felician.edu, NJ
Fortis Institute, www.fortis.edu, NJ
Georgian Court University, www.georgian.edu, NJ
Kean University, www.kean.edu, NJ
Mercer County Community College, www.mccc.edu, NJ
Middlesex County College, www.middlesexcc.edu, NJ
Monmouth University, www.monmouth.edu, NJ
Montclair State University, www.montclair.edu, NJ
New Jersey City University, www.njcu.edu, NJ
New Jersey Institute of Technology, www.njit.edu, NJ
Ocean County College, www.ocean.edu, NJ
Princeton University, www.princeton.edu, NJ
Princeton Theological Seminary, www.ptsem.edu, NJ
Ramapo College of New Jersey, www.ramapo.edu, NJ
Raritan Valley Community College, www.raritanval.edu, NJ
Rider University, www.rider.edu, NJ
Rowan University, www.rowan.edu, NJ
Rutgers University, www.rutgers.edu, NJ
Seton Hall University, www.shu.edu, NJ
Stenotech Career Institute, www.stenotech.edu, NJ
Stevens Institute of Technology, www.stevens.edu, NJ
Stockton College, www.stockton.edu, NJ
Sussex County Community College, www.sussex.edu, NJ
The College of New Jersey, www.tcnj.edu, NJ
Thomas Edison State College, www.tesc.edu, NJ
William Paterson University, www.wpunj.edu, NJ
County College of Morris, www.ccm.edu, NJ
Camden County College, www.camdencc.edu, NJ
Passaic County Community College, www.pccc.edu, NJ
Ross University, www.rossu.edu, NJ

New Mexico
Central New Mexico, www.cnm.edu, NM
Eastern New Mexico University, www.enmu.edu, NM
New Mexico Highlands University, www.nmhu.edu, NM
New Mexico State University, www.nmsu.edu, NM
New Mexico State University Alamogordo, www.nmsua.edu, NM
New Mexico Institute of Mining & Technology, www.nmt.edu, NM
Northern New Mexico College, www.nnmc.edu, NM
San Juan College, www.sanjuancollege.edu, NM
Southwestern College, www.swc.edu, NM
University of New Mexico, www.unm.edu, NM
University of the Southwest, www.usw.edu, NM

Nevada
College of Southern Nevada, www.csn.edu, NV
Great Basin College, www.gbcnv.edu, NV
Pima Medical Institute, www.pmi.edu, NV
Sierra Nevada College, www.sierranevada.edu, NV
Truckee Meadows Community College, www.tmcc.edu, NV
University of Nevada Las Vegas, www.unlv.edu, NV
University of Nevada Reno, www.unr.edu, NV
Western Nevada College, www.wnc.edu, NV

New York
Adelphi University, www.adelphi.edu, NY
University at Albany, www.albany.edu, NY
Alfred University, www.alfred.edu, NY
The American Musical & Dramatic Academy, www.amda.edu, NY
ASA College, www.asa.edu, NY
Bard College, www.bard.edu, NY
Barnard College, www.barnard.edu, NY
Binghamton University, www.binghamton.edu, NY
The College at Brockport, www.brockport.edu, NY
University at Buffalo, www.buffalo.edu, NY

Buffalo State University, www.buffalostate.edu, NY
Cazenovia College, www.cazenovia.edu, NY
Clarkson University, www.clarkson.edu, NY
Clinton Community College, www.clinton.edu, NY
The College of New Rochelle, www.cnr.edu, NY
Cobleskill University, www.cobleskill.edu, NY
Colgate University, www.colgate.edu, NY
Columbia University in the City of New York, www.columbia.edu, NY
Concordia College New York, www.concordia-ny.edu, NY
The Cooper Union, www.cooper.edu, NY
Cornell University, www.cornell.edu, NY
Cortland College, www.cortland.edu, NY
The City University of New York, www.cuny.edu, NY
The College of Westchester, www.cw.edu, NY
Daemen College, www.daemen.edu, NY
Dominican College, www.dc.edu, NY
Delhi State University of New York, www.delhi.edu, NY
Dowling College, www.dowling.edu, NY
D'Youville College, www.dyc.edu, NY
Erie Community College State University of New York, www.ecc.edu, NY
Elim Bible Institute, www.elim.edu, NY
Elmira College, www.elmira.edu, NY
Empire State College, www.esc.edu, NY
College of Environmental Science & Forestry, www.esf.edu, NY
Farmingdale State College, www.farmingdale.edu, NY
Fashion Institute of Technology, www.fitnyc.edu, NY
Finger Lakes Community College, www.flcc.edu, NY
Fordham University, www.fordham.edu, NY
Fredonia University, www.fredonia.edu, NY
Five Towns College, www.ftc.edu, NY
Geneseo University, www.geneseo.edu, NY
Globe Institute of Technology, www.globe.edu, NY
The General Theological Seminary, www.gts.edu, NY
Hamilton College, www.hamilton.edu, NY
Hartwick College, www.hartwick.edu, NY
Herkimer College, www.herkimer.edu, NY
Hofstra University, www.hofstra.edu, NY
Hudson Valley Community College, www.hvcc.edu, NY
Hobart & William Smith Colleges, www.hws.edu, NY
Institute of Design & Construction, www.idc.edu, NY
Iona College, www.iona.edu, NY
Ithaca College, www.ithaca.edu, NY
The Jewish Theological Seminary, www.jtsa.edu, NY
The Juilliard School, www.juilliard.edu, NY
Keuka College, www.keuka.edu, NY
Lehman College, www.lehman.edu, NY
Le Moyne, www.lemoyne.edu, NY
Lim College, www.limcollege.edu, NY
Long Island University, www.liu.edu, NY
Manhattan College, www.manhattan.edu, NY
Marist College, www.marist.edu, NY
Metropolitan College of New York, www.mcny.edu, NY
Mercy College, www.mercy.edu, NY
Marymount Manhattan College, www.mmm.edu, NY
Monroe Community College, www.monroecc.edu, NY
Morrisville State College, www.morrisville.edu, NY
Mount Saint Marry College, www.msmc.edu, NY
Icahn School of Medicine at Mount Sinai, www.mssm.edu, NY
Manhattanville College, www.mville.edu, NY
Nazareth College, www.naz.edu, NY
Nassau Community College, www.ncc.edu, NY
New Paltz, www.newpaltz.edu, NY
The New School, www.newschool.edu, NY
Niagara University, www.niagara.edu, NY
Nyack College, www.nyack.edu, NY
New York College of Health Professions, www.nycollege.edu, NY
New York Film Academy, www.nyfa.edu, NY

New York Institute of Technology, www.nyit.edu, NY
New York University, www.nyu.edu, NY
State University of New York at Oneonta, www.oneonta.edu, NY
State University of New York at Oswego, www.oswego.edu, NY
Pace University, www.pace.edu, NY
Paul Smith's College, www.paulsmiths.edu, NY
State University of New York at Plattsburgh, www.plattsburgh.edu, NY
State University of New York at Potsdam, www.potsdam.edu, NY
Pratt Institute, www.pratt.edu, NY
Purchase College, www.purchase.edu, NY
Rochester Institute of Technology, www.rit.edu, NY
Roberts Wesleyan College, www.roberts.edu, NY
University of Rochester, www.rochester.edu, NY
Rensselaer Polytechnic Institute, www.rpi.edu, NY
The Sages Colleges, www.sage.edu, NY
Saint Bonaventure University, www.sbu.edu, NY
The New York Conservatory for Dramatic Arts, www.sft.edu, NY
Siena College, www.siena.edu, NY
Saint John Fisher College, www.sjfc.edu, NY
Skidmore College, www.skidmore.edu, NY
Sarah Lawrence College, www.slc.edu, NY
Saint Bernard's School of Theology & Ministry, www.stbernards.edu, NY
Saint John's University, www.stjohns.edu, NY
Saint Lawrence University, www.stlawu.edu, NY
Stony Brook University, www.stonybrook.edu, NY
Stony Brook Medicine, www.stonybrookmedicine.edu, NY
The College of Saint Rose, www.strose.edu, NY
State University of New York, www.suny.edu, NY
State University of New York at Adirondack, www.sunyacc.edu, NY
State University of New Institute of Technology, www.sunyit.edu, NY
Jamestown Community College, www.sunyjcc.edu, NY
Orange County Community College, www.sunyorange.edu, NY
Rockland Community College, www.sunyrockland.edu, NY
Suffolk County Community College, www.sunysuffolk.edu, NY
Westchester Community College, www.sunywcc.edu, NY
Syracuse University, www.syr.edu, NY
Tompkins Cortland Community College, www.tc3.edu, NY
The Touro College & University System, www.touro.edu, NY
Touro College Jacob D. Fuchsberg Law Center, www.tourolaw.edu, NY
Union College, www.union.edu, NY
Upstate Medical University, www.upstate.edu, NY
United States Military Academy West Point, www.usma.edu, NY
Utica College, www.utica.edu, NY
Vassar College, www.vassar.edu, NY
Wagner College, www.wagner.edu, NY
Wells College, www.wells.edu, NY
Yeshiva University, www.yu.edu, NY
Canton State University of New York, www.canton.edu, NY
Excelsior College, www.excelsior.edu, NY
Culinary Institute of America, www.ciachef.edu, NY

Ohio

Ashland University, www.ashland.edu, OH
Aultman College of Nursing & Health Sciences, www.aultmancollege.edu, OH
Belmont College, www.belmontcollege.edu, OH
Bowling Green State University, www.bgsu.edu, OH
Baldwin Wallace University, www.bw.edu, OH
Capital University, www.capital.edu, OH
Case Western Reserve University, www.case.edu, OH

Cincinnati College of Mortuary Science, www.ccms.edu, OH
Cedarville University, www.cedarville.edu, OH
Central State University, www.centralstate.edu, OH
Cincinnati State Technical & Community College, www.cincinnatistate.edu, OH
Central Ohio Technical College, www.cotc.edu, OH
Columbus State Community College, www.cscc.edu, OH
Cleveland State University, www.csuohio.edu, OH
Western Reserve University, www.cwru.edu, OH
Defiance College, www.defiance.edu, OH
Denison University, www.denison.edu, OH
The University of Findlay, www.findlay.edu, OH
Franklin University, www.franklin.edu, OH
Heidelberg University, www.heidelberg.edu, OH
Hiram College, www.hiram.edu, OH
Hocking College, www.hocking.edu, OH
John Carroll University, www.jcu.edu, OH
Kettering College, www.kc.edu, OH
Kent State University, www.kent.edu, OH
Kenyon College, www.kenyon.edu, OH
Lakeland Community College, www.lakelandcc.edu, OH
Lima Central Catholic High School, www.lcchs.edu, OH
Lorain County Community College, www.lorainccc.edu, OH
Malone University, www.malone.edu, OH
Marietta College, www.marietta.edu, OH
Miami University, www.miamioh.edu, OH
University of Mount Union, www.mountunion.edu, OH
Mount Saint Joseph University, www.msj.edu, OH
Muskingum University, www.muskingum.edu, OH
Mount Vernon Nazarene University, www.mvnu.edu, OH
North Central State College, www.ncstatecollege.edu, OH
Oberlin College & Conservatory, www.oberlin.edu, OH
Ohio University, www.ohio.edu, OH
Ohio Dominican University, www.ohiodominican.edu, OH
Ohio State University, www.osu.edu, OH
Ohio Northern University, www.onu.edu, OH
Otterbein University, www.otterbein.edu, OH
Owens Community College, www.owens.edu, OH
Ohio Wesleyan University, www.owu.edu, OH
University of Rio Grande, www.rio.edu, OH
Shawnee State University, www.shawnee.edu, OH
Sinclair Community College, www.sinclair.edu, OH
Tiffin University, www.tiffin.edu, OH
Cuyahoga Community College, www.tri-c.edu, OH
The University of Akron, www.uakron.edu, OH
University of Cincinnati, www.uc.edu, OH
University of Cincinnati Blue Ash, www.ucblueash.edu, OH
University of Cincinnati Clermont, www.ucclermont.edu, OH
University of Dayton, www.udayton.edu, OH
Urbana University, www.urbana.edu, OH
Ursuline College, www.ursuline.edu, OH
University of Toledo, www.utoledo.edu, OH
Walsh University, www.walsh.edu, OH
Wilmington College, www.wilmington.edu, OH
Wittenberg University, www.wittenberg.edu, OH
The College of Wooster, www.wooster.edu, OH
Wright State University, www.wright.edu, OH
Xavier University, www.xavier.edu, OH
Youngstown State University, www.ysu.edu, OH
Ohio State University, www.osu.edu, OH

Oklahoma
Cameron University, www.cameron.edu, OK
Connors State College, www.connorsstate.edu, OK
East Central University, www.ecok.edu, OK
Langston University, www.langston.edu, OK
Mid-America Christian University, www.macu.edu, OK
Meridian Technology Center, www.meridiantech.edu, OK
Northeastern State University, www.nsuok.edu, OK
Northwestern Oklahoma State University, www.nwosu.edu, OK
Oklahoma Christian University, www.oc.edu, OK
Oklahoma City Community College, www.occc.edu, OK
Oklahoma City University, www.okcu.edu, OK
Oklahoma State University, www.okstate.edu, OK
Oral Roberts University, www.oru.edu, OK
Oklahoma State University Institute of Technology, www.osuit.edu, OK
Oklahoma State University, www.osuokc.edu, OK
The University of Oklahoma, www.ou.edu, OK
The University of Oklahoma Health Sciences Center, www.ouhsc.edu, OK
Rose State College, www.rose.edu, OK
Rogers State University, www.rsu.edu, OK
Southeastern Oklahoma State University, www.se.edu, OK
Southwestern Christian University, www.swcu.edu, OK
Southwestern Oklahoma State University, www.swosu.edu, OK
Tulsa Community College, www.tulsacc.edu, OK
University of Central Oklahoma, www.uco.edu, OK
University of Science & Arts of Oklahoma, www.usao.edu, OK
University of Tulsa, www.utulsa.edu, OK
Western Oklahoma State College, www.wosc.edu, OK

Oregon
Blue Mountain Community College, www.bluecc.edu, OR
Clatsop Community College, www.clatsopcc.edu, OR
Central Oregon Community College, www.cocc.edu, OR
Columbia School of English, www.cs.edu, OR
Concordia University Portland Oregon, www.cu-portland.edu, OR
Eastern Oregon University, www.eou.edu, OR
George Fox University, www.georgefox.edu, OR
Lane Community College, www.lanecc.edu, OR
Lewis & Clark, www.lclark.edu, OR
Linfield College, www.linfield.edu, OR
Linn-Benton Community College, www.linnbenton.edu, OR
Marylhurst University, www.marylhurst.edu, OR
National College of Natural Medicine, www.ncnm.edu, OR
Oregon Health & Science University, www.ohsu.edu, OR
Oregon State University, www.oregonstate.edu, OR
Pacific University Oregon, www.pacificu.edu, OR
Portland Community College, www.pcc.edu, OR
Portland State University, www.pdx.edu, OR
Reed College, www.reed.edu, OR
Rogue Community College, www.roguecc.edu, OR
Southwestern Oregon Community College, www.socc.edu, OR
Southern Oregon University, www.sou.edu, OR
University of Oregon, www.uoregon.edu, OR
University of Portland, www.up.edu, OR
Warner Pacific College, www.warnerpacific.edu, OR
Willamette University, www.willamette.edu, OR
Western Oregon University, www.wou.edu, OR

Pennsylvania
Allegheny College, www.allegheny.edu, PA
Alvernia University, www.alvernia.edu, PA
Arcadia University, www.arcadia.edu, PA
Baptist Bible College & Seminary, www.bbc.edu, PA
Butler County Community College, www.bc3.edu, PA
Bloomsburg University, www.bloomu.edu, PA
Bryn Mawr College, www.brynmawr.edu, PA
Bucknell University, www.bucknell.edu, PA
Bucks County Community College, www.bucks.edu, PA
California University of Pennsylvania, www.calu.edu, PA
Carlow University, www.carlow.edu, PA
Community College of Allegheny County, www.ccac.edu, PA

Community College of Philadelphia, www.ccp.edu, PA
Cedar Crest College, www.cedarcrest.edu, PA
Chatham University, www.chatham.edu, PA
Chestnut Hill College, www.chc.edu, PA
Clarion University, www.clarion.edu, PA
Carnegie Mellon University, www.cmu.edu, PA
Delaware County Community College, www.dccc.edu, PA
Delaware Valley College, www.delval.edu, PA
Dickinson College, www.dickinson.edu, PA
Drexel University, www.drexel.edu, PA
Drexel University College of Medicine, www.drexelmed.edu, PA
Duquesne University, www.duq.edu, PA
Eastern University, www.eastern.edu, PA
Edinboro University, www.edinboro.edu, PA
Elizabethtown College, www.etown.edu, PA
Evangelical Seminary, www.evangelical.edu, PA
Franklin & Marshall College, www.fandm.edu, PA
Saint Francis University, www.francis.edu, PA
Grove City College, www.gcc.edu, PA
Geneva College, www.geneva.edu, PA
Gettysburg College, www.gettysburg.edu, PA
Harrisburg Area Community College, www.hacc.edu, PA
Haverford College, www.haverford.edu, PA
Holy Family University, www.holyfamily.edu, PA
Indiana University of Pennsylvania, www.iup.edu, PA
Thomas Jefferson University, www.jefferson.edu, PA
Juniata College, www.juniata.edu, PA
Keystone College, www.keystone.edu, PA
King's College, www.kings.edu, PA
Kutztown University, www.kutztown.edu, PA
Lackawanna College, www.lackawanna.edu, PA
Lafayette College, www.lafayette.edu, PA
Lancaster County Career & Technology Center, www.lancasterctc.edu, PA
Lancaster Theological Seminary, www.lancasterseminary.edu, PA
La Roche College, www.laroche.edu, PA
La Salle University, www.lasalle.edu, PA
Lehigh Carbon Community College, www.lccc.edu, PA
Lake Erie College of Osteopathic Medicine, www.lecom.edu, PA
Lehigh University, www.lehigh.edu, PA
Lock Haven University, www.lhup.edu, PA
The Lincoln University, www.lincoln.edu, PA
Lansdale School of Business, www.lsb.edu, PA
Lebanon Valley College, www.lvc.edu, PA
Lycoming College, www.lycoming.edu, PA
Manor College, www.manor.edu, PA
Mansfield University, www.mansfield.edu, PA
Marywood University, www.marywood.edu, PA
Montgomery County Community College, www.mc3.edu, PA
Mercyhurst University, www.mercyhurst.edu, PA
Messiah College, www.messiah.edu, PA
Millersville University, www.millersville.edu, PA
Misericordia University, www.misericordia.edu, PA
Moravian College, www.moravian.edu, PA
Mount Aloysius College, www.mtaloy.edu, PA
Muhlenberg College, www.muhlenberg.edu, PA
Neumann University, www.neumann.edu, PA
Northampton Community College, www.northampton.edu, PA
Pennsylvania Gunsmith School, www.pagunsmith.edu, PA
Philadelphia College of Osteopathic Medicine, www.pcom.edu, PA
Pennsylvania College of Technology, www.pct.edu, PA
Philadelphia University, www.philau.edu, PA
University of Pittsburgh, www.pitt.edu, PA
Penn State University, www.psu.edu, PA
Reading Area Community College, www.racc.edu, PA
Robert Morris University, www.rmu.edu, PA
Saint Vincent Seminary, www.saintvincentseminary.edu, PA
Salus University, www.salus.edu, PA
The University of Scranton, www.scranton.edu, PA
Shippensburg University, www.ship.edu, PA
Saint Joseph's University, www.sju.edu, PA
Slippery Rock University, www.sru.edu, PA
Saint Vincent College, www.stvincent.edu, PA
Susquehanna University, www.susqu.edu, PA
Swarthmore College, www.swarthmor.edu, PA
Temple University, www.temple.edu, PA
The American College of Financial Services, www.theamericancollege.edu, PA
Thiel College, www.thiel.edu, PA
University of the Arts, www.uarts.edu, PA
University of Pennsylvania, www.upenn.edu, PA
University of the Sciences in Philadelphia, www.usciences.edu, PA
Valley Forge Christian College, www.vfcc.edu, PA
Villanova University, www.villanova.edu, PA
Washington & Jefferson College, www.washjeff.edu, PA
Westmoreland County Community College, www.wccc.edu, PA
West Chester University, www.wcupa.edu, PA
Westminster College, www.westminster.edu, PA
Widener University, www.widener.edu, PA
Wilkes University, www.wilkes.edu, PA
Wilson College, www.wilson.edu, PA
York College of Pennsylvania, www.ycp.edu, PA
Pennsylvania Academy of the Fine Arts, www.pafa.edu, PA
East Stroudsburg University, www.esu.edu, PA
Ursinus College, www.ursinus.edu, PA
DeSales University, www.desales.edu, PA
Lancaster Bible College, www.lbc.edu, PA
Cheyney University of Pennsylvania, www.cheyney.edu, PA

Rhode Island
Brown University, www.brown.edu, RI
Bryant University, www.bryant.edu, RI
Community College of Rhode Island, www.ccri.edu, RI
Johnson & Wales University, www.jwu.edu, RI
New England Institute of Technology, www.neit.edu, RI
Providence College, www.providence.edu, RI
The University of Rhode Island, www.uri.edu, RI
Rhode Island College, www.ric.edu, RI
Rhose Island School of Design, www.risd.edu, RI
Roger Williams University, www.rwu.edu, RI
University of Rhode Island, www.uri.edu, RI

South Carolina
Centura College, www.centura.edu, SC
The Citadel Military College of South Carolina, www.citadel.edu, SC
Columbia International University, www.ciu.edu, SC
Clemson University, www.clemson.edu, SC
Coastal Carolina University, www.coastal.edu, SC
College of Charleston, www.cofc.edu, SC
Coker College, www.coker.edu, SC
Columbia College South Carolina, www.columbiasc.edu, SC
Florence-Darlington Technical College, www.fdtc.edu, SC
Francis Marion University, www.fmarion.edu, SC
Forrest College, www.forrestcollege.edu, SC
Furman University, www.furman.edu, SC
Lander University, www.lander.edu, SC
Limestone College, www.limestone.edu, SC
Midlands Technical College, www.midlandstech.edu, SC
Medical University of South Carolina, www.musc.edu, SC
Newberry College, www.newberry.edu, SC
North Greenville University, www.ngu.edu, SC
Orangeburg-Calhoun Technical College, www.octech.edu, SC

Presbyterian College, www.presby.edu, SC
University of South Carolina, www.sc.edu, SC
South Carolina State University, www.scsu.edu, SC
Sinte Gleska University, www.sintegleska.edu, SC
Spartanburg Methodist College, www.smcsc.edu, SC
TriCounty Technical College, www.tctc.edu, SC
University of South Carolina Aiken, www.usca.edu, SC
University of South Carolina Beaufort, www.uscb.edu, SC
University of South Carolina Upstate, www.uscupstate.edu, SC
Winthrop University, www.winthrop.edu, SC
Wofford College, www.wofford.edu, SC
York Technical College, www.yorktech.edu, SC
Bob Jones University, www.bju.edu, SC
Anderson University, www.andersonuniversity.edu, SC
Black Hills State University, www.bhsu.edu, SD
Dakota State University, www.dsu.edu, SD
Dakota Wesleyan University, www.dwu.edu, SD
Mount Marty College, www.mtmc.edu, SD
Northern State University, www.northern.edu, SD
South Dakota School of Mines & Technology, www.sdsmt.edu, SD
South Dakota State University, www.sdstate.edu, SD
University of South Dakota, www.usd.edu, SD
University of Sioux Falls, www.usioxfalls.edu, SD
Western Dakota Technical Institute, www.wdt.edu, SD

Tennessee

Austin Peay State University, www.apsu.edu, TN
Belmont University, www.belmont.edu, TN
Bryan College, www.bryan.edu, TN
Christian Brothers University, www.cbu.edu, TN
Carson-Newman University, www.cn.edu, TN
Columbia State Community College, www.columbiastate.edu, TN
Cumberland University, www.cumberland.edu, TN
DeVry University, www.devry.edu, TN
East Tennessee State University, www.etsu.edu, TN
Freed-Hardeman University, www.fhu.edu, TN
Fisk University, www.fisk.edu, TN
Huntington College of Health Sciences, www.hchs.edu, TN
Hiwassee College, www.hiwassee.edu, TN
Johnson University, www.johnsonu.edu, TN
Jackson State Community College, www.jscc.edu, TN
Lee University, www.leeuniversity.edu, TN
Lincoln Memorial University, www.lmunet.edu, TN
The LeMoyne-Owen College, www.loc.edu, TN
The University of Memphis, www.memphis.edu, TN
Milligan College, www.milligan.edu, TN
Middle Tennessee State University, www.mtsu.edu, TN
Nashville State Community College, www.nscc.edu, TN
Pellissippi State Community College, www.pstcc.edu, TN
Rhodes College, www.rhodes.edu, TN
Roane State Community College, www.roanestate.edu, TN
Southern College of Optometry, www.sco.edu, TN
Sewanee The University of the South, www.sewanee.edu, TN
Southern Adventist University, www.southern.edu, TN
The University of Tennessee, www.tennessee.edu, TN
Southwest Tennessee Community College, www.tn.edu, TN
Tennessee State University, www.tnstate.edu, TN
Tennessee Technological University, www.tntech.edu, TN
Tennessee Wesleyan College, www.twcnet.edu, TN
University of Tennessee Chattanooga, www.utc.edu, TN
University of Tennessee Health Science Center, www.uthsc.edu, TN
University of Tennessee Knoxville, www.utk.edu, TN
University of Tennessee Martin, www.utm.edu, TN
University of Tennessee Space Institute, www.utsi.edu, TN
Union University, www.uu.edu, TN

Vanderbilt University, www.vanderbilt.edu, TN
Volunteer State Community College, www.volstate.edu, TN
King University, www.king.edu, TN

Texas

Abilene Christian University, www.acu.edu, TX
Alamo Colleges, www.alamo.edu, TX
Alvin Community College, www.alvincollege.edu, TX
Angelo State University, www.angelo.edu, TX
Austin Community College District, www.austincc.edu, TX
Austin College, www.austincollege.edu, TX
Austin Graduate School of Theology, www.austingrad.edu, TX
Baylor University, www.baylor.edu, TX
Blinn College, www.blinn.edu, TX
Brazosport College, www.brazosport.edu, TX
Brookhaven College, www.brookhavencollege.edu, TX
Baptist Health System School of Health Professions, www.bshp.edu, TX
Career Point College, www.careerpointcollege.edu, TX
Cedar Valley College, www.cedarvalleycollege.edu, TX
Coastal Bend College, www.coastalbend.edu, TX
College of the Mainland, www.com.edu, TX
Concordia University Texas, www.concordia.edu, TX
Central Texas College, www.ctcd.edu, TX
Culinary Institute LeNotre, www.culinaryinstitute.edu, TX
Dallas Baptist University, www.dbu.edu, TX
Del Mar College, www.delmar.edu, TX
Dallas Nursing Institute, www.dni.edu, TX
El Paso Community College, www.epcc.edu, TX
East Texas Baptist University, www.etbu.edu, TX
Galen College of Nursing, www.galencollege.edu, TX
Galveston College, www.gc.edu, TX
Grayson College, www.grayson.edu, TX
Houston Baptist University, www.hbu.edu, TX
Houston Community College, www.hccs.edu, TX
Hill College, www.hillcollege.edu, TX
Howard College, www.howardcollege.edu, TX
Howard Payne University, www.hputx.edu, TX
Lamar University, www.lamar.edu, TX
Lamar State College – Port Arthur, www.lamarpa.edu, TX
Lubbock Christian University, www.lcu.edu, TX
LeTourneau University, www.letu.edu, TX
Lamar Institute of Technology, www.lit.edu, TX
Lone Star College System, www.lonestar.edu, TX
Lamar State College – Orange, www.lsco.edu, TX
McLennan Community College, www.mclennan.edu, TX
McMurry University, www.mcm.edu, TX
Midland College, www.midland.edu, TX
Midwestern State University, www.mwsu.edu, TX
National American University, www.national.edu, TX
North Central Texas College, www.nctc.edu, TX
North American University, www.northamerican.edu, TX
North Lake College, www.northlakecollege.edu, TX
Odessa College, www.odessa.edu, TX
Ogle School, www.ogleschool.edu, TX
Our Lady of the Lake University, www.ollusa.edu, TX
Panola College, www.panola.edu, TX
Patty Hands Shelton School of Nursing, www.phssn.edu, TX
Prairie View A&M University, www.pvamu.edu, TX
Rice University, www.rice.edu, TX
Richland College, www.richlandcollege.edu, TX
San Jacinto College, www.sanjac.edu, TX
Schreiner University, www.schreiner.edu, TX
Stephen F. Austin State University, www.sfasu.edu, TX
Sam Houston State University, www.shsu.edu, TX
Southern Methodist University, www.smu.edu, TX
South Plains College, www.southplainscollege.edu, TX
South Texas College, www.southtexascollege.htp TX

Southwestern University, www.southwestern.edu, TX
Seminary of the Southwest, www.ssw.edu, TX
South Texas College of Law, www.stcl.edu, TX
Saint Edward's University, www.stedwards.edu, TX
Saint Mary's University, www.stmarytx.edu, TX
University of Saint Thomas, www.stthom.edu, TX
Texas A&M Health Science Center, www.tamhsc.edu, TX
Texas A&M International University, www.tamiu.edu, TX
Texas A&M University, www.tamu.edu, TX
Texas A&M University Commerce, www.tamuc.edu, TX
Texas A&M University Corpus Christi, www.tamucc.edu, TX
Texas A&M University Kingsville, www.tamuk.edu, TX
Texas A&M University Texarkana, www.tamut.edu, TX
Tarleton State University, www.tarleton.edu, TX
Texas Christian University, www.tcu.edu, TX
Temple College, www.templejc.edu, TX
Tyler Junior College, www.tjc.edu, TX
Trinity University, www.trinity.edu, TX
Texas State Technical College, www.tstc.edu, TX
Texas Southern University, www.tsu.edu, TX
Texas Tech University, www.ttu.edu, TX
Texas Tech University Health Sciences Center, www.ttuhsc.edu, TX
Texas Woman's University, www.twu.edu, TX
Texas Chiropractic College, www.txchiro.edu, TX
Texas State University, www.txstate.edu, TX
University of Dallas, www.udallas.edu, TX
University of Houston, www.uh.edu, TX
University of Houston Clear Lake, www.uhcl.edu, TX
University of Houston Downtown, www.uhd.edu, TX
University of the Incarnate Word, www.uiw.edu, TX
University of Mary Hardin-Baylor, www.umhb.edu, TX
University of North Texas, www.unt.edu, TX
University of North Texas Health Science Center, www.unthsc.edu, TX
University of Texas Arlington, www.uta.edu, TX
University of Texas Brownsville, www.utb.edu, TX
University of Texas Dallas, www.utdallas.edu, TX
University of Texas at El Paso, www.utep.edu, TX
University of Texas at Austin, www.utexas.edu, TX
University of Texas Health Science Center Houston, www.uth.edu, TX
University of Texas Health Science Center San Antonio, www.uthscsa.edu, TX
University of Texas Medical Branch at Galveston, www.utmb.edu, TX
University of Texas Pan American, www.utpa.edu, TX
University of Texas of the Permian Basin, www.utpb.edu, TX
University of Texas at San Antonio, www.utsa.edu, TX
University of Texas Southwestern Medical Center, www.utsouthwestern.edu, TX
University of Texas at Tyler, www.online.uttyler.edu/ TX
Valley Grande Institute, www.vgi.edu, TX
Victoria College, www.victoriacollege.edu, TX
Wayland Baptist University, www.wbu.edu, TX
Weatherford College, www.wc.edu, TX
West Texas A&M University, www.wtamu.edu, TX

U.S. Virgin Islands
University of the Virgin Islands, www.uvi.edu, USVI

Utah
Brigham Young University, www.byu.edu, UT
Dixie State University, www.dixie.edu, UT
Salt Lake Community College, www.slcc.edu, UT
Snow College, www.snow.edu, UT
Southern Utah University, www.suu.edu, UT
Utah State University, www.usu.edu, UT
University of Utah, www.utah.edu, UT
Utah Valley University, www.uvu.edu, UT
Weber State University, www.weber.edu, UT

Virginia
Averett University, www.averett.edu, VA
Christendom College, www.christendom.edu, VA
Christopher Newport University, www.cnu.edu, VA
Dabney S. Lancaster Community College, www.dslcc.edu, VA
Eastern Mennonite University, www.emu.edu, VA
Eastern Virginia Medical School, www.evms.edu, VA
Ferrum College, www.ferrum.edu, VA
Germanna Community College, www.germanna.edu, VA
George Mason University, www.gmu.edu, VA
Hampden-Sydney College, www.hsc.edu, VA
The Institute for the Psychological Sciences, www.ipsciences.edu, VA
James Madison University, www.jmu.edu, VA
Liberty University, www.liberty.edu, VA
Longwood University, www.longwood.edu, VA
Marymount University, www.marymount.edu, VA
New River Community College, www.nr.edu, VA
Norfolk State University, www.nsu.edu, VA
Northern Virginia Community College, www.nvcc.edu, VA
Old Dominion University, www.odu.edu, VA
Radford University, www.radford.edu, VA
Randolph College, www.randolphcollege.edu, VA
Rappahannock Community College, www.rappahannock.edu, VA
Regent University, www.regent.edu, VA
Reynolds Community College, www.reynolds.edu, VA
University of Richmond, www.richmond.edu, VA
Randolph-Macon College, www.rmc.edu, VA
Roanoke College, www.roanoke.edu, VA
Sentara College of Health Sciences, www.sentara.edu, VA
Stratford University, www.stratford.edu, VA
Shenandoah University, www.su.edu, VA
Southern Virginia University, www.svu.edu, VA
Southwest Virginia Community College, www.sw.edu, VA
Tidewater Community College, www.tcc.edu, VA
Thomas Nelson Community College, www.tncc.edu, VA
University of Mary Washington, www.umw.edu, VA
University of Virginia's College at Wise, www.uvawise.edu, VA
Virginia's Community Colleges, www.vccs.edu, VA
Virginia Commonwealth University, www.vcu.edu, VA
Virginia Highlands Community College, www.vhcc.edu, VA
Virginia Institute of Marine Science, www.vims.edu, VA
University of Virginia, www.virginia.edu, VA
Virginia Western Community College, www.virginiawestern.edu, VA
Virginia International University, www.viu.edu, VA
Virginia State University, www.vsu.edu, VA
Virginia Polytechnic Institute & State University, www.vt.edu, VA
Virginia Union University, www.vuu.edu, VA
Virginia Wesleyan College, www.vwc.edu, VA
Washington & Lee University, www.wlu.edu, VA
The College of William & Mary, www.wm.edu, VA

Vermont
Castleton State College of Vermont, www.castleton.edu, VT
Champlain College, www.champlain.edu, VT
Green Mountain College, www.greenmtn.edu, VT
Johnson State College, www.jsc.edu, VT
Middlebury College, www.middlebury.edu, VT
New England Culinary Institute, www.neci.edu, VT

Norwich University, www.norwich.edu, VT
School for International Training, www.sit.edu, VT
Saint Michael's College, www.smcvt.edu, VT
University of Vermont, www.uvm.edu, VT
University of Vermont, www.uvm.edu, VT
Vermont Law School, www.vermontlaw.edu, VT
Vermont Technical College, www.vtc.edu, VT
Bennington College, www.bennington.edu, VT

Washington
Bellevue College, www.bellevuecollege.edu, WA
Big Bend Community College, www.bigbend.edu, WA
Cascadia Community College, www.cascadia.edu, WA
Centralia College, www.centralia.edu, WA
Charter College, www.chartercollege.edu, WA
Clark College, www.clark.edu, WA
Central Washington University, www.cwu.edu, WA
DigiPen Institute of Technology, www.digipen.edu, WA
Edmonds Community College, www.edcc.edu, WA
Everett Community College, www.everettcc.edu, WA
The Evergreen State College, www.evergreen.edu, WA
Eastern Washington University, www.ewu.edu, WA
Faith Evangelical College & Seminary, www.faithseminary.edu, WA
Gonzaga University, www.gonzaga.edu, WA
Green River Community College, www.greenriver.edu, WA
Highline College, www.highline.edu, WA
Mukogawa Fort Wright Institute, www.mfwi.edu, WA
North Seattle College, www.northseattle.edu, WA
Olympic College, www.olympic.edu, WA
Peninsula College, www.pencol.edu, WA
Perry Technical Institute, www.perrytech.edu, WA
Pacific Lutheran University, www.plu.edu, WA
Renton Technical College, www.rtc.edu, WA
Seattle Central College, www.seattlecentral.edu, WA
Seattle University, www.seattleu.edu, WA
Shoreline Community College, www.shoreline.edu, WA
Seattle Institute of Oriental Medicine, www.siom.edu, WA
Skagit Valley College, www.skagit.edu, WA
South Seattle College, www.southseattle.edu, WA
Spokane Falls Community College, www.spokanefalls.edu, WA
Seattle Pacific University, www.spu.edu, WA
Saint Martin's University, www.stmartin.edu, WA
University of Puget Sound, www.pugetsound.edu, WA
University of Washington, www.uw.edu, WA
University of Washington Bothell, www.uwb.edu, WA
Walla Walla University, www.wallawalla.edu, WA
Whitman College, www.whitman.edu, WA
Whitworth University, www.whitworth.edu, WA
Washington State University, www.wsu.edu, WA
Wenatchee Valley College, www.wvc.edu, WA
Walla Walla Community College, www.wwcc.edu, WA
Western Washington University, www.wwu.edu, WA
Yakima Valley Community College, www.yvcc.edu, WA
University of Washington, www.washington.edu, WA

Wisconsin
Alverno College, www.alverno.edu, WI
Carroll University, www.carrollu.edu, WI
Carthage College, www.carthage.edu, WI
Chippewa Valley Technical College, www.cvtc.edu, WI
Edgewood College, www.edgewood.edu, WI
Gateway Technical College, www.gtc.edu, WI
The Institute of Beauty & Wellness, www.ibw.edu, WI
Lawrence University, www.lawrence.edu, WI
Madison Area Technical College, www.madisoncollege.edu, WI
Marquette University, www.marquette.edu, WI
Milwaukee Area Technical College, www.matc.edu, WI
Medical College of Wisconsin, www.mcw.edu, WI
Milwaukee Institute of Art & Design, www.miad.edu, WI
Moraine Park Technical College, www.morainepark.edu, WI
Milwaukee School of Engineering, www.msoe.edu, WI
Northland College, www.northland.edu, WI
Northcentral Technical College, www.ntc.edu, WI
Northeast Wisconsin Technical College, www.nwtc.edu, WI
Silver Lake College of the Holy Family, www.sl.edu, WI
Saint Norbert College, www.snc.edu, WI
Cardinal Stritch University, www.stritch.edu, WI
University of Wisconsin Colleges, www.uwc.edu, WI
University of Wisconsin Eau Claire, www.uwec.edu, WI
University of Wisconsin Extension, www.uwex.edu, WI
University of Wisconsin Green Bay, www.uwgb.edu, WI
University of Wisconsin La Crosse, www.uwlax.edu, WI
University of Wisconsin Milwaukee, www.uwm.edu, WI
University of Wisconsin Oshkosh, www.uwosh.edu, WI
University of Wisconsin Platteville, www.uwplatt.edu, WI
University of Wisconsin River Falls, www.uwrf.edu, WI
University of Wisconsin Stevens Point, www.uwsp.edu, WI
University of Wisconsin Superior, www.uwsuper.edu, WI
University of Wisconsin Whitewater, www.uww.edu, WI
Viterbo University, www.viterbo.edu, WI
Waukesha County Technical College, www.wctc.edu, WI
University of Wisconsin, Madison, www.wisc.edu, WI
Wisconsin Indianhead Technical College, www.witc.edu, WI
Wisconsin Lutheran College, www.wlc.edu, WI
Wisconsin Technical College System, www.wtcsystem.edu, WI
Western Technical College, www.westerntc.edu, WI

West Virginia
American Public University System, www.apus.edu, WV
Concord University, www.concord.edu, WV
Eastern West Virgina Community & Technical College, www.easternwv.edu, WV
Fairmont State University, www.fairmontstate.edu, WV
Marshall University, www.marshall.edu, WV
Ohio Valley University, www.ovu.edu, WV
Pierpont Community & Technical College, www.pierpont.edu, WV
Shepherd University, www.shepherd.edu, WV
University of Charleston, www.ucwv.edu, WV
West Liberty University, www.westliberty.edu, WV
Wheeling Jesuit University, www.wju.edu, WV
West Virginia Northern Community College, www.wvncc.edu, WV
West Virginia State University, www.wvstateu.edu, WV
West Virginia University, www.wvu.edu, WV
West Virginia Wesleyan College, www.wvwc.edu, WV

Wyoming
Casper College, www.caspercollege.edu, WY
Central Wyoming College, www.cwc.edu, WY
National Outdoor Leadership School, www.nols.edu, WY
Northwest College, www.northwestcollege.edu, WY
Northern Wyoming Community College District, www.sheridan.edu, WY
University of Wyoming, www.uwyo.edu, WY

About the Authors

Jonathan Machtig works as a Chess Department Director for Star Education. Star Education provides after-school programs for 10,000 California-based students K-12. Jonathan's hobbies include reading, music and chess. Jonathan attended Musician's Institute in Los Angeles and Salt Lake School for the Performing Arts.

Brett Machtig serves on the Normandale College Business Advisory Committee as well as The National Security Forum for the United States Department of Defense. Brett is the founding partner of The Capital Advisory Group and has written more than 22 books on finance, history, negotiation, and art. His hobbies include history, collecting antique books, and a lifetime of study.

www.brettmachtig.com
brett@cagcos.com

Publications Available by Brett Machtig

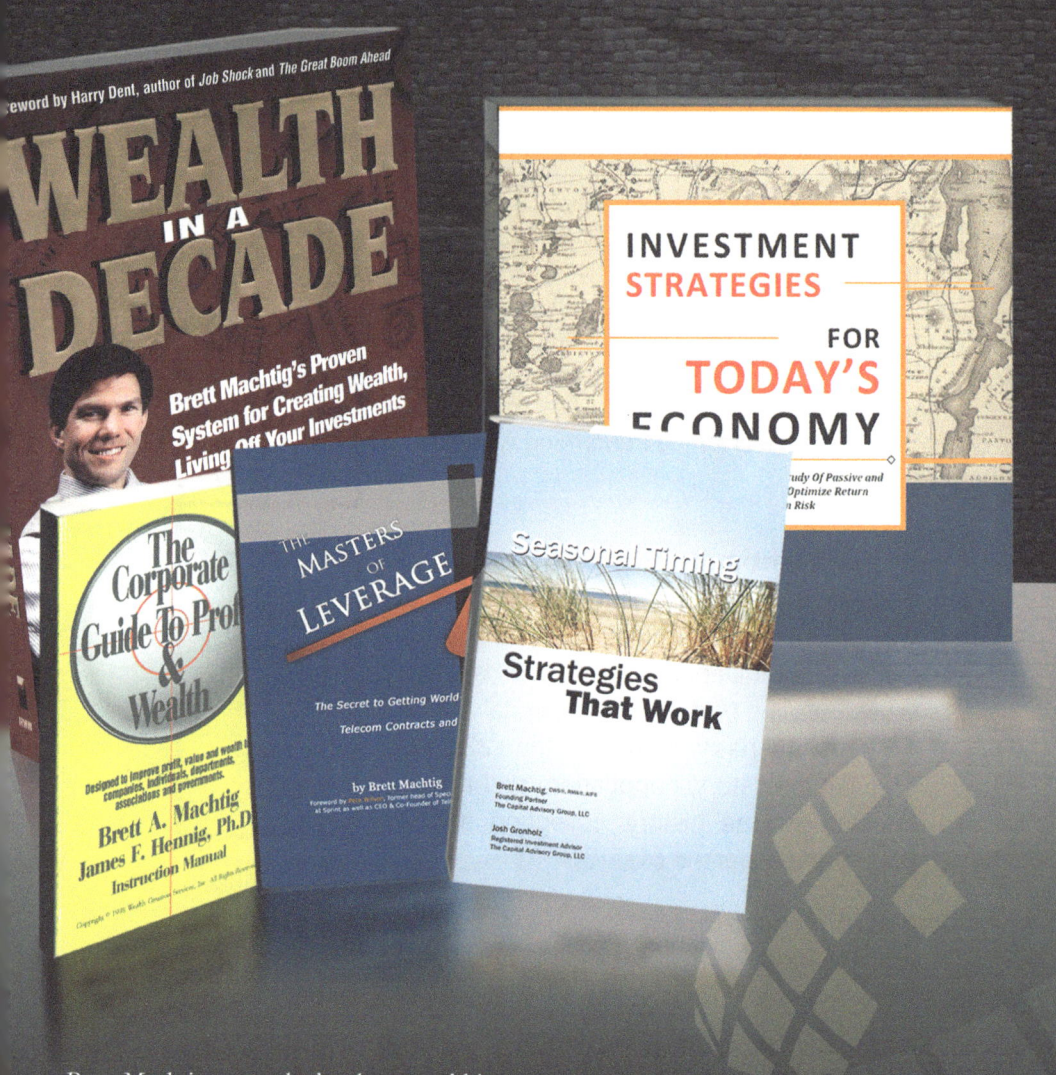

Brett Machtig wrote the book on wealth!
Wealth in a Decade (Irwin McGraw Hill 1996) was praised by the
LA TIMES as "The Personal Book of the Year"

Among Machtig's more recent books, you'll find **Your Guide to Financial Freedom** (MGI Publications 2010), **Investment Strategies that Work** (MGI Publications 2015) and **A Twenty-Something's Guide to Financial Freedom** (MGI Publications 2015) in stores, as well as on line through Amazon.com and i-Tunes.

265

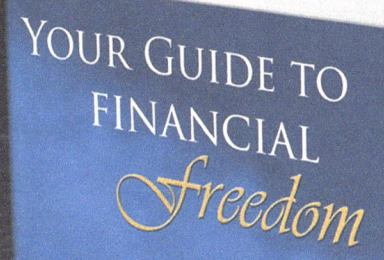

See our latest book on Amazon:

"The Secret Killer of President John F. Kennedy"
by Ashley Machtig & Brett Machtig

© 2022 by MGI Publications, Jonathan Machtig and Brett Machtig. All rights reserved.

Published 2022. First Printing March 2022.

No part of this publication may be reproduced, distributed, or transmitted in any form or by any means, including photocopying, recording, or other electronic or mechanical methods, without the prior written permission of the publisher, except in the case of brief quotations embodied in critical reviews and certain other noncommercial uses permitted by copyright law.